LEGAL RIGHTS
OF THE CATASTROPHICALLY ILL AND INJURED:

A FAMILY GUIDE
Second Edition

JOSEPH L. ROMANO, ESQUIRE
COMMONWEALTH BANK PLAZA
2 WEST LAFAYETTE STREET
NORRISTOWN PA 19401-4725
(610) 279-3900
(800) 331-4134
FAX 610-279-6265

WebSite: http://www.josephromanolaw.com/
Email: Info@josephromanolaw.com

- Philadelphia PA
  (215) 854-0225

- Pittsburgh PA
  (412) 471-7788

- Lancaster PA
  (717) 392-2019

- Allentown PA
  (610) 437-2644

- Wilkes-Barre PA
  (570) 829-4220

- Camp Hill PA
  (717) 731-8297

Mr. Romano, along with qualified co-counsel, represents clients throughout the United States

This book is dedicated to individuals, families, and medical providers who advocate for the rights of the catastrophically ill and injured.

INTRODUCTION

" THE LAWS ASSIST THOSE WHO ARE VIGILANT,
NOT THOSE WHO SLEEP ON THEIR RIGHTS"

Legal Maxim

Whenever there is a castastrophic injury or illness, family members are faced not only with the monumental task of identifying short-term medical insurance benefits, but must also identify long-term benefits. Insurance regulations, independent medical examinations, exclusions, forms and more forms, peer review, insurance companies' refusal to authorize a second medical opinion - When will it all end?

It would be ideal if insurance companies, the courts, and state and federal governmental agencies promptly determined whether you or your loved one is entitled to benefits. Unfortunately, anyone who has attempted to obtain benefits knows that "the wheels of justice and the administrative process turn very slowly". Relying upon insurance companies, the courts, and state and federal agencies to "do the right thing" often results in frustration and delay.

Throughout the course of this book, you will find one issue constantly emphasized—that you must have an attorney working with you in the early stages of hospitalization and recovery. I have heard it said that this is insensitive, and that during this time families can only focus on the medical needs of their loved ones. As an attorney who has worked for twenty years to help families at what is probably the most difficult time they will ever encounter, it is my opinion that the earlier I am asked to assist both the patient and the family, the greater likelihood there is in obtaining maximum short-term and long-term medical benefits for use in the rehabilitation process.

If you are reading this book while a loved one is in an acute-care facility, you will discover that the day of discharge comes very quickly, and that you need to be prepared for the next step—rehabilitation and recovery. To find these sources for payment is not an overnight process. This requires active planning with your family, doctor, attorney, and health care team. You need to adopt a team approach to be sure that the rehabilitation care recommended by the doctor is not thwarted by your health insurance company and the governmental process. People find it very difficult to accept the fact that health insurance companies and the government constantly challenge a doctor's expertise, even when they know that the doctor is focused on the best interest of the patient while their only interest is cost containment.

My clients are people... People who have suffered tragedy, and are now rebuilding their lives. Fortunately, medical and rehabilitation advances can make this possible in cases that previously had little hope. Unfortunately, the cost of acute care, sub-acute care, rehabilitation care, nursing care, and long-term care is astronomical.

Adequate "planning for the future" requires a clear understanding of the rights of the catastrophically ill and injured. I hope this book provides the information and practical strategies to advocate for your rights and those of your loved ones. Be vigilant! Don't sleep on your rights! You can make a difference!

Joseph L. Romano

On October 23, 1997, **THE WALL STREET JOURNAL** published a special section entitled *Health and Medicine*. Mr. Romano was profiled in this section in the following article:

THE PATIENTS

TO THEIR DEFENSE

Lawyer Joseph Romano helps clients get health insurers to pay up. If they win, he wins big.

"What people don't realize is that obtaining health-insurance benefits is an adversarial process"
– Joseph Romano

By Elizabeth Seay

Most liability lawyers simply guide accident victims through the courts. Joseph Romano is a liability lawyer with a modern day twist: He also guides his clients through the mazes of managed care.

When insurers won't pay for treatments, Mr. Romano advises, negotiates and appeals the decisions. In some cases, he even persuades nurses, rehabilitation centers and other long-term health-care providers to treat his clients at no charge while he pursues personal-injury suits that he hopes will pay the doctors back. To get care, "you have to be aggressive, and use the law to help you," says the 44-year-old attorney.

Sign of the Times

A law practice like Mr. Romano's, at Rosenstein & Romano, the Norristown, Pa., law firm where he is a partner, could have sprung up only in today's health-care environment, doctors say. Dazzling but costly improvements in medical technology—such as artificial skin for burn victims and programs to stimulate brain activity in coma patients—are allowing injured people to live longer or recover more fully.

At the same time, the insurance system has become more cost-conscious, forcing patients to scrap for every penny. So more people are turning to lawyers to help them with everything from reading contracts to taking insurers to court when they are denied care.

"A lot of patients feel vulnerable and perceive that advocacy can help them," says Arthur Caplan, director of the center for bioethics at the University of Pennsylvania. "I think lawyers of this sort have a future in doing these battles."

Mr. Romano provided his brand of full-service law to Mary Ann Golobek of Bensalem, Pa. When her husband, David, suffered severe brain injuries in an auto accident on his way to work, his auto insurer, Harleysville Group Inc., balked at paying for any of the treatment amid questions over which of Mr. Golobek's insurance policies—auto or workers' comp—was responsible for coverage. With her husband's care in limbo, and treatment programs unwilling to even evaluate him without a commitment to pay, Ms. Golobek hired Mr. Romano.

"I was getting desperate, thinking I had thousands of dollars [in bills] at my house after five or six days, and I had nowhere to turn," says Ms. Golobek, a 39-year-old nursing instructor.

In negotiations with Harleysville, Mr. Romano established that the company was the primary insurer, but it couldn't cover all the treatment. The policy has a limit of $50,000 a year— for care that cost about $100,000 a year, covering such things as medical supervision speech therapy, physical therapy and psychological care.

So Mr. Romano got Beechwood Rehabilitation Services in Langhorne, Pa., to treat Mr. Golobek on contingency,while Mr. Romano sued the owners of the truck that allegedly caused the accident. If he loses, Mr. Romano won't get paid, and the doctors will get only the $50,000 a year from Harleysville. If he wins or reaches a settlement, Mr. Romano keeps a third of the payment, and the rest goes toward the family's medical bills.

Harleysville officials declined to comment on the case, citing their involvement in pending litigation against another of Mr. Golobek's insurers. Beechwood wouldn't discuss the financial arrangements in Mr. Golobek's case, but confirmed that it sometimes takes a patient without immediate payment while a liability case is pending.

Convincing Argument

It isn't easy to get doctors to wait for pay. But Mr. Romano, universally described as aggressive and articulate, makes a convincing argument. In the case of Destine Weightman, a child who suffered brain damage when she nearly drowned in a pool, Mr. Romano asked Bayada Nursing Agency of Moorestown, N.J., to care for the child. Mr. Romano described to the home-care group a strong case he was filing against the apartment complex that owned the pool and the company that provided the lifeguard. He also pointed out that "if the case is successful, [Bayada would] get paid dollar for dollar. A normal health-insurance company negotiates people down."

In the end, says Bayada's founder, Mark Baiada, "we did it to help the child." As for the risk, he adds that today plenty of insurers refuse to pay for care. "We are at risk in many cases," he says. "Every time you're dealing with insurance companies, you're in an unsure world."

In Destine's case, the risk paid off. Mr. Romano and co-counsel Shanin Specter won a sizable $24.3 million personal-injury verdict in 1995, though the amount was later reduced to $19 million. Bayada got its payment and some good publicity, and Mary and Robert Weightman, of Norristown, got funds to care for their daughter, now seven, for the rest of her life.

Of course, such service from a lawyer rarely comes without a price, and Mr. Romano makes a comfortable living from his practice. He and Mr. Specter, for example, divided $3 million from the Weightman case. Such fees—30% of the settlement—are standard, says Mr. Romano, who still lives in the unpretentious town where he grew up but these days drives a 1994 Mercedes S300.

Going It Alone

When it comes to routine medical disputes, some people believe that lawyers shouldn't be involved. "Lawyers are the last people who can mediate well," says Jeffrey O'Connell, a professor at the University of Virginia's law school. "They like to fight." Other lawyers note that state health commissions and nonprofit groups can provide advocates for a lot less money than lawyers charge.

Mr. Romano agrees that patients can do plenty of things on their own, without a lawyer, to appeal treatment decisions. To start with: while most people are issued a booklet with a sketch description of benefits, they can demand, and are entitled to have, the master provider agreement, the document containing the fine print of the whole policy.

The master agreement defines such terms as "medical necessity," "durable medical equipment" and "custodial care." It also spells out in greater detail the limits on coverage—for instance, specifying 10 days of outpatient therapy for certain injuries, or allowing coverage for a regular wheelchair but not a motorized one. In one case Mr. Romano tried, an insurance company denied a claim for injuries a patient suffered while riding an off-road all-terrain vehicle. The patient's family didn't know the master agreement contained a specific exclusion for injuries from ATVs.

Patients can also ask for the names and qualifications of the health plan's experts who decide which treatments are warranted. They also can ask how many times these doctors or others have made such decisions and how many times they have ruled in favor of the insurer.

If the system is set up to deny benefits arbitrarily, Mr. Romano says, the insurer is acting in bad faith—and can be taken to court. "By doing all this, you increase the chances that they're going to decide in your favor," he says. "If they turn the decision down, you're ready for the appeal."

The most important thing to understand, he says, is that patients need an advocate—if not a lawyer, a family member—to look out for their interests in the managed-care process. "All these people who are hired by managed care do not owe a duty to the patient," he says. "What people don't realize is that obtaining health-insurance benefits is an adversarial process."

'A Good Neuro-Lawyer'

Mr. Romano says he spends half of his time on activities to educate the public. A fiery orator and self-appointed expert on managed care, Mr. Romano has written many articles and given hundreds of speeches on benefits. (He says he usually waives his speaking fees.) He gives patients and audiences a book he published on the legal rights of the catastrophically ill and injured, and runs a toll-free fax service to field inquiries from families, doctors and other lawyers.

While all this educational work undoubtedly makes for good publicity—Mr. Romano estimates that he generates as much as a third of his referrals from such efforts. Many other lawyers and even doctors say the work is indeed valuable. "He's a good neuro-lawyer," says George Zitney, head of the Brain Injury Association, where Mr. Romano attended seminars on brain injuries and now helps train other lawyers. Brain injuries are an important part of Mr. Romano's practice, because they can affect victims in mysterious ways, which may be difficult for managed care decision makers to fully understand.

"My wife tells me my life is consumed by the law," says Mr. Romano, who took no summer vacation this year. He says he works 80-hour weeks and spends much of his free time reading up on medical cases. He has no children. "I always say my children are my cases," he says.

Mr. Romano traces his interest in fighting the powerful to his childhood. He grew up in Norristown, a small, largely blue-collar city outside Philadelphia. His father was a milkman while his mother worked at a school cafeteria. He got his first job at 11 as a golf caddy, and continued working through his teens as a waiter.

After putting himself through Ohio Northern law school in Ada, Ohio, he started out as a trial lawyer in 1977. "A small individual can be David and slay Goliath because of the jury system, and that always appealed to me, to represent the David," he says.

One Sunday, Mr. Romano saw a TV public service announcement for what was then called the Brain Injury Foundation. "I ran and got a pencil," he says, and soon began attending the foundation's seminars to learn more about the field.

Such training helps Mr. Romano argue against doctors in cases like Dennis Blanton's. An auto accident had left Mr. Blanton with severe head injuries and hearing problems. But his auto insurer, Erie Insurance Group of Erie, Pa., declined to pay for hearing aids, saying Mr. Blanton's hearing loss was insignificant and unrelated to his accident.

Mr. Romano asked Erie to review the decision, hired brain-injury specialists to evaluate Mr. Blanton and sent the specialists' reports to the independent doctor carrying out the review. The result: Erie agreed to pay for the hearing aids.

Erie declined to comment on the specifics of the case. "From a general insurance standpoint, I see a lot of instances where people don't need to hire a lawyer to settle their claim," says Keith Lane, vice president of corporate communications at Erie. "It adds cost, it adds time, and it takes money away from their settlements."

But Mr. Blanton disagrees. "A layperson cannot get through the insurance system," He says.

In addition to shepherding Mr. Blanton through the system, Mr. Romano sued the driver of the car that hit Mr. Blanton and got a settlement from that driver's insurer—also, coincidentally, Erie.

Since then, Mr.Blanton has made progress. Formerly a "walking dictionary" who disdained his computer spell-checker, he lost his spelling ability in his accident—but now he has learned how to spell again. He believes it is thanks to Mr. Romano that he has had the help of specialists in cognitive and eye therapy and round-the-clock care.

"The gift that Joe had was he knew my rights," says Mr. Blanton. "I would never have known what to do, especially in my condition."

Ms. Seay is a special writer for The Wall Street Journal in New York

LEGAL RIGHTS OF THE CATASTROPHICALLY ILL AND INJURED:

A FAMILY GUIDE
Second Edition

TABLE OF CONTENTS

v

I. IDENTIFYING LEGAL RIGHTS AND BENEFITS

After a catastrophic injury or illness occurs, the person or the person's family is confronted with a number of serious problems requiring qualified professional advice. Among the most significant questions asked by the families are:

Who is responsible to pay my medical bills and the cost of long-term care?

Can managed care, Medicare, Medicaid, automobile insurance or the worker's compensation carrier deny payment for the medical treatment my treating doctor recommends?

How do I know if our family member, who has a traumatic brain injury, needs a court-appointed guardian?

What should I do if the school district will not pay special education benefits when my ill or injured child returns to school?

What is the procedure to apply for Social Security Disability benefits, Supplemental Security Income benefits (SSI), Medicare, and Medicaid benefits?

What is the appeals procedure?

If there is more than one health insurance source, how do we determine which insurance policy pays first, and how can we be sure that the health insurance company is paying the maximum benefits available under the policy?

Are there time limits for applying for state and federal medical benefits?

How do I compile the evidence necessary to prove that the catastrophically ill or injured person is entitled to additional rehab, a longer hospital stay, a motorized wheelchair, home modifications, or other specific benefits?

How do we determine if the injury was caused by the negligence of some other person or corporation, and whether or not a personal injury claim seeking compensation should be pursued? What are the time limits for pursuing a personal injury claim?

This is not a "how-to" manual and is not intended as a substitution for qualified and experienced professional advice. You should consult a qualified attorney to discuss the specific facts and circumstances of your matter and your questions pertaining to medical and legal reimbursement.

1

A.   WHEN SHOULD I CONSULT AN ATTORNEY?

After a catastrophic injury occurs, the person and his family can benefit by consulting an attorney. Aside from answering legal questions and doing necessary legal work, the attorney may be able to provide options and offer suggestions (such as how to obtain help in paying medical expenses) that the family of the injured person was not aware of. Families should obtain prompt advice concerning guardianship, Social Security disability benefits, SSI (Supplemental Security Income) benefits, worker's compensation benefits, and COBRA. Many attorneys, particularly those concentrating on the personal injury field of the law, offer free initial interviews to clients. It is extremely important to contact a qualified attorney as soon as possible after a serious accident or injury so that your questions can be answered by a competent professional who can help you choose the best medical facilities and doctors to treat the particular medical problems of the injured individual.

If your questions involve a particular field of law, don't hesitate to ask the attorney whether he has extensive experience in that field of law. If not, the attorney may refer you to another attorney who does have experience in representing persons who have suffered serious and catastrophic injuries.

B.   HOW CAN AN ATTORNEY HELP?

The most common problem for families of catastrophically ill or injured persons is determining how to pay for past and continued medical treatment and care. The cost of acute, sub-acute and long-term care for the catastrophically ill or injured is astronomical and continues to escalate. Most lay persons, health care providers, and even many attorneys, are not aware of the countless medical benefits to which catastrophically ill and injured individuals are entitled. Medicare and Medicaid (state medical assistance coverage) are so restrictive that it is next to impossible to understand the complicated eligibility requirements without competent legal assistance.

If you have private health insurance it is difficult to determine what your health insurance policy will pay for without first obtaining the entire policy and reviewing it carefully. It is vital that an attorney assist you in coordinating all the potential sources of health care benefits, such as private health insurance, state and governmental assistance, programs offered through the Office of Vocational Rehabilitation (OVR), and special education benefits for children.

C.   WHERE DO I BEGIN TO FIND AN ATTORNEY?

Support Groups may be able to provide to the catastrophically ill or injured persons and their families preliminary assistance. It is common for the spouse and family of a seriously ill or injured individual to be physically and mentally exhausted from efforts to cope with the situation. Besides assisting the ill or injured person and his or her family in identifying resources that may be of help, most members of advocacy associations have ill or injured family members of their own, or are themselves recovering from injuries, and can provide understanding and support to those undergoing a similar experience. In many instances, the best therapy may be simply talking to someone who knows exactly how you feel, and who can provide the assurance that you are not alone.

You should be prepared to spend an extensive amount of time in the selection process of the attorney you hire. It is one of the most important decisions you will make. You should compile a list of names of attorneys you want to interview or speak with concerning your case, and schedule a telephone or in-person meeting with each attorney. You should not be deterred if you are unable to find an appropriate attorney nearby. An experienced attorney in other parts of the state, or even from another state, can coordinate with local counsel to insure that the injured person is properly represented.

To compile your list, you can ask for names of qualified attorneys from physicians and rehabilitation professionals who routinely treat individuals with catastrophic injuries; speak with individuals who are catastrophically ill or injured, and their family members, who attend local support group meetings at rehabilitation facilities in your area; contact local and state brain injury associations, spinal cord injury associations, burn foundations, etc.; and call state and national bar associations, who can often provide names of attorneys who handle catastrophic illness and injuries. As you search for an attorney who is experienced in representing individuals who are catastrophically ill and injured and their families, the same names will often be mentioned in your contacts with many different sources.

I often advise prospective clients to follow their instincts. No matter who you hire, you must be comfortable that the attorney you choose is going to do everything possible to see that you are fairly compensated. You have to feel that the attorney you hire is totally committed to your case.

D.   **HOW SOON AFTER A CATASTROPHIC INJURY OR ILLNESS SHOULD I HIRE AN ATTORNEY?**

Civil Law (the law of Torts) exists to compensate individuals and their families for illness, injuries, and losses which were caused by defective products, negligence, recreational injuries (swimming pool accidents), negligence of the driver of an automobile, or some other form of misconduct or failure to act. If you or a member of your family have sustained a catastrophic injury, you should consult with an attorney who has experience in this area of the law to determine whether a personal injury claim should be pursued.

Because evidence can be lost or discarded and witnesses' memories can fade, you should review the facts of your case with an experienced attorney as soon as possible. The facts and circumstances surrounding the accident should be investigated on behalf of the injured person by a trained investigator, engineer, or accident reconstructionist, to determine what caused the accident, to take photographs of the scene before certain landmarks are destroyed or altered, to examine and protect physical evidence, and to properly canvass the area of the accident scene to locate potential witnesses.

The goal in a personal injury claim is to compensate the injured person for both his out-of-pocket expenses, such as medical bills and lost earnings, and for the pain, suffering and disability that the injured person has endured and is likely to endure in the future.

E.   *WHAT QUESTIONS SHOULD I ASK AN ATTORNEY?*

The selection of an attorney can have significant long-term implications. This is a decision which will require consideration of many factors. You will likely have many questions to ask a prospective attorney. The questions listed below are intended as a guide for your information-gathering. In a catastrophic injury or illness case, it is always best to interview one or more attorneys before making your final choice.

How many catastrophically ill or injured individuals have you represented in the past, and how many are you currently representing?

What percentage of your practice is limited to representing catastrophically ill or injured individuals?

How many of your cases have resulted in substantial verdicts or settlements for catastrophically ill or injured individuals? Ask for specifics.

What is your involvement with spinal cord or brain injury associations, Cerebral Palsy Foundation, Phoenix Society, or other local or national organizations that advocate for the catastrophically ill or injured?

Have you spoken before any groups, or written any articles or books concerning legal issues affecting the catastrophically ill or injured population?

Based on the information you have about my situation/ case, what is your opinion of my case?

Is your firm capable and willing to advance the expenses necessary to investigate, prepare, and present my case?

What additional information about my case do you need to know, and how do you propose to obtain it?

F.   HOW DO I PAY FOR LEGAL ASSISTANCE?

Fees should be discussed with your attorney at the initial conference. In cases involving personal injury, a contingent fee agreement is used, in which the lawyer agrees to accept a fixed percentage of the recovery arising out of a settlement or lawsuit. You pay contingent fees only if the lawyer handles the case successfully. If you win the case, the lawyer's fee comes out of the money awarded to you. If you lose, neither you nor the lawyer will get any money. Also, in most states, you will not have to repay the lawyer for the basic operating costs and expenses advanced by the attorney to prepare your case, such as expert's fees, medical record copying, court filing fees, etc.

You can prevent misunderstandings concerning fees by insisting that all fee agreements be in writing, and that you receive a copy of any contingent fee agreement or fee agreement letter for your records.

Some legal services can be performed on an hourly basis. Examples of this type of work are: drafting a will, having a guardian appointed, and reviewing a health insurance policy.

G.   WHAT CAN I DO IF I HAVE ALREADY RETAINED AN ATTORNEY?

If you find yourself in the position of having hired an attorney who displays either inexperience, lack of skill, or disinterest in handling your claim, it is wise to consider changing attorneys, to get a second or third opinion about the handling of your case. A contingency fee retainer agreement, which is used in personal injury cases, does not bind a client to the attorney initially selected. Attorneys can be changed, subject to local and state bar association guidelines. Many clients refrain from doing so out of the misplaced fear that their legal fees will consequently increase. Attorney's fees are not increased, however, but are allocated between the initial and new attorney, either by their agreement or by court determination at the conclusion of the case.

CONCLUSION

The cases which an attorney is already handling are important evidence of his or her commitment to the representation of persons with catastrophic illness and injuries. Lawyers tend to concentrate on the type of cases about which they care. The absence of traumatic brain injury, spinal cord, amputation, burn, or other types of catastrophic illness or injury cases in an attorney's office evidences lack of experience or lack of interest in handling complex litigation involving catastrophic injuries.

Because of the abundance of attorneys, it requires special effort to find experienced and competent counsel for catastrophically ill and injured individuals and their families. You will be successful if you spend the time to research, ask many questions, speak with and/or interview a few attorneys, and choose an attorney who is committed to representing you and your family.

II. TIMETABLE - STATUTE OF LIMITATIONS, ADULTS AND MINORS

A.   *TIME DEADLINE*

As with any legal claim, personal injury claims must be initiated within a certain period of time. This period varies, depending upon the facts of the case and the state where the injury or accident occurred. If the case is not commenced before the deadline, the court will refuse to hear it. You should consult an attorney immediately to discuss the particular facts of your case, regardless of how much time has elapsed since the injury.

B.   *STATUTE OF LIMITATIONS - ADULTS*

Generally, in Pennsylvania and most states, an adult (a person over 18) must file a lawsuit against any responsible parties within two years of the date of the injury. Therefore, most injury claims must be filed within two years from the date of the injury, or the injured person is forever barred from bringing a claim against a person or insurance company to recover monetary damages for the injury.

C.   *ARE THERE ANY EXCEPTIONS TO THE TWO YEAR STATUTE OF LIMITATIONS RULE FOR ADULTS?*

Yes, the statute of limitations can be extended for adults if the injured person lacks knowledge of the relationship between the injury and the cause of the injury. This is known as the "***discovery rule***" and essentially refers to situations where the injured person does not discover that he or she may have been injured as a result of the omission or commission of certain persons or entities until many years after the illness or injury. An example would be the Dalkon Shield or IUD cases. In these circumstances the "discovery rule" will allow the statute of limitations to be extended beyond the general rule of two years from the date of the accident.

You should be cautioned that the courts will strictly abide by the time period in most states, including Pennsylvania. Do not rely upon the fact that the statute of limitations may be extended beyond the two year period, as the "discovery rule" is very complex and depends on the particular facts and circumstances of each case.

The prudent approach is to contact an attorney who is familiar with the rules of civil procedure in your particular state and obtain guidance immediately after the injury occurs, and not assume that the time period will be extended under the facts and circumstances of your particular case.

## D.	MUST A MINOR FILE SUIT WITHIN TWO YEARS FROM THE DATE OF THE INJURY?

In Pennsylvania, prior to June 30, 1984, a minor who was injured or had a claim had to file suit or bring the claim within two years of the date of the accident. Therefore, prior to June 30, 1984, the statute of limitations was the same for both adults and minors.

In Pennsylvania, after June 30, 1984, a minor child injured in any type of accident or case in which he or she has the right to bring suit has two years from the date he or she reaches majority, or 18 years of age, in which to file a lawsuit or bring about a civil action.

An example will illustrate the new Minor Statute of Limitations rule: Assume that on June 1, 1980, Tom Jones is one year old, and is hit by a truck. Under the old law, prior to June 30, 1984, Tom Jones' parents would have to initiate a claim of action or file a suit before June 1, 1982. Under the new statute, if Tom Jones is one year old and is injured on June 1, 1985, he will have two years from the time he reaches age eighteen to bring a claim; that is, seventeen years until he reaches eighteen plus two years after he reaches eighteen years of age, or an additional nineteen years, to file a claim.

The legislature passed this particular provision of the law to protect a minor's rights, since often the full extent of a minor's injuries are not known until many years after the accident. One example of an injury which is not known until many years after the accident is a developmentally delayed learning disability in children.

Granting parents of a minor two years from the date the minor reaches eighteen years of age to bring a claim allows both the treating professionals, the attorney, and the courts time to properly evaluate the medical and legal needs of the minor at the time the minor reaches majority.

Not all states have a Minor's Statute of Limitations law that is as broad as Pennsylvania's. You should examine the Minor Statute of Limitations law that applies to the facts and circumstances of your case, in your state, immediately after a serious accident or injury occurs.

## E.	WHAT ARE THE SPECIFIC REQUIREMENTS FOR NOTICE AGAINST A MUNICIPALITY, COUNTY, BOROUGH OR STATE?

Most states require that a notice be sent to a municipality or governmental unit that a suit may be filed against them by an injured individual or his representative. The time period in which the notice must be given varies from state to state. Pennsylvania law requires that a notice must be sent to a municipality or governmental unit that suit may be filed against them within six months of the date of the injury. The six-month notice must be given, whether or not the individual injured in the accident is an adult or a minor. If the injured person is a minor, or in a coma, or otherwise incapacitated, the six-month notice requirement must be met by the parent, other family member, or the court-appointed guardian.

The Pennsylvania Legislature requires the six-month municipal or governmental unit notice so that the municipality, etc., will have sufficient time to investigate the causes of the accident. Many municipalities now have their own trained investigators, who look for skid marks, evidence, witnesses, etc.

Therefore, as soon as possible after a serious accident, and prior to sending the six-month notice letter to the municipality, the facts and circumstances surrounding the accident should be investigated on behalf of the injured person by a trained investigator and engineer to determine what caused the accident, to take photographs of the scene before certain landmarks are destroyed, to examine physical evidence, and to properly canvass the area of the accident scene to locate potential witnesses.

F. **WHAT IS THE STATUTE OF LIMITATIONS FOR A PERSON WHO IS INCAPACITATED OR IN A COMA?**

The statute of limitations for a person who is in a coma or otherwise incapacitated is two years from the date of the injury, unless the person is a minor, in which case the new minor's statute previously discussed would apply.

Arguments have been made that the requirement that a person who is an adult and incapacitated or in a coma must file a lawsuit within two years of the date of the accident or injury is unfair. Quite often the guardians or family members are unaware of the time limitations, and are normally deeply involved in the rehabilitation process during the early stages of the injury.

Since Pennsylvania's legislature and courts have chosen to require that an incapacitated person's lawsuit be filed within two years from the date of his or her injury or illness, it is imperative that family members and the court-appointed guardians thoroughly investigate the accident or occurrence and identify the potential sources of benefits immediately after a catastrophic injury or illness has occurred.

Although it is understandable that family members and health care providers focus their concern on the immediate medical needs of the individual, a thorough legal investigation of the case will usually produce additional sources for medical benefits and future rehabilitation. I have attempted to clarify and stress the need for a prompt inquiry into whether or not there are sources of medical benefits which can be recovered and a determination of whether or not all legal time requirements have been met.

III. DURABLE POWER OF ATTORNEY

A. POWER OF ATTORNEY - LIMITED RIGHT

A Power of Attorney is a right which is given by one competent individual to another, granting that person the right to do a specific act for the competent individual, such as write checks, open bank accounts, sign legal documents, etc. A power of Attorney ceases if the competent individual revokes the Power or Attorney, or becomes incapacitated, unless that person has executed a Durable Power of Attorney.

B. DURABLE POWER OF ATTORNEY - BROADER RIGHT

A durable power of attorney is a specific document in which a competent individual, prior to his or her incapacitation, names another person to act on his or her behalf at such time as that individual becomes unable to manage his or her own affairs. The person named in the durable power of attorney will serve as the guardian of the individual without the necessity of petitioning the court to have the individual declared incapacitated in the event of a medical disability.

Durable power of attorneys are underused. A durable power of attorney should be signed by every competent patient who is catastrophically ill or injured. If the durable power of attorney is signed and the patient's medical condition deteriorates, it will not be necessary to file a petition with the court to seek a formal guardianship. Hospitals and health care providers are required under the **Patient Self-determination Act** to discuss the use of a durable power of attorney with patients and their families. Unfortunately, most health care facilities do not take the time to have a social worker or patient advocate sit down and explain why the signing of a durable power of attorney would be beneficial.

Managed care, HMO's, and the "health care landscape", mandates prompt decision-making by injured persons, or their family members. Incorporating a properly executed durable power of attorney into a patient's medical records will aid in this process. Discharge planning will not be delayed while a formal guardianship is being pursued in the courts.

C. *SAMPLE DURABLE POWER OF ATTORNEY FORM*

POWER OF ATTORNEY

KNOW ALL MEN BY THESE PRESENTS, that I, _____
_____, have constituted, made and appointed, and
by these Presents do constitute, make and appoint _____
_____ my true and lawful attorney:

1.   To ask, demand, sue for, recover and receive all sums of money, debts, goods, merchandise, chattels, effects and things of whatsoever nature or description which are now or hereafter shall be or become owing, due, payable, or belonging to me in or by any right whatsoever, and upon receipt thereof, to make, sign, execute and deliver such receipts, releases or other discharges for the same, respectively as [**he/she**] shall think fit.

2.   To deposit any moneys which may come into [**his/her**] hands as such attorney with any bank or banker, either in my or [**his/her**] own name, and any of such money or any other money to which I am entitled which now is or shall be so deposited to withdraw as [**he/she**] shall think fit; to sign mutual savings bank and federal savings and loan association withdrawal orders; to sign and endorse checks payable to my order and to draw, accept, make endorse, discount, or otherwise deal with any bills of exchange, checks, promissory notes or other commercial or mercantile instruments; to borrow any sum or sums of money on such terms and with such security as [**he/she**] may think fit and for that purpose to execute all notes or other instruments which may be necessary or proper; and to have access to any and all safe deposit boxes registered in my name.

3.   To sell, assign, transfer and dispose of any and all stocks, bonds, including U.S. Savings Bonds, loans, mortgages, or other securities registered in my name; and to collect and receipt for all interest and dividends due and payable to me.

4.   To invest in my name in any stock, shares, bonds, securities or other property real or personal, and to vary such investments as [**he/she**] in [**his/her**] sole discretion, may deem best; and to vote at meetings of shareholders or other meetings of any corporation or company and to execute any proxies or other instruments in connection therewith.

5.   To enter into and upon all and singular my real estate, and to let, manage, and improve the same or any part thereof, and to repair or otherwise improve or alter, and to insure any buildings thereon; to sell, either at public or private sale or exchange any part or parts of my real estate or personal property for such consideration and upon such terms as [**he/she**] shall think fit, and to execute and deliver good and sufficient deeds or other instruments for the conveyance or transfer of the same, with such covenants of warranty or otherwise as [**he/she**] shall see fit, and to give good and effectual receipts for all or any part of the purchase price or other consideration; and to mortgage; including purchase money mortgage, and to execute bonds and warrants and all other instruments and documents in connection therewith and relating thereto, and such power shall not be in limitation of any other powers herein set forth.

6.   To contract with any person for leasing for such periods, at such rents and subject to such conditions as [**he/she**] shall see fit, all or any of my said real estate; to let any such person into possession thereof; to execute all such leases and contracts as shall be necessary or proper in that behalf; to give notice to quit to any tenant or occupier thereof; and to receive and recover from all tenants and occupiers thereof or of any part thereof all rents, arrears of rent, and sums of money which now are or shall hereafter become due and payable in respect thereof; and also on nonpayment thereof or of any part thereof to take all necessary or proper means and proceedings for determining the tenancy or occupation of such tenants or occupiers, and for ejecting the tenants or occupiers and recovering the possession thereof.

7.   To commence, prosecute, discontinue or defend all actions or other legal proceedings touching my estate or any part whatsoever, or touching any matter in which I or my estate may be in any wise concerned; to settle, compromise, or submit to arbitration any debt, demand or other right or matter due me or concerning my estate as [**he/she**], in [**his/her**] sole discretion, shall deem best and for such purpose to execute and deliver such releases, discharges or other instruments as [**he/she**] may deem necessary and advisable; and to satisfy mortgages, including the execution of a good and sufficient release, or other discharge of such mortgage.

8.   To execute, acknowledge and file Federal, State and local income tax and personal property tax returns.

9.   To engage, employ and dismiss any agents, clerks, servants or other persons as [**he/she**] in [**his/her**] sole discretion, shall deem necessary and advisable.

10.   In general, to do all other acts, deeds, matters and things whatsoever in or about my estate, property and affairs and things herein, either particularly or generally described, as fully and effectually to all intents and purposes as I could do in my own proper person if personally present, giving to my said attorney power to make and substitute under [**him/her**] an attorney or attorneys for all purposes herein described, hereby ratifying and confirming all that the said attorney or substitute or substitutes shall do therein by virtue of these presents.

11.   In addition to the powers and discretion herein specially given and conferred upon [**him/her**] and not withstanding any usage or custom to the contrary, to have the full power, right and authority to do, perform and to cause to be done and performed all such acts, deeds, matters and things in connection with my property and estate as [**he/she**] in [**his/her**] sole discretion, shall deem reasonable, necessary and proper, as fully, effectually and absolutely as if [**he/she**] were the absolute owner and possessor thereof.

12.   This Power of Attorney shall not be invalidated or affected by my subsequent disability or incapacity.

IN WITNESS WHEREOF, I have hereunto set my hand and seal this_____ day of _____ , **[year]**.

_____(Seal)

Witness:

_____

STATE OF   :
                            SS.
COUNTY OF   :

On this ____ day of _____ , **[year]**, before me, a Notary Public, came the above-named _____, and acknowledged the within Power of Attorney to be **[his/her]** act and deed, and desired the same to be recorded as such.

Witness my hand and seal, the day and year aforesaid.

_____
               Notary Public

My commission expires:

13

IV. GUARDIANSHIP

A.   *QUESTIONS AND ANSWERS; PRACTICAL PROBLEMS AND PROCEDURES*

In some states, unlike Pennsylvania, the courts still use the term "incompetent" when an individual is unable to manage his own affairs and money, rather than the term adopted in Pennsylvania, "an incapacitated person". The guardianship procedures in most states, and the most commonly asked questions posed by family members and health care providers are discussed below.

1.   *What is a guardianship?*

Guardianship is a legal relationship between one individual (the guardian) and an incapacitated individual (the ward) which gives the guardian the right and the duty to act on behalf of the incapacitated party in making decisions which affect that person's life. Unless the guardianship is limited by the court in some way, the guardian will manage all of the incapacitated party's personal, legal and financial affairs.

2.   *When do I need a guardian?*

A guardian is necessary when an individual suffers a catastrophic injury, illness , or is otherwise so disabled that the individual is unable to make responsible decisions concerning his medical, legal and financial needs and manage his daily affairs.

3.   *Why is a guardian needed?*

A guardian has the legal responsibility of safeguarding the incapacitated person's welfare.

If the person handling the incapacitated party's affairs is not a court-appointed guardian, and this person dies, becomes himself disabled because of illness or injury, or chooses not to continue to assist the incapacitated party, orderly and timely transfer of responsibilities to another person can be difficult to accomplish to insure that someone will act in the incapacitated party's behalf.

However, if a guardian has been appointed by the court, and that guardian ceases to act for any of the above reasons, the court will promptly replace that person with another court-appointed guardian, to assure that all the rights and benefits due the incapacitated person are continued without interruption.

Some of the various responsibilities and functions of a guardian are:

a.   Consult with the treating doctors concerning proper medical treatment and placement, if necessary;

b.   Legally give authorization for inspection of medical records by signing a release of medical information for:

    (1)   Medical Assistance;

    (2)   Worker's compensation insurance companies;

    (3)   Social Security Disability;

    (4)   Medicare/Medicaid;

    (5)   Blue Cross/Blue Shield;

    (6)   HMO's;

    (7)   Others.

c.   Legally refuse or limit access to the incapacitated party's medical records in order to protect the individual's right to continuing health care and insurance benefits[1];

d.   Open bank accounts and write checks;

e.   Keep records of all financial transactions;

f.   Safeguard the incapacitated party's assets;

g.   Legally speak for the incapacitated party as an advocate for that individual's best interest;

h.   Apply for governmental benefits, Social Security Disability, Supplemental Security Income and state medical benefits;

i.   Apply for no-fault benefits;

j.   Safeguard continuity of health care;

k.   Set up proper Trust and Estate planning;

l.   In an injury case, retain an attorney to investigate the cause of the accident, seeking catastrophic health care benefits;

m.   Institute legal action to protect the incapacitated party's rights against:

    (1)   the insurance company, for payment of proper medical benefits;

    (2)   the party who caused the accident, seeking catastrophic health care benefits; or

---

1 This will be better explained in the Managed Care Section.

(3)   the school district, for failing to provide required special education benefits for minor children;

n.   Meet notification requirements under applicable state laws to protect the incapacitated party's right to seek catastrophic health care benefits;

o.   Use evidence of a declaration of incapacitation by the court in obtaining governmental benefits and catastrophic health care benefits from insurance companies.

4.   *Who should be appointed guardian?*

a.   *Spouse, Family Member.*

Generally, I believe the guardian should be a family member who is responsible and will work in the incapacitated individual's best interests. Usually, a husband, wife, parent, or next-of-kin is appointed guardian by the court. The court will not appoint someone guardian unless that person is over 18 years of age and the court feels that the person will act in the best interests of the incapacitated individual.

b.   *Bank.*

It is sometimes a good idea to have co-guardians; often the family member is the guardian of the person, and the professional or a bank is the guardian of the estate. Banks are often used as guardians of the estate where there are substantial assets to be invested or a minor is involved. Each set of circumstances should be discussed with your attorney and with the family members involved, to determine which person or persons would be the best guardian for the incapacitated individual.

5.   *What is the procedure for appointing a guardian?*

a.   *Costs, Jurisdiction, Contents of Petition.*

If you decide that appointment of a guardian is required, a petition must be filed in the orphans' court in the county in which the disabled individual resides. The petition must state certain information, which varies from county to county, but essentially it requires information concerning the relationship of the proposed guardian to the incapacitated individual, financial information of the incapacitated individual, facts and circumstances which led to the particular injury or illness, and medical documentation.

Upon receiving a petition for the appointment of a guardian, the orphans' court will hold a hearing to determine if there is sufficient medical documentation to appoint a guardian. Most courts will require that the treating doctor testify in person concerning medical aspects of the case. However, some courts will not require the doctor to testify and will appoint a guardian if the doctor files a notarized medical report or deposition with the court.

Most attorneys will charge an hourly rate or an agreed-upon fee for filing a guardianship petition and attending a guardianship hearing. If you cannot afford an attorney's legal services, you should still obtain a consultation with an attorney familiar with guardianship matters and possibly that attorney can refer you to a Legal Aid Society or non-profit foundation that could assist you in filing the guardianship papers at a nominal cost.

6. *Is it necessary for the incapacitated individual to appear in court?*

The requirements to have a guardian appointed vary, but generally if the treating doctor states that it would be against the best interest of the incapacitated individual to appear in court, the court will usually not require his or her appearance. Sometimes the judge will want to visit the incapacitated individual to discuss the appointment of the guardian, especially if the individual is able to communicate his or her wishes to the judge.

7. *Is a guardianship revocable?*

Yes, a guardianship is revocable. The incapacitated individual, or anyone acting on his or her behalf, may ask the probate court at any time to remove the guardian or revoke the guardianship. Medical documentation of the treating doctor is necessary to revoke a guardianship.

8. *Do parents have to petition the court for legal guardianship of their minor child?*

No, it is not necessary for the parent to petition the court to be appointed guardian if the incapacitated individual is under 18 years of age. Parents are the natural guardians of their minor children and it only becomes necessary for a parent to file the petition with the court requesting appointment as guardian once the child reaches the age of 18. As soon as possible after an injury occurs, a parent should discuss with an attorney the steps that should be taken to protect the welfare of the child, such as the proper drafting of Wills, estate planning, investigation of special education benefits, and circumstances of how the injury occurred.

It is often very difficult for a family member to think about the issue of guardianship, but it is crucial that this matter be discussed as soon as possible with the family, your doctors, and your attorney, so that the interests of the incapacitated individual are protected.

9.   *What is the legal test to determine if a person is incapacitated?*

As previously mentioned, the legal test to determine whether or not a person is incapacitated in Pennsylvania is an adult whose "ability to receive and evaluate information effectively and communicate decisions in any way is impaired to such a significant extent that he is partially or totally unable to manage his financial resources or meet essential requirements for his physical health and safety".

The decision of whether or not a person meets the legal test for incapacity is made by a judge, based on medical documentation from the treating physician. It is not necessary that the doctor's report be obtained from a psychiatrist. The court will accept a report or testimony from any medical doctor who has examined the patient and can give an opinion, based upon reasonable medical certainty, as to whether or not a guardian is necessary.

10.   *Why is the term "incapacitated person" used?*

The word "incapacitated person" is a "legal term of art" which means that the court has determined that the individual can no longer manage his or her own affairs, and needs a guardian. Many times, clients or families will inquire as to whether or not they can be appointed as guardian by the court for their family member without a determination of incapacity being made by the court. This is not possible, as state guardianship laws require that an adult individual be declared incapacitated before a guardian can be appointed by the court.

11.   *Is it difficult to have a person declared incapacitated?*

Courts are reluctant to declare a person incapacitated unless it is absolutely necessary and is based upon proper medical documentation.

12.   *How can I be sure a guardian is necessary?*

Each case must be judged on its own facts. I recommend that the treating doctor meet with the social worker, case worker, interested family members, proposed guardian, and attorney to discuss whether or not everyone agrees that a guardian is necessary. This approach alleviates court battles and enables the attorney to present unanimous opinion on behalf of the treating professionals and interested family members that a guardian is needed in a particular case. Since, as I indicated earlier, the courts are reluctant to declare a person incapacitated, a consistent approach with comprehensive medical information will insure that a particular court will appoint a guardian without delay.

13. *What are some of the factors that the court uses to determine who to appoint as a guardian?*

a. Relationship to alleged incapacitated person: Example: Spouse, brother, parent, etc.

b. Age: The proposed guardian must be over eighteen.

c. Educational and financial background of the proposed guardian.

d. Health of guardian.

e. Geographical proximity.

f. Adverse interests: The guardian is not permitted to have any adverse interest to the alleged incapacitated person. For example, the proposed guardian is not permitted to have any litigation pending against the alleged incapacitated person. The proposed guardian, if that person is a spouse, will not be appointed if there is a divorce pending against the alleged incapacitated person.

14. *Will the court appoint a guardian for a specific period of time?*

a. *Temporary guardian.*

If there is a medical or legal emergency, the court will appoint a temporary guardian pending a hearing to determine whether or not a permanent guardian is necessary.

b. *Permanent guardian.*

Normally the court will appoint a permanent guardian for an indefinite period of time and will revoke the guardianship once it is not medically necessary.

15. *Who is appointed a guardian if no family members or friends are qualified to serve as guardian?*

The court has the power to appoint anyone as guardian in this case, and often will appoint an attorney or a bank to serve as guardian where there are no qualified relatives or friends.

In Pennsylvania, the Legislature has adopted a guardianship support section, see Section IV, Guardianship, B, 10, page 24.

16. *Who should file the guardian petition with the court when there are no family members available to file the petition?*

In these cases a request should be made to the Legal Aid office in the county where the individual resides, since they will often provide free legal counsel and file a guardianship petition. Legal Aid attorneys should not request that they themselves be appointed as guardian, but should only be filing the petition with the court asking the judge to appoint an appropriate guardian for the person, based on medical evidence.

17. *Must family members receive notice of guardianship proceedings?*

There is usually one court proceeding, at which time the judge hears evidence, and all family members must receive notice of that hearing by certified mail. This gives interested family members the opportunity to testify in court, ask any questions that they may have, or to provide the court with relevant information concerning the health of the alleged incapacitated individual.

18. *What happens if a court-appointed guardian dies, becomes ill, or changes his or her mind concerning serving as guardian?*

In all of these cases, the court will appoint another guardian. This is a simple procedure and can be accomplished by requesting that the court, which appointed the original guardian, appoint a substitute guardian.

19. *Can the assets of an incapacitated person be protected in any way by the court?*

a. *Bond.*

The court can require a guardian to post a bond, insuring that the assets will be protected in the event they are lost, misappropriated, or improperly handled.

b. *Accounting.*

Each court will set its own procedure requiring periodic accounting statements which must be prepared by the court-appointed guardian. The statement lists any monies that have been received, any disbursements or checks that have been written on the guardianship account, and the balance of funds remaining in the account.

20. *Must the court approve a settlement of a lawsuit for an individual who has a court-appointed guardian?*

Yes, the court must approve any settlement of a lawsuit for an individual who has a court-appointed guardian. The reason is that the court must determine if a particular settlement is in the best interests of the incapacitated person. The court continues to assume jurisdiction over all financial matters involving an individual who has a court-appointed guardian until the guardianship has been revoked. Based upon medical information, it must be shown that the person is able to manage his or her affairs and money.

The issue of guardianship is sometimes avoided because it is an emotional issue, but it is crucial that family members and professionals discuss the issue of guardianship with each other as soon as possible after the catastrophic illness or injury occurs, in order that the best interests of the disabled individual are protected.

B.   *PENNSYLVANIA GUARDIANSHIP LAW*

1.   *Purpose of Guardianship Law Containment Provisions.*

The purpose of the guardianship changes are to "promote the general welfare of all citizens by establishing a system which permits incapacitated persons to participate as fully as possible in all decisions which affect them; which assists these persons in meeting the essential requirements for their physical health and safety, protecting their rights, managing their financial resources and developing or regaining their abilities to the maximum extent possible; and which accomplishes these objectives through the use of the least restrictive alternatives..." It is important to find appropriate individuals or entities willing to serve as guardians".

2.   *Incapacitated—not incompetent.*

Many family members in the past found the word "incompetent" to be worrisome and demeaning, and they confused the guardianship proceedings with the mental health system. There was a misconception that once an individual was declared "incompetent" the incompetency decree could not be revoked.

The previous definition of an "incompetent" was an individual unable to manage his property, liable to dissipate it or become the victim of designing persons, or lacking sufficient capacity to make or communicate responsible decisions concerning his person. Under the new provisions, the term "incapacitated" or "incapacitated person" has been substituted for the term "incompetent".

An "incapacitated person" is an adult whose "ability to receive and evaluate information effectively and communicate decisions in any way is impaired to such a significant extent that he is partially or totally unable to manage his financial resources or meet essential requirements for his physical health and safety".

This new definition of incapacity retains the concept of a separate guardian of the estate and a guardian of the person.

3.   *Evidence required at guardianship hearing.*

In order to begin guardianship proceedings, a petition must now be given to the alleged incapacitated person in "simple language". Notice of the hearing shall indicate the date, time and place of the hearing;

purpose and seriousness of the proceeding; description of the rights that can be lost; and the incapacitated person's right to request counsel.

The petition must include reasons why a guardianship is sought, a description of the functional limitations and physical and medical condition of the alleged incapacitated person, and the steps that have been taken to find a less restrictive alternative. The court in its order must specify the duties that the guardian has powers to accomplish, i.e. medical decisions, check writing, etc.

Detailed testimony must be presented in person or by deposition establishing the nature, extent of disabilities, mental, emotional and physical condition, behavior, and social skills.

The evidentiary test has been changed from "good cause shown" to "clear and convincing evidence"; this requires a higher degree of proof.

The alleged incapacitated person must be present at the hearing unless the court, upon the deposition, testimony or sworn statement of a physician or licensed psychologist, is satisfied that the person would be harmed by his or her presence.

4.   *Right to counsel and independent medical examination.*

As under the previous guardianship rules, anyone may file a Petition requesting that a guardian be appointed for an incapacitated person. The petitioner is required to notify the court at least seven days prior to a hearing if counsel has not been retained by or on behalf of the incapacitated person. In some cases, counsel for the alleged incapacitated person will be appointed by the court. If the person is unable to pay for counsel or for the cost of a court-appointed independent medical evaluation, the court shall order the county to pay for these costs.

5.   *Who may be appointed guardian?*

The court may appoint as guardian a qualified individual, a corporate fiduciary, a non-profit corporation, the newly recognized guardianship support agency, or a county agency. In the case of residents of state facilities, the court may also appoint, as guardian of the estate only, the guardian office at the appropriate state facility.

A guardian of the person or estate of an incapacitated person may be appointed by the court of the county in which the incapacitated person is domiciled, is a resident, or is residing in a long term care facility. A guardian may also be appointed by the court of any county where an asset of the incapacitated person is located.

The court shall consider and make specific findings of fact concerning the nature of any condition or disability which impairs the individual's capacity to make and communicate decisions; the extent of the individual's capacity to make and communicate decisions; the need for guardianship services in light of such factors as the availability of family,

22

friends and other support to assist the individual in making decisions, and the existence, if any, of any advance directives such as a Durable Power of Attorney; and the duration of the guardianship.

6. _Limited guardian and plenary (total) guardian of the person and of the estate._

Upon a finding that the person is only partially incapacitated, the court shall enter an Order appointing a limited guardian of the person. The powers of the limited guardian may include general care, maintenance and custody of the incapacitated person; designating the place for the person to live; assurance that the person receives the proper training, education, medical, psychological, social and vocational services.

The court may only appoint a plenary (total) guardian of the person upon a finding that the person is totally incapacitated.

A limited or plenary guardian of the person would have authority to make all decisions for the incapacitated person except those decisions pertaining to the incapacitated person's assets or income. Only a guardian of the estate would have the authority to make decisions concerning the incapacitated person's assets and income. The court may appoint either a limited guardian of the estate or a plenary (total) guardian of the estate, and shall specify the portion of assets or income over which the guardian of the estate is assigned powers and duties.

A person with a plenary guardian shall be incapable of making a Will, contract or gift.

7. _Emergency guardian._

An "emergency guardian", previously called a "temporary guardian" may now be appointed under appropriate circumstances. Usually, an emergency guardian is appointed by the court when there is some legal or medical urgency. The emergency guardian is appointed for a period of time up to 72 hours. The emergency order can be extended for a period of no more than 20 days from the expiration of the initial emergency order; however, this is decided on a case by case basis.

8. _Revocation of incapacity decree._

The **Pennsylvania Guardianship Law** provides for review hearings in the event of a significant change in a person's capacity, a change in the need for guardianship services, or a guardian's failure to perform duties in the best interest of the incapacitated person.

9.   _Record keeping and reporting._

The Act requires that each guardian file a detailed report with the court at least once within the first twelve months of appointment, and at least annually thereafter, attesting to certain information concerning the economic, mental and physical well being of the incapacitated person.

10.   _Guardianship support._

The Act creates guardianship support agencies to provide guardianship services when there are no family members willing to serve as the court-appointed guardian. A guardian support agency may be available to serve as either guardian of the estate or the person, or both. If a guardian support agency is appointed, it is not necessary that a specific individual of the guardian support agency be designated by the court. These support agencies are available to assist courts, guardians, petitioners and others, in all aspects of guardianships, including providing information on available alternatives to potential petitioners and filing petitions for guardianship. Recipients of guardianship services shall be charged by the agency for services based on their ability to pay. The provisions state that "guardianship support agencies shall make every effort to minimize cost, including minimizing personnel costs through the use of volunteers".

11.   _Miscellaneous provisions._

In the past, it was very difficult to have a guardianship hearing in any forum other than a county court house. The new Act allows a hearing to be held, with court approval, at the institutional residence of the alleged incapacitated person.

A guardian may not, without orphans' court approval, consent to an abortion, sterilization, psychosurgery, electroconvulsive therapy or the removal of a healthy body organ. Neither may a guardian prohibit a marriage, consent to a divorce, nor consent to the performance of any experimental, biomedical, behavioral or medical procedure.

C.   SAMPLE DOCTOR'S LETTER RE: INCAPACITATION

"In Re: (_Joseph Smith_)

Dear Mr. Romano:

(_Joseph Smith_) is a _(30 year old male)_ who was involved in a(n) _(type of accident)_ on (_date of accident_). (_Mr. Smith_) was admitted to (_name of hospital_) on (_date of admission_) for intensive rehabilitation for a (_closed head injury, etc._), which (_he_) sustained in the accident of (_date of accident_).

I am a medical doctor who has practiced (*medicine, psychiatry, psychology, etc.*) since 19__: (*List any special qualifications and training with respect to evaluating persons with incapacities.*)

(*Joseph Smith*) is presently suffering from the following medical problems; (*memory disorders, seizures, paralysis, etc.*), and is an incapacitated person. (*Mr. Smith*) has a (*tracheostomy, respirator, gastro-feeding tube, etc.*).

A description of (*Mr. Smith's*) functional limitations and physical and mental condition are as follows: (*describe*). The medical diagnosis of (*Mr. Smith's*) injury is (*closed head injury with frontal lobe brain damage, anoxia, etc.*) In my judgment, and based upon my training, experience and acquaintance with (*Mr. Smith*), I believe the probability that (*his*) incapacities may significantly lessen or change is _____. The prognosis for (*Mr. Smith*) is (*poor/guarded, etc.*)

(*KEY LANGUAGE*)

On the basis of my examination and treatment of (*Mr. Smith*) on _____, 19__, it is my medical opinion based upon reasonable medical certainty that (*Joseph Smith*) lacks the ability to receive and evaluate information effectively and communicate decisions in any way, and is impaired to such a significant extent that (*he*) is totally unable to manage (*his*) financial resources or meet essential requirements for (*his*) physical health and safety and is, therefore, incapacitated. (*Mr. Smith*) requires a guardian of the person and of the estate.

I would recommend that a guardian be named by the court to provide to (*Mr. Smith*) the services necessary to meet (*his*) essential requirements for physical health and safety, and to manage (*his*) financial resources.

It is my opinion, based upon reasonable medical certainty, that (*Mr. Smith's*) presence at the incapacity hearing would be harmful to (*his*) physical or mental condition.

Very truly yours,

John Jones, M.D."

V. GUARDIAN AD LITEM

A.   *WHAT IS A GUARDIAN AD LITEM?*

A Guardian Ad Litem is usually an attorney who is appointed by the court to advocate for the best interests of a child. For example, if a child only has one living parent, and that parent is driving an automobile under the influence of alcohol, hits a tree and catastrophically injures the minor child who is a passenger - a claim for insurance benefits could be brought on behalf of the minor child against the insurance company that insured the natural parent. A suit cannot be filed by the natural parent since the parent would have to bring a claim against themselves, but can be filed by an attorney appointed by the court to advocate the best interests of the child. The independent person appointed by the court is a Guardian Ad Litem.

B.   *WHEN IS A GUARDIAN AD LITEM NECESSARY?*

A Guardian Ad Litem is necessary when there is a conflict between parents and children, when there is no one who is adequately representing the interests of the injured child, or in certain domestic proceedings, such as custody cases, visitation and abuse proceedings. As indicated above, in personal injury matters involving catastrophically injured children, a Guardian Ad Litem protects the interests of the catastrophically injured child by filing a claim for insurance benefits against anyone responsible for causing the accident. Often, the natural parents are deceased or unavailable and in these cases, the court will appoint a Guardian Ad Litem to protect the best interests of the injured child. A Petition for the appointment of a Guardian Ad Litem is usually filed with the court by an attorney, interested family member or child welfare department.

C.   *WHAT ARE THE DUTIES OF A GUARDIAN AD LITEM?*

The duties of a Guardian Ad Litem are:

1.   Legally advocate for the child's best interests;

2.   In an accident case, retain an attorney to investigate the cause of the accident and seek catastrophic health care benefits;

3.   Institute legal action to protect the child's rights;

4.   Seek special education benefits;

5.   Meet notification requirements under applicable state law to protect the child's rights to seek catastrophic health care benefits;

6.   Attend domestic, custody and child abuse hearings;

7.   Thoroughly examine all records, meet with treating doctors, and present relevant information to the court for the court to determine what is in the best interest of the child.

CONCLUSION

Determining competency issues will enable healthcare providers to identify the decision-makers and to treat with legal authority. The court-appointed guardian will be able to apply for state, federal and other benefits, and to focus on discharge planning issues at the time of admission and not the day before discharge.

VI. PATIENTS' RIGHTS

As we approach the 21st century, it is necessary for the role of health care professionals to evolve with the current changes in the nation's health care system. The medico-legal issues on which health care professionals need to focus to insure the protection of patients' rights are the issues of the patient's right of self-determination and informed consent, guardianship, living wills, and the patient's right-to-life/right-to-die decisions.

A. *PATIENT SELF-DETERMINATION ACT*

As of December 1, 1991, the **Patient Self-Determination Act** required health care facilities to advise newly admitted patients of their right to accept or refuse treatment should they become gravely ill. This Act applies to most health care providers—hospitals, skilled nursing facilities, home-health agencies, hospices and prepaid organizations—that accept Medicaid or Medicare.

Patients are entitled by law to state their wishes in documents known as "advance directives". The most common of these are living wills and healthcare proxies (also known as a "Durable Power of Attorney"). According to a 1996 study by the Gallup Organization, only about 20% of adults have living wills or durable powers of attorney.

A living will outlines the life-prolonging treatment a patient would choose should he or she become unable to make medical decisions. With healthcare proxies, patients designate someone to make health care decisions for them.

The Act requires health care providers to do the following:
1. Provide adult patients with written notice of (1) their state law regarding a patient's right to consent to, or refuse, care and to formulate advance directives regarding health care, and (2) the relevant policies of the particular institution;

2. Inquire whether the patient has executed an advance directive and document the response in the medical record;

3. Educate the staff on these issues;

4. Insure compliance with any state law applicable to any advance directives (such as durable power of attorney, living will, etc.);

5. Maintain written policies and procedures implementing the above requirements.

In many hospitals, admissions personnel make the initial inquiry about whether a patient has advance directives. Some facilities provide patients or their families with written or videotaped information, or more extensive interviews with a nurse, doctor, social worker or patient advocate.

The *Patient Self-Determination Act* does not require a competency determination but a health care provider would be prudent to first determine the issue of competency before discussing authority to treat, living wills and healthcare directives.

A facility or health care provider may not require that patients execute advance directives as a condition of admission or treatment.

B.   *LIVING WILL*

1.   **Pennsylvania Advance Directive for Health Care Act -** Living Will Law

Pennsylvania's action on living wills became important when the federal government passed the *Patient Self-Determination Act* on December 1, 1991. This Act requires hospitals and nursing homes that accept Medicare to inform patients about state laws on living wills legislation and health care directives.

On April 16, 1992, a living will statute was enacted in Pennsylvania. The *Pennsylvania Advance Directive for Health Care Act* provides an opportunity for individuals to contemplate issues of death and dying while they are still competent and able to state their preferences in writing. The Act states that "all competent adults have a qualified right to control decisions relating to their medical care, subject to certain interests of society, such as the maintenance of ethical standards in the medical profession and the preservation and protection of human life." The Act also acknowledges that "modern medical technological procedures make it possible to prolong life beyond natural limits" and that "the application of some procedures to individuals suffering a difficult and uncomfortable process of dying may cause them to lose patient dignity and secure only the continuation of a precarious and burdensome life." In the event an individual does not have a written health care directive, *Cruzan* and Pennsylvania case law are still applicable to those who make verbal declarations regarding the withholding and withdrawal of life-sustaining procedures.

2.   Definitions

The *Advance Directive for Health Care Act* - Living Will Bill sets forth important definitions, as follows:

a.   Incompetent

Someone is "incompetent" when they lack the sufficient capacity to make and communicate decisions concerning themselves. As indicated, the burden of making a determination as to incompetency rests with an "attending physician."

b.   Terminal Condition

Someone is in a "terminal condition" when they have "an incurable and irreversible medical condition in an advanced state caused by injury, disease or physical illness which will, in the opinion of the attending physician, to a reasonable degree of medical certainty, result in death."

c.   Permanently Unconscious

Someone is "permanently unconscious" when they have "a medical condition that has been diagnosed in accordance with currently accepted standards and with reasonable medical certainty as a totally irreversible loss of consciousness and capacity for interaction with the environment. The term includes a persistent vegetative state or irreversible coma."

d.   Life-Sustaining Treatment

Any medical procedure or intervention which "will serve only to prolong a process of dying or to maintain the patient in a state of permanent consciousness" is a "life-sustaining treatment." The administration of nutrition and hydration, euphemistically labeled food and water by some, is one of the seven categories of procedures, alluded to above, and is specifically spelled out in this definition to avoid any doubt or misunderstanding.

e.   Revocation

A declarant may revoke his or her writing at any time and in any manner, including orally, by communicating such an intention to the "attending physician" or other "health care provider," or to a witness of the revocation which is made in writing. It should be noted that a revocation can be made "without regard to the declarant's (current) mental or physical condition."

f.   Attending Physician, Health Care Provider, Medical Command Physician

An "attending physician" is a physician who has the primary responsibility for the treatment care of declarant. A "health care provider" is a state licensed or certified person, defined to include both individuals and institutions, and personnel, such as a "medical command physician." defined and recognized under the *Emergency Medical Services Act* of July 3, 1985 (P.L. 164, No. 45).

3. *Who may execute a Living Will?*

Any individual of sound mind who is 18 years of age or older, or who has graduated from high school or is married, may execute a declaration governing the initiation, continuation, withdrawing or withdrawal of life-sustaining treatment. The declaration must be voluntarily executed by the declarant or other authorized person and must be witnessed by two individuals, each of whom is 18 years of age or older. A sample Advance Health Care Declaration is contained in the Act.

4. *What can a person include in his or her Living Will?*

The declaration may not only include specific treatment directions, but a person may also designate another individual to make health care decisions for him or her if he or she becomes incapacitated and is determined either to be in a "terminal condition" or to be "permanently unconscious".

5. *When does a Living Will become effective?*

A Living Will becomes effective when a copy of the declaration is provided to the person's attending physician, and when the physician thereafter determines that the individual is incapacitated and either in a terminal condition or a state of permanent unconsciousness.

If the doctor determines that the individual is incapacitated and unable to congnitively sign an Advance Health Care Declaration, then a petition should be filed with the court to have a guardian of the person and guardian of the estate appointed. The court-appointed guardian would then have the authority to make decisions concerning the withholding and withdrawal of life sustaining procedures, subject to the approval of the court.

An attending physician is the physician who has the responsibility for the treatment and care of the declarant. When the declaration becomes effective, both the attending physician and any other health care provider must, except for reasons of "conscience", act in accordance with the patient's previously stated declarations. If the attending physician or other health care provider, for reasons of "conscience", cannot comply with the declaration, notice must be given to the patient's surrogate, family or guardian or other representative. The attending physician or other health care provider must make every reasonable effort to assist in the transfer of the patient/client to another physician or health care provider who will comply with the declaration.

The withholding or withdrawal of life-sustaining treatment in accordance with the provisions of the Act, does not, for any purpose, constitute suicide or homicide. No hospital, physician, or other health care provider shall require any person to execute a declaration as a condition

31

for being insured, receiving health care services, or charging different rates or fees.

6. *Should a Living Will be made a part of a Declarant's Medical Records?*

Attending physicians are required to make a Living Will a part of the patient's medical records. The Act contains a liability section that provides that no physician or other health care provider who complies with the Health Care Directive Act and Living Will Declaration shall be subject to criminal or civil liability.

An attending physician has a duty to confirm either a terminal condition or state of permanent unconsciousness by obtaining a second opinion from another physician.

7. *Are there specific guidelines in Pennsylvania when a pregnant woman has a Living Will?*

Notwithstanding the existence of a declaration or direction to the contrary, life-sustaining treatment, nutrition and hydration must be provided to a pregnant woman who is incompetent and has a terminal condition and is permanently unconscious unless, to a reasonable degree of medical certainty as certified on the patient's medical record by the attending physician and an obstetrician who has examined the patient, life-sustaining treatment, nutrition and hydration: (a) will not maintain the pregnant woman in such a way as to permit the continuing development and live birth of the unborn child; (b) will be physically harmful to the pregnant woman; or (c) would cause pain to the pregnant woman which cannot be alleviated by medication.

Conclusion

The **Advance Directive for Health Care Act** sets forth clear guidelines for families and the health care community which allow everyone to contemplate death and dying and health care issues while they are still competent. Signing an Advance Health Care Declaration will remove all questions and doubt from family members and the health care community in regard to the treatment wishes of the individual. All persons should have a Will, an Advance Directive for Health Care Declaration (Living Will), and a Durable Power of Attorney.

8. *Sample Living Will*

I,_____, being of sound mind, wilfully and voluntarily make this declaration to be followed if I become incompetent. This declaration reflects my firm and settled commitment to refuse life-sustaining treatment under the circumstances indicated below.

I direct my attending physician to withhold or withdraw life-sustaining treatment that serves only to prolong the process of my dying, if I should be in a terminal condition or in a state of permanent unconsciousness.

I direct that treatment be limited to measures to keep me comfortable and to relieve pain, including any pain that might occur by withholding or withdrawing life-sustaining treatment.

In addition, if I am in the condition described above, I feel especially strong about the following forms of treatment:

I ( ) do ( ) do not want cardiac resuscitation.
I ( ) do ( ) do not want mechanical respiration.
I ( ) do ( ) do not want tube feeding or any other artificial or invasive form of nutrition (food) or hydration (water).
I ( ) do ( ) do not want blood products.
I ( ) do ( ) do not want any form of surgery, or invasive diagnostic tests.
I ( ) do ( ) do not want kidney dialysis.
I ( ) do ( ) do not want antibiotics.

I realize that if I do not specifically indicate my preference regarding any of the forms of treatment listed above, I may receive that form of treatment.

Other instructions:

I ( ) do ( ) do not want to designate another person as my surrogate to make medical treatment decisions for me if I should be incompetent and in a terminal condition or in a state of permanent unconsciousness.
Name and address of surrogate (if applicable): _____
_____,
_____

Name and address of substitute surrogate (if surrogate designated above is unable to serve):
_____,
_____

I made this declaration on the _____ day of
_____ (month), _____ (year).

Declarant's signature:
_____

Declarant's address:
_____

The declarant or the person on behalf of and at the direction of the declarant knowingly and voluntarily signed by his writing by signature or mark in my presence.

Witness's signature: _____

Witness's address:

_____

Witness's signature: _____

Witness's address:

_____

C.   *INFORMED CONSENT*

As early as the 18th century, a physician was legally obligated to obtain a patient's consent. If a physician did not obtain a patient's consent, the patient had a remedy which was compensable under the intentional tort theory of battery. A battery is harmful or offensive bodily contact with a patient without the consent of the patient. Traditionally, the key element to prove a battery was not the intent of the physician but the absence of patient consent.

1.   *What is the doctrine of informed consent?*

It is a well established legal principal that health care professionals, including paramedics and emergency medical technicians, are responsible for making adequate disclosures of information to the patient and obtaining the patient's informed consent. The basis of the doctrine of informed consent is that the patient has a right to determine what shall be done with his or her own body.

2.   *What must be discussed with a patient in order for a patient to give "Informed Consent"?*

The health care professional should discuss:

    a.   Diagnosis

    b.   Nature and purpose of treatment

    c.   The desired outcome

    d.   The hazards or risk of the medication, treatment or proposed health care

    e.   Chances of success or failure

    f.   Alternative procedures which could achieve the desired medical result

    g.   Likely medical consequences without any treatment at all

3.   *What is Actual Consent?*

Actual consent is when a health care professional has explained the risks, alternative procedures, and expected consequences to a competent adult, to the parent of a minor child for the child, or to the court-appointed guardian of an individual who has been declared incapacitated, and then the consent form is signed.

4.   *What is Implied Consent?*

Implied consent is a legal theory that evolved because ill or injured individuals were unable to grant a health care professional actual consent. The most common situation where the court will use the doctrine of implied consent is an emergency situation. Health care professionals, paramedics and emergency medical technicians (EMT's) can transport an individual to a facility and treat an adult, minor, or any individual in an emergency without anyone's consent, since in an emergency a patient's consent is implied.

5.   *When does an emergency exist?*

Generally, an emergency exists when a patient is suffering from a life-threatening disease or injury that requires immediate treatment.

6.   *Can an individual refuse medical care?*

A competent adult has the right to accept or refuse medical care. There is no clear-cut answer to the question of whether or not a paramedic or EMT should transport someone to a hospital if they refuse or request not to be transported. Generally, if the patient is of clear mind, not under the influence of drugs or alcohol, and appears to understand the EMT or paramedic, the health care professional has to decide at the scene what is the best course of action.

In most jurisdictions, a health care professional administering emergency treatment at an accident scene will abide by the wishes of the patient if he or she is minimally injured and refuses to be transported to a hospital for observation. If it is clear that an individual is under the influence of drugs or alcohol, or is in a life threatening medical emergency but refuses to be transported to the nearest hospital for medical treatment, the police should be called to assist. Remember, consent will be implied where a patient is suffering from a life-threatening disease or injury that requires immediate treatment, even if the individual patient is refusing to give verbal consent.

7.   *Can a minor receive medical treatment or paramedic services without the consent of a parent?*

A minor can be provided medical treatment in an emergency situation without a parent's consent.

8.   *Can a person who is unconscious or comatose receive medical treatment or paramedic services?*

When there is a life-threatening emergency, health care professionals can provide medical services and treatment to an individual who is unconscious or comatose, since consent is implied.

9.   *How long does an emergency last? How long can health care professionals provide treatment in an emergency situation?*

There is no clear-cut rule as to how long an emergency lasts. It could last from a few days to a week, and during this time medical personnel are permitted to give necessary treatment to the patient at an acute care facility. If it becomes evident that an adult will remain in a coma for a long period of time, the family members should be advised that it will be necessary to have the court appoint a guardian for the comatose individual.

Paramedics, EMT's, and first responders should be cautioned to document their records of all trips. The records should indicate:

a.   Whether the person was unconscious or conscious;

b.   That all procedures were explained to the individual and consent was given;

c.   If the person refused transport and/or treatment, document why you believed this was "informed consent";

(1)   The person did not appear to be under the influence of drugs or alcohol;

(2)   That the patient said he or she was not knocked unconscious;

(3)   That the patient indicated that he or she was not in any pain;

(4)   That the person indicated that he or she did not want to go to the hospital and the reason why.

Because emergency medical personnel can make hundreds of "trips" per year, it will be difficult, without properly documented records, for a paramedic or EMT to support a particular decision concerning the issue of consent.

36

D.   RIGHT-TO-DIE

1.   Overview

The **Right to Die** and to decline medical treatment is embodied in the XIVth Amendment Due Process clause of the Constitution. You have the right to control what happens to your body. The right to die has been codified in the United States Constitution. You have the right to decline medical treatment. Therefore, the right to die arises from three places: A common law right of self-determination; the U.S. Constitution; the doctrine of informed consent.

2.   Review of Cases: Karen Quinlan; Nancy Cruzan

a.   **Karen Quinlan case** - Karen Quinlan lapsed into a coma. Her parents requested the New Jersey court to authorize the discontinuance of the use of a mechanical respirator to sustain the vital processes of their daughter, who was in a persistent vegetative state. The court authorized the removal of the respirator, since Ms. Quinlan had expressly evidenced during her life that she not be sustained by artificial means. In **Quinlan**, the court stated that individuals must have expressed their wishes with regard to medical treatment, hydration and nutrition, while they are living. It is not sufficient that a patient wishes to die, or that he or she agrees with the termination of life, if the patient did not expressly indicate his or her wishes before death. The court also indicated that before it would authorize the removal of a respirator or life-sustaining medical treatment, the patient must be in an irreversible, persistent, vegetative state.

Usually, a neurologist or other qualified doctor will be required to testify in court that the person is in a persistent vegetative state. In most cases, more than two medical opinions are obtained.

b.   **Nancy Cruzan case** - The United States Supreme Court upheld a state's authority to stop the removal of food, water, or other life-prolonging treatment from permanently unconscious patients whose wishes are unknown or unclear. The court upheld Missouri's authority to keep Nancy B. Cruzan, a 32 year old comatose woman, alive despite her parents' desire to withdraw a surgically implanted feeding tube. The woman suffered severe head injuries when she was thrown from her car in a crash, and never regained consciousness. The only treatment provided was a gastrotomy tube through which she received food and water.

The court ruled that the Constitution does not forbid any state from preserving the life of an incompetent person unless a surrogate produces "clear and convincing" proof that the patient would have wanted to die rather than live in a vegetative state. While the court did not state that there is a Constitutional right to die, it suggested such a right may exist for those individuals who have made a clear declaration of their intention in a document such as a Living Will.

3.   *Pennsylvania cases*

a.   ***Jane Doe*** - Competent individual - Right to remove life support system.

A Pennsylvania court had never decided the issue of whether a hospital may remove a life-support system from a patient who is competent, but terminally ill, until 1987.

In September 1987, the Philadelphia Court of Common Pleas faced this issue, based on the following facts: an adult, mature, competent woman had been a patient in a hospital since January 21, 1987. She suffered from ALS, commonly referred to as Lou Gehrig's disease. The medical evidence was clear that the patient was terminally ill.

The patient requested that the life-support system be removed. Her family agreed with her decision, but the hospital wanted the court to decide the complex legal issues involved before it complied with the patient's decision.

On August 26, 1987, Judge Samuel M. Lehrer ruled that the hospital and physician could remove the life-support system from the patient suffering from ALS.

It is very helpful to look specifically at some of the court's conclusions of law in this case. The court stated the following:

(1)   "The refusal of medical treatment or the discontinuance of medical treatment by a person is a common law right to self-determination and a right of privacy under the U.S. Constitution Amendment XIV."

(2)   "Such right is not absolute. It is subject to the state's interest in the preservation of life, protection of and for innocent third parties, prevention of suicide, and maintenance of the ethical integrity of medical practice."

(3)   "A person who is <u>competent</u> and asserts or requests a refusal of medical treatment or its continuance, has standing to bring an action for appropriate relief in his or her own name." (Emphasis added)

(4)   "Mental competence for such purposes involves the following determinations: (1) does the patient understand his/her current condition; (2) is the patient able to make independent decisions about his/her welfare and medical treatment; (3) does the patient understand what would happen if the current condition goes untreated; (4) does the patient understand what the proposed treatment consists of; (5) does the patient understand the complications, benefits and risks of the pro-

posed treatment, and finally; (6) overall, does the patient have the ability to perceive the world realistically, think clearly and make a judgment of the above mentioned considerations with an accurate understanding of the consequences of such conduct both physically and emotionally to himself/herself, his/her family, and his/her loved ones."

The court ruled the following:

(5)   "Jane Doe is competent to make an informed, intelligent and independent decision concerning her mode of treatment, its refusal and discontinuance."

(6)   "Based on the findings of fact in this case, no state interest as above set forth nor any combination thereof is paramount to Jane Doe's right to privacy and self determination."

(7)   "The denial of Jane Doe's choice by any agency of the Commonwealth or by this court would constitute a violation of her right to due process under the U.S. Constitution, Amendment XIV, and under the Pennsylvania Constitution, Article 1."

(8)   "The removal or discontinuance of the ventilator or any other life-support system, by the physician and/or hospital or any other person designated by either of them is not conduct which aids or abets the commission of a suicide prohibited by 18 Pa.C.S.A. 2505 (Purdon 1973) nor is it criminal conduct violative of any other criminal statute in or of this Commonwealth."

(9)   "The removal or discontinuance of the ventilator or any other life-support system by the physician and/or hospital or any other person designated by either of them is not conduct which constitutes the crimes of criminal homicide under 18 Pa. C.S.A. 2501 et seq (Purdon 1973) or any other conduct defined as a crime in or of this Commonwealth."

(10)   "No civil liability attaches or shall attach, neither under the statute or case law of this Commonwealth, on the part of the physician or hospital or any person designated by either of them by reason of the removal or discontinuance of the ventilator or any other life-support system."

This case is helpful, as it provides guidelines for the legal and health care communities when a competent individual wishes a life-support system withdrawn.

b.   ***Ragona*** - Right to remove life-support system from an Incompetent Individual.

Ruth Ragona was age 64 when she suffered a massive stroke in February 1990, and as a result she lapsed into a coma. An artificial feeding tube was inserted to sustain her life, and her family filed a request that the artificial feeding tube be withdrawn. Four certified neurologists testified that Ruth Ragona was in a persistent vegetative state with absolutely no likelihood of recovery. For the first time in Pennsylvania, the Lackawanna Court in a 1990 decision recognized the right to die in Pennsylvania for an incompetent individual. Essentially in **_Ragona_**, the court held that Mrs. Ragona was in a persistent vegetative state and the family had met its burden of proving by clear and convincing evidence that she had expressed her wishes during her lifetime that she did not want to be kept alive by artificial means. Mrs. Ragona had written and requested a living will document after reading and listening to stories about the **_Cruzan_** case. Although Mrs. Ragona never had time to execute the living will document for which she had written, the fact that she had requested this document was clear evidence of her intent. In addition, Mrs. Ragona's family testified that she had clearly expressed her intent not to be kept alive by artificial means numerous times prior to lapsing into a persistent vegetative state.

c. **_Fiori_** - Right of a substituted decision-maker to remove life-support system from an incapacitated individual.

Daniel Joseph Fiori suffered his injuries in 1972, when he was 20 years old. In 1976, his condition deteriorated while he was being treated in a long-term care facility. Fiori never regained consciousness, and slipped into a persistent vegetative state. His mother, Rosemarie Sherman, had attempted to have the nursing home where Fiori was a patient, withdraw her son's feeding tube. Fiori's mother believed that her son, who was physically active, would not have wanted to exist living in the coma, and decided on that basis that his treatment should be stopped. Because Fiori had left no living will, the nursing center where he resided, demanded a court order before it would allow his feeding tube to be removed. The lower court ruled that no such order was necessary. It found that if two doctors determined Fiori's condition would not improve, his mother could make the decision on her own (the "substituted judgment doctrine").

On April 2, 1996, a unanimous Supreme Court ruled that "A close family member is well-suited to the role of substituted decision maker." This ruling makes Pennsylvania the 25th state to have a law or legal precedent permitting close relatives to make life-sustaining treatment decisions, with the consent of two qualified physicians, for an individual who is incapacitated and in a persistent vegetative state.

4. _Guidelines: The terminally ill do not have a constitutional right to physician-assisted suicide_

Attempting to make medical and legal decisions for a catastrophically ill or injured person is a difficult process. Certain guidelines should be followed:

a. The competency of a patient must be determined before any medical treatment is rendered, and this issue should be re-evaluated as a patient's medical condition changes;

b. In the absence of a Durable Power of Attorney, a guardian should always be appointed for the incapacitated person. Medical professionals can place themselves in a difficult position if they provide medical services to an incapacitated person without authority from the patient or a court-appointed guardian;

c. In most states, a competent individual does have the right to remove life-support systems and refuse hydration and nutrition;

d. In most states, life-support systems can be withdrawn from an incapacitated individual if the petitioners have met the burden to prove by clear and convincing evidence that the person is in a persistent vegetative case and by evidence that the person, during his or her lifetime, decided not to be kept alive by artificial means;

e. In many states, including Pennsylvania, the courts have adopted a "substituted judgment doctrine" which permits a close relative, with the consent of two physicians, to make life-sustaining treatment decisions for an individual who is incapacitated;

f. All individuals who are competent should execute a will, a durable power of attorney, and a living will.

Throughout the nation there are approximately 10,000 patients in a persistent vegetative state who are being kept alive with medical technology. Unfortunately, only about 20% of U.S. citizens have Living Wills. The *Cruzan* and *Ragona* decisions underscore the need for a living will, durable power of attorney, and court-appointed guardian. Because of the increasing use and sophistication of medical technology, the legal and medical communities face the issues of Resuscitate vs. Do Not Resuscitate, custodial care vs. rehabilitation, quality of life decisions concerning future care, and when to remove life-support systems. The court's decisions in *Quinlan*, *Cruzan*, *Ragona*, and *Fiori* are a first step toward promulgating standards for the medical/legal community in the right-to-life/right-to-die area.

In 1997, in a unanimous decision, the United States Supreme Court ruled that terminally ill patients do not have a constitutional right to physician-assisted suicide. The court did give states the leeway to enact laws that would allow patients to end their lives. According to a recent poll by the American Medical Association, 50% of those surveyed said they favored doctor-assisted suicide. The recent Supreme Court decision to uphold state laws banning assisted suicide will not end the debate about the right-to-die. Indeed, Oregon voters, the only group in the nation to vote for allowing assisted suicide, voted in favor of this on the ballot in November 1997. Justice Sandra Day O'Connor while agreeing there is no broad-based constitutional right to assisted suicide, defined a "narrower question" of "whether a mentally competent person who is experiencing great suffering has a constitutional cognizable interest in controlling the circumstances of his or her imminent death." The Supreme Court's decision will not end efforts to legalize the practice of physician-assisted suicide, nor alter the real-life dilemmas faced by catastrophically ill and injured persons and their families.

E.   **PATIENT'S BILL OF RIGHTS**

1.   _Pennsylvania Patient's Bill of Rights_

The following are minimal provisions for the Patient's Bill of Rights:

- A patient has the right to respectful care given by competent personnel.

- A patient has the right, upon request, to be given the name of his attending physician, the names of all other physicians directly participating in his care, and the names and functions of other health care persons having direct contact with the patient.

- A patient has the right to every consideration of his privacy concerning his own medical care program. Case discussion, consultation, examination, and treatment are considered confidential and should be conducted discreetly.

- A patient has the right to have all records pertaining to his medical care treated as confidential except as otherwise provided by law or third party contractual arrangements.

- A patient has the right to know what hospital rules and regulations apply to his conduct as a patient.

- The patient has the right to expect emergency procedures to be implemented without unnecessary delay.

- The patient has the right to good quality care and

high professional standards that are continually maintained and reviewed.

- The patient has the right to full information in layman's terms, concerning his diagnosis, treatment, and prognosis, including information about alternative treatments and possible complications. When it is not medically advisable to give such information to the patient, the information shall be given on his behalf to the patient's next of kin or other appropriate person.

- Except for emergencies, the physician must obtain the necessary informed consent prior to the start of any procedure or treatment, or both.

- A patient or, in the event the patient is unable to give informed consent, a legally responsible party, has the right to be advised when a physician is considering the patient as a part of a medical care research program or donor program, and the patient, or legally responsible party, must give informed consent prior to actual participation in such a program. A patient, or legally responsible party, may, at any time, refuse to continue in any such program to which he has previously given informed consent.

- A patient has the right to refuse any drugs, treatment, or procedure offered by the hospital, to the extent permitted by law, and a physician shall inform the patient of the medical consequences of the patient's refusal of any drugs, treatment or procedure.

- A patient has the right to assistance in obtaining consultation with another physician at the patient's request and own expense.

- A patient has the right to medical and nursing services without discrimination based upon race, color, religion, sex, sexual preference, national origin, or source of payment.

- The patient who does not speak English should have access, where possible, to an interpreter.

- The hospital shall provide the patient, or patient designee, upon request, access to all information contained in his medical records, unless access is specifically restricted by the attending physician for medical reasons.

- The patient has the right to expect good management techniques to be implemented within the hospital considering effective use of the time of the patient and to avoid the personal discomfort of the patient.

- When medically permissible, a patient may be transferred to another facility only after he or his next of kin or other legally responsible representative has received complete information and an explanation concerning the needs for and alternatives to such a transfer. The institution to which the patient is to be transferred must first have accepted the patient for transfer.

- The patient has the right to examine and receive a detailed explanation of his bill.

- The patient has a right to full information and counseling on the availability of known financial resources for his health care.

- A patient has the right to expect that the health care facility will provide a mechanism whereby he is informed upon discharge of his continuing health care requirements following discharge and the means for meeting them.

- A patient cannot be denied the right of access to an individual or agency who is authorized to act on his behalf to assert or protect the rights set out in this section.

- A patient has the right to be informed of his rights at the earliest possible moment in the course of his hospitalization.

See 28 PA Code 103.22.

F.   *PARENTS' BILL OF RIGHTS*

The Parent Task Force of the Research and Training Center in Rehabilitation and Childhood Trauma has developed a Parents' Bill of Rights based on their experiences. This Bill of Rights indicates that parents of injured children have the right to:

- Be able to take care of yourself first in order to be able to care for your child.

- Ask questions.

- Receive information clearly and in words you can understand.

- Be a member of the rehabilitation team.

- Be with your child during testing or examination if your child requests it or is frightened.

- Have a role in evaluating the value of a risky or intrusive procedure and the discomfort and possible risks to your child.

- Be angry and to act appropriately.

- Know the financial costs of care and the benefits and limits of your insurance.

- Ask for independent professional advice before agreeing to any financial settlements with insurers or other third parties.

- Be informed of all choices for rehabilitation programs and have the opportunity to visit them and participate in the selection process.

- Participate in the discharge planning process and the development of continuing care plans.

VII. YOU AND YOUR MEDICAL RECORDS

A. *CONFIDENTIALITY*

Physician-patient confidentiality is required in the Hippocratic oath. That oath requires the physician to pledge:

"Whatever in connection with my professional practice, or not in connection with it, I see or hear, in the life of men, which ought not be spoken of abroad, I will not divulge, as reckoning that all should be kept secret."

According to a 1993 poll by Harris and Associates, 85% of the public believe that protecting the confidentiality of health records is absolutely essential. Despite the fact that the public considers confidentiality a top priority, many health care advocates argue that as a result of the policies of managed care organizations and the computerization of medical records, confidentiality is eroding. Today, patients are generally required to sign blanket authorizations, giving the insurer access to any confidential medical information. Catastrophically ill or injured individuals and their families must insist that their treating health care professionals not discuss their care with insurers, rehabilitation nurses, case managers, governmental agencies, employers, or anyone requesting information, without first obtaining a specific, detailed medical release from patients or their court-appointed guardian or representative.

B. *YOUR RIGHT TO YOUR MEDICAL RECORDS*

Although it is generally conceded that the hospital or physician are the owners of your medical records, both common law and Pennsylvania law have recognized your right as a patient to have access to your own medical records.

Unfortunately, only fourteen states have established the right of patients to get both hospital and doctor's records. In Pennsylvania, you must be given access to, or copies of, your medical records in accordance with the Pennsylvania Patient's Bill of Rights, 28 Pa. Code 103.21-103.24.

According to a policy statement of the 1985 Joint Committee on the Accreditation of Hospitals, medical records are to be kept "confidential, secure, current, authenticated, legible, and complete." The Joint Committee report stated that hospital records should contain, at a minimum, the following data:

1. The patient's identification information;

2. The patient's duly executed consent to treatment;

3.   The patient's medical history;

4.   Reports and results of laboratory tests;

5.   Diagnostic orders;

6.   Therapeutic orders;

7.   Observation of the patient's condition;

8.   Reports of medical action taken and the findings from consultations;

9.   Pre-operative, operative, and post-operative reports;

10.   Medical conclusions including provisional diagnosis, primary diagnosis and final diagnosis;

11.   Clinical resumes;

12.   Autopsy reports;

13.   Discharge summaries.

Numerous studies have indicated the advantages of permitting a patient free and complete access to medical records. According to a study conducted by the Medical Center Hospital of Vermont, when patients are permitted free and complete access to their medical records, cooperation between physician and patient was markedly increased, and patient anxiety was reduced. 80% of patients who had access to their records were more careful about following recommendations for medication after seeing them in writing, and 97% worried less about their health care.

C.   *MEDICAL RELEASES*

Laws governing access by third parties to your medical records vary from state to state. Some states prohibit certain government agencies and law enforcement officials from obtaining medical information without patient authorization, a subpoena or a court order. Unfortunately, some hospitals or facilities will release information to insurance companies and other third parties without a proper, specific authorization from the patient.

In Pennsylvania, unless otherwise provided by law, access to medical records is limited to authorized medical personnel in the absence of consent by the patient. If a patient is admitted to a hospital, he gives permission by implication for all medical personnel involved with his treatment to see his medical records. In addition, a patient's records can be reviewed by hospital committees which are constituted to monitor the care of patients.

Hospitals, doctors, or other health care facilities should not release patient's records without a properly signed, currently dated, authorization signed by either the patient or his legally appointed representative.

If your family member or relative is involved in a serious accident or illness and you do not want information released to a newspaper or other source, you should advise the hospital at the initial intake interview so that the records may be marked accordingly: "Not to release information without specific consent of patient, parent, or court-appointed guardian".

Unless the patient or his representative specifically denies the medical institution permission to release this information, certain biographical and chronological information provided to a hospital by a patient may be considered "not confidential" and could be released to police, government agencies or the press.

Other information may be available to police or government agencies whether or not the patient consents. This information would include dangerous communicable diseases, poisonings, child abuse, and gunshot wounds.

You should be wary of signing a release allowing an insurance company to have unlimited access to your medical records. The best approach is to ask the insurance company what specific information they need from the hospital or your treating physician, then either you or your attorney can obtain that information from your doctor, and forward it to the appropriate insurance company.

You have the ultimate responsibility to review your medical records for accuracy and limit access by unauthorized persons. By accepting this responsibility and participating in your medical care, you will increase communication between you and your doctor, and become an active part of the health care team.

D.   *PSYCHOLOGICAL / PSYCHIATRIC MEDICAL RELEASES*

Most health care facilities will require that a special psychological/psychiatric medical release be obtained from the patient, parent or court-appointed guardian before releasing records relating to mental health treatment.

E.   *X-RAYS, CAT SCANS*

X-rays and CAT scans are a part of an individual's medical record and must be kept with a person's file or stored separately so that a patient can have prompt access. On request, a patient, parent or court-appointed guardian must be provided the original x-rays, CAT scans or duplicate copies. A hospital can charge a reasonable cost for the reproduction of the x-rays, CAT scans, etc. Some hospitals indicate that they will only release x-rays, CAT scans or medical records to another doctor or hospital. This is not a proper policy since an individual's complete medical file must be provided to the patient who desires these records.

F.   *VIDEO TAPES*

Hospitals, especially rehabilitation facilities, are videotaping occupational therapy sessions, speech therapy sessions and cognitive retraining. Video tapes are a part of a patient's medical records and must be released to the patient upon request. As with x-rays and CAT scans, the hospital may keep the original video tape but they must provide a copy of the video tape to the patient, parent or court-appointed guardian at a reasonable cost. Many facilities are having difficulty storing video tapes because they use a single video tape to tape three or four patients. This is not a wise procedure. If one of the patients request a copy of the video tape, then the hospital will have to go to the expense of editing the video tape. Some hospitals are destroying video tapes after an individual leaves their facility. This is improper since the video tape is an integral part of the patient's medical record. A hospital would not usually destroy a CAT scan or x-ray but some do not realize the importance of a video tape. Often hospitals "tape over" the therapy sessions after the individual is discharged or has been transferred to another facility.

G.   *COPYING MEDICAL RECORDS*

A patient, parent or court-appointed guardian has the right to a copy of all their medical records. The medical facility should provide these medical records to the patient or his representative in a prompt manner. Sometimes there are excessive delays in providing medical records to a patient or a patient's representative. This can cause difficulty when a patient is obtaining a second opinion or the family is trying to arrange discharge planning. When this occurs, patients and families are often apprehensive that they are not receiving complete medical records.

The hospital or treating medical practitioner is entitled to reimbursement for the cost of copying medical records. Individuals can designate a medical copying service as their representative to actually copy the medical records, and this can often expedite the procedure.

VIII. FAMILY AND MEDICAL LEAVE ACT

A.   *QUESTIONS AND ANSWERS*

1.   *What is the Family and Medical Leave Act of 1993? When did it become effective?*

The **Family and Medical Leave Act of 1993** is federally mandated legislation that allows qualifying individuals to take reasonable leave from their employment "for medical reasons, for the birth or adoption of a child, and for the care of a child, spouse or parent who has a serious health condition." The Act took effect in February of 1994 for all qualified individuals.

2.   *Who is affected by the Family and Medical Leave Act?*

The Act applies to qualifying employers and qualifying employees. A "qualifying employer" has at least 50 employees who have worked at least 20 work-weeks during the current or preceding calendar year. A "qualifying employee" works at a site with at least 50 other employees. The employee must have worked for the employer for at least 12 months, and worked at least 1,250 hours during the 12-month period prior to the requested leave.

3.   *What length of leave is a qualified employee entitled to under the Act?*

A qualified employee is entitled to a total of 12 weeks of unpaid leave per year for either family or medical reasons.

4.   *Can the employer require that an employee use paid vacation time or other paid leave as part of the mandatory 12 weeks under the Act?*

An employer may require that an employee use paid vacation time or other paid leave as part of the mandatory 12 weeks, i.e. if an employee has five weeks of paid vacation time, then the employer would only have to allow the employee seven additional unpaid weeks.

5.   *Must an employer continue to provide health insurance benefits for the employee during either medical or family leave?*

The employer must continue to provide health insurance benefits at the same level as when the employee was working.

6.   *Must the employer return the employee to the same position at the end of either medical or family leave?*

The employer must either return the employee to his or her previous position, or offer the employee "a substantially similar position". The "substantially similar position" must offer responsibility and compensation similar to the position held prior to the medical or family leave.

7.   *Are there any situations in which the employer is not required to reinstate an employee who was on medical or family leave?*

Under the Act, the employer may deny reinstatement to an employee whose salary is among the top 10% of salaries within the company, if reinstating the employee will cause serious economic harm to the employer. The employee must receive notice that he or she will not be reinstated and the employer is required to continue to provide health insurance coverage for up to 12 weeks.

8.   *Can the 12 weeks of medical or family leave be broken up or must it be taken at one time?*

Family leave must be taken at one time unless the employer agrees to intermittent family leave. Medical leave can be taken intermittently or broken up without the approval of the employer.

9.   *What must an employee do in order to request family leave?*

An employee must provide the employer advance notice at least 30 days prior to commencement of family leave.

The Act does not appear to permit employers to require a medical certification for family leave, although certification is required for medical leave.

10.   *When is an employee entitled to medical leave under the Family and Medical Leave Act?*

An employee is entitled to medical leave if there is:

•   A "serious health condition" of an employee's child, parent, or spouse; or

•   A "serious health condition" that renders an employee incapable of performing his or her job.

11.   *How is "serious health condition" defined?*

A "serious health condition" is defined as an illness, injury, impairment or physical or mental condition that involves in-patient hospital care or continual treatment by a healthcare provider.

12. *If an employee needs medical leave due to a "serious health condition, can he/she work part-time?*

Yes, employees are entitled to a reduced work schedule, i.e. fewer hours per week or per work day.

13. *How does an employee prove a "serious health condition"?*

The employer may require certification by a health care provider. The certification must contain the following:

- The date the condition began;

- The estimated duration of the medical condition;

- Appropriate medical facts;

- If medical leave is for an employee's own health condition, the certification must state the length of time the employee will be unable to perform job functions;

- If medical leave is for an employee's child, spouse or parent, certification must contain a statement explaining why the employee is needed to provide care for that person, and the length of time the need will exist;

- If the employee requests intermittent leave, the certification must state the medical reasons why intermittent leave is necessary.

14. *Can an employer challenge the validity of a healthcare provider's certification?*

Yes, the employer can require a second opinion, which must be at the employer's expense. If the opinion of the treating health care provider and the second opinion conflict, the employer can require a third opinion, again, at the employer's expense. The third opinion must be rendered by a healthcare provider agreed upon by both the employer and the employee. The employer can require that periodic updates of status be supplied by the employee, stating when the employee will return to work. The employer can also require subsequent certification regarding the employee's health, on a "reasonable basis".

15. *How is a "healthcare provider" defined by the Act?*

A healthcare provider can be a physician or any other type of caregiver designated by the Secretary of Labor.

16. *Can an employee who was not reinstated by his/her employer also get the benefit of COBRA?*

Yes, during the three months in which the employer is required to maintain health insurance for the employee who is on medical or family leave, this time period may be counted towards the 18 month continuation mandated by COBRA. Under this circumstance, since the employer maintained healthcare benefits for three months, the non-reinstated employee would have the right to 15 months of additional health insurance benefits under COBRA coverage at his or her own expense. The employer may recover the premiums that were paid by the employer for maintaining coverage for the employee during any period of unpaid leave.

17. *Does an employee have the right to make a claim under either the family or medical provisions of this Act for violations of this Act?*

An employee can sue an employer who is in violation of the Act. Suit may be filed in either federal or state court. An employee has two years from the date of the alleged violation to file suit. If the violation of the Act is willful, the employee has three years from the date to file suit.

18. *What damages may the employee recover for violation of the Family and Medical Leave Act?*

If the employer wrongfully terminates an employee, the employer may be liable for lost wages, salary, unemployment benefits, plus interest. If an employee is wrongfully denied leave under the Act, the employer will be liable for the out-of-pocket costs actually incurred by the employee, such as child care expenses (not to exceed an amount equal to 12 weeks of the employee's salary plus interest). The Court can provide "double damages" as an incentive for employers to comply with the Act. In addition, the Act provides that an employee who wins his or her claim may recover Court costs and attorney's fees.

CONCLUSION

The Family and Medical Leave Act is working across the country without causing the hardships for businesses that critics had feared. The Commission on Family and Medical Leave, a bipartisan commission created by Congress to monitor and report on the impact of the law, found that:

- **Between 1.5 million and 3 million people took family or medical leave between January 1994 an July 1995, or less than 4 percent of eligible workers.**

- Employer costs increased in the administrative area, but more than 90 percent of employers surveyed reported no change, or only small increases in benefits, hiring or other costs.

- The most difficult problem for businesses was employees taking intermittent leave.

- Overall, 86.4 percent of employers said there was no noticeable effect on business productivity.

- 60 percent of people taking leave did so for their own health problems. About 23 percent took leave to care for a sick parent, spouse or other relative.

- The average length of leave is 10 days, and 90 percent of all leave is within the 12-week limit established in the law.

IX. SPECIAL EDUCATION AND YOUR SCHOOL DISTRICT: WHAT ARE YOUR CHILDREN'S RIGHTS?

The *Education For All Handicapped Children Act,* Public Law 94-142, (EHA), which was later renamed the *Individuals With Disabilities Education Act, (IDEA),* mandates that all states make available to handicapped children a "free appropriate public education" and extensive "due process" procedures. This federal act and the regulations of the United States Department of Education establish procedures by which handicapped children are evaluated, their classifications are determined, and an appropriate program of special education and "related services" is developed and implemented. The program developed for each individual handicapped child is known as an *Individualized Education Program* (IEP), and must be developed jointly by school officials and parents. Every state is required to follow the EHA and its regulations; therefore, the process for obtaining special education services is substantially similar in all states. Consequently, while the descriptions in this section utilize terminology found in Pennsylvania law, the basic principles will generally also be applicable (although sometimes with different terminology) in the states of New Jersey, Delaware, Maryland, etc.

The federal government has reduced its contribution to the states for special education, even though the costs continue to escalate. In Pennsylvania, more than 296,000 students received some type of special education benefits.

A. WHAT ARE YOUR CHILDREN'S RIGHTS?

1. *Who is eligible for special education?*

All children who are physically and/or mentally impaired and who, because of their impairments, require special attention in order to learn are eligible for special education benefits.

2. *What age must a child be to receive special education benefits?*

a. Children from birth to 3 years old

Children below age 3 are eligible for early intervention services if they have a developmental delay or have a physical or mental disability that is likely to result in developmental delay. The term "developmental delay" includes delays in physical development, language and speech, cognitive, emotional or social development, or in self-help skills. Services to children from birth to 3 years old who meet these criteria are provided through the Mental Health/Mental Retardation System (MH/MR) of the Department of Public Welfare.

Early intervention services can include: Occupational, physical, speech and language therapies, specialized learning instruction, and psychological services. Other assistance can be provided on a case-by-case basis. Early intervention services can be provided in a specialized facility, at a day care center, or in a child's home.

b.   Children ages 3 to 5

Most of the rules that apply to school age children with disabilities also apply to pre-schoolers ages 3 to 5. An evaluation of the pre-schooler is performed in a similar manner by the multi-disciplinary team and a report recommending whether or not the child is eligible for services and what particular services are needed is sent to the school district and the parents. The multi-disciplinary team evaluation must look at the child's developmental levels and physical development to determine if the child has a disability or is developmentally delayed. Re-evaluations must be done each year for children ages 3 to 5 rather than every two years, since the needs of the child at this age change frequently.

3.   *What is an IEP (Individualized Educational Program)?*

An IEP (Individualized Educational Program) is a program which a school district must develop for a child once the child has been identified as "exceptional" by the local school district. An "exceptional" child is defined under the standards for special education set forth by the Department of Education as a student, who has at least one of the following physical, emotional, or mental conditions:

a.   Brain Damaged

Brain damage is an injury to the brain which causes severe behavior and learning disorders. Persons whose behavior and learning disorders are primarily the result of visual, hearing, or motor handicaps, mental retardation, emotional factors, or of environmental disadvantage are not brain-injured. Brain damage does not include the condition known as minimal brain dysfunction.

b.   Hearing Impaired

A hearing loss which ranges from mild (hard of hearing) to profound (deaf) is described as that which interferes with the development of the communication process and results in failure to achieve the full educational potential.

c.   Learning Disability

A deficiency in the acquisition of basic learning skills, including but not limited to, the ability to reason, think, read, write, spell or to do mathematical calculations is considered a learning disability.

d.   Mentally Gifted

Refers to a student with outstanding intellectual and creative ability and an I.Q. of 130 or higher.

e.   Mentally Retarded

Impaired mental development which adversely affects a person's educational performance.

(1)   *Educable mentally retarded* is a condition where, due to intellectual functioning, the student's I.Q. is below average (I.Q. below 80), or the student has a problem with learning in a standard educational setting.

(2)   *Trainable mentally retarded* is a condition used to describe a person with an I.Q. score lower than 55.

(3)   *Severely and profoundly mentally retarded* is used to describe a student with an I.Q. score lower than 30.

f.   Physically Handicapped

Orthopedic and/or other health impairments of sufficient magnitude to limit a person's classroom accommodation and educational performance.

g.   Severely Multi-Handicapped

Persons who are diagnosed as having two or more of the following severe conditions: Blind, brain-damaged, cerebral palsy, deaf, emotional disturbance, muscular dystrophy, and severely mentally retarded.

In this category, "brain-damaged" is defined as those persons who manifest severe behavior and learning disorders resulting from severe insult to the brain as identified by a neurological evaluation.

h.   Socially and Emotionally Disturbed

Those students who display unacceptable behavior characteristics in an extreme manner over a long period of time.

i.   Speech and Language Impaired

Communication disorders of impaired language, voice, fluency or articulation to such a degree that academic achievement is invariably affected and the condition is significantly handicapping to the affected person.

j.   Visually impaired

Visual impairment which adversely affects a person's educational performance.

To have a child classified as "exceptional" under the above categories, parents should have qualified medical professionals document the specific problems a child is experiencing. Objective tests, such as CAT scans, hearing tests, EEG's (electroencephalogram), current I.Q. tests, and other tests are invaluable evidence in documenting that your child is "exceptional" and entitled to an individualized educational program.

4.   *What must be included in your child's IEP?*

Each IEP must contain information in the following areas:

a.   The child's current educational levels.

b.   Annual goals and short-term learning outcomes that respond to the individual needs of the student.

c.   The specific special education services and programs to be provided to the student.

d.   The type, amount and frequency of the related services needed by the student.

e.   The date services and programs will begin, and how long they will continue.

f.   If the student has a disability, the amount of time the child will spend in programs and activities with regular education students.

g.   The tests or other procedures used to tell if the student is achieving goals and learning outcomes.

h.   If the student is in a regular educational classroom for part of the day, what modifications, if any, such as wheelchairs, ramps, etc. are needed for the child to succeed in that class? Additionally, the educational team may recommend that your child take untimed tests, or have another student take class notes.

5.   *Who evaluates the child to determine if he or she is "exceptional"?*

Depending on the type of physical, emotional, or mental condition that has to be evaluated, the school district will have your child seen by an appropriate specialist, certified school psychologist or psychiatrist or other doctor to determine whether or not your child's particular difficulties meet the requirements for "exceptionality".

The school district must pay the cost of their doctor's evaluation, but it is a good idea to have an independent evaluation performed by a specialist of your choice to determine the extent of your child's emotional, physical, or mental deficiencies. Generally, you must pay for the cost of your independent evaluation by the doctor of your choice. Since you may not agree with the findings of the school district's doctors, it is essential that you have medical documentation to support your belief that your child meets the definitions for "exceptionality". Your evidence, by way of a report from your independent evaluator, can be used at a hearing to contest the school district's findings.

6. *What happens after the doctor's evaluation?*

The result of the evaluation must be reviewed by a multi-disciplinary team, which determines whether or not the child is "exceptional". If a determination of "exceptionality" is made, then the parents are notified in writing that the child is "exceptional".

After a child is determined to be "exceptional", an IEP conference is held to document and describe all the educational, mental, and other needs of the child so that they can be incorporated into the IEP conference report. The IEP for each person assigned to special education shall include:

a. A statement of the person's present level of educational performance;

b. A statement of annual goals which describes the expected behaviors to be achieved through the implementation of the person's individualized education program;

c. A statement of short-term instructional objectives;

d. A statement of specific educational services to be provided to the child, including a description of (1) all special education and related services required to meet the unique needs of the child, (2) any special instructional media and materials to be provided, and (3) the type of physical education program in which the child will participate;

e. A description of the extent to which the child will be able to participate in the regular educational programs;

f. The projected date for initiation and the anticipated duration of services; and

g. Appropriate objective criteria, evaluation procedures and schedules for determining, on at least an annual basis, whether the instructional objectives are being realized.

The IEP conference results in the development of a written individualized educational program. The IEP report is a legally enforceable document in that the school district must provide exactly those services that the IEP sets forth. Parents may be represented by an attorney at the IEP conference and should have their school psychologist or appropriate doctor present medical evidence to support the programs they are requesting to be included in the final decision of the IEP conference.

7. *What benefits must a school district pay for a child ? What are related services?*

Related services are defined as those special education services which are required to assist a handicapped child to benefit from special education. The list of related services which must be provided by the school district at no cost to parents or guardians are as follows:

a. Transportation

(1) Transportation to and from school;

Depending upon the child's specific medical condition and special education needs, the child may need to be transported by a school bus, van, or car, or receive tokens for use on public transit.

(2) Transportation in the school building;

If the child needs help to move in and around the school building or school grounds, such assistance must be provided.

b. Specialized equipment

Specialized equipment, such as wheelchairs, lifts, adaptive devices, and ramps, must also be made available by the school district;

c. Developmental - corrective and supportive services;

d. Speech pathology

e. Audiology

f. Psychological services

g. Physical therapy

h. Occupational therapy

i. Recreation

j. Medical and counseling services

The concept of "related services" is broad enough to allow attorneys to use this in advocating for the benefit of their clients.

Pennsylvania has adopted Special Education Regulations and Standards. These Regulations and Standards provide that each special education student's yearly Individualized Educational Program (IEP) must determine whether that student requires one or more related services. The new regulations list several examples of related services, and recognize that additional unnamed related services must be required in order to allow a particular student to benefit from his or her special education program. The listed examples of related services include "transportation, speech pathology, audiology, psychological services, physical therapy, occupational therapy, social work services, school health services, early identification/assessment, medical services for diagnoses or evaluation, parent counseling/education, recreation, counseling services, developmental services, corrective services, and other support services".

Although the list of potential related services is extensive, it must be remembered that a special education student is entitled only to such related services as are required to allow the student to receive an "appropriate education" (a special education program which provides "educational benefit" to the student). Unfortunately, the level of "benefit" which a student must attain in order to render his or her special education program "appropriate" is less than precise. However, the courts have rejected attempts by school districts to equate the terms "appropriate education" or "educational benefit" with "lack of regression", "minimal progress" or "trivial educational progress". The courts have indicated that an appropriate education must, at the very least, involve a program which is designed and implemented in such a manner as to permit "meaningful" educational progress in relation to the student's educational potential. Therefore, if a student requires one or more related services in order to attain meaningful educational benefit (and thus to receive an appropriate education), the school district is responsible for providing such related services. In applying these standards, the courts have sometimes ordered school districts to provide unusual or extensive related services.

While the new Pennsylvania special education regulations and standards regarding related services were designed to mirror the requirements of federal law, Congress thereafter amended the EHA in October, 1990, to include the additional related services of "rehabilitation counseling".

Although school districts have frequently refused to provide such devices as wheelchairs, computer services, hearing aids and glasses for exceptional students who require such items in order to benefit from their educational program, the new IDEA amendments clearly call such school district policies into serious question. Moreover, the United States

Department of Education, Office of Special Education, has recently issued a major policy ruling which indicates that school districts must provide such assistive equipment as wheelchairs, computers and augmentative communication devices for use during school hours regardless of the parents' ability to pay. The full extent of this entitlement remains to be seen, but it is clear that school districts can no longer presumptively deny particular forms of related services or assistive technology devices to students with disabilities. They must fully consider each student's needs for _all_ related services or assistive devices on a case-by-case basis. This process needs to be done during the development of the student's IEP, to determine whether such services or devices are necessary to allow effective participation in educational programs.

In **_Irving Independent School District v. Tatro_**, 468 U.S. 883, 104 S.Ct. 3371, 82 L.Ed.2d 664 (1984), the United States Supreme Court addressed the issue of whether a procedure known as *clean intermittent catheterization* (CIC) was a "related service" which a school district must provide to a handicapped child. CIC involves the insertion of a catheter into the urethra to drain the bladder; the procedure was described by the court as "a simple one that may be performed in a few minutes by a lay person with less than an hour's training", 104 S.Ct. at 3374.

In light of the decision in the **_Tatro_** case, it is useful to compile cases which have examined related services and their specific results, as follows:

- Also holding CIC to be a related service;

- Psychotherapy is a related service;

- Constant in-school nursing care for life-threatening respiratory condition not a related service where the required procedures are outside the skills of a typical school nurse;

- Repositioning of a suction tube in child's throat is a related service;

- Psychological services are related services;

- Transportation is a related service;

- Placement of student in emotionally-required small class of 6-8 pupils is related service;

- Upholding hearing officer's determination that school district need pay for only a limited number of trips home for a residentially-placed handicapped child;

- Cued speech interpreter required as related services for hearing-impaired child;

- Psychiatric hospitalization is not a related service;

- Psychotherapy is a related service even if performed by a psychiatrist.

8. _What type of classes must a school district provide to meet your child's special education needs?_

The appropriate class for your child depends on the amount and type of special education or related services your child needs. The school district may choose from the following:

a. Home-bound instruction - Teacher must see the student for 5 or more hours a week, usually at the child's home.

b. A regular class for the entire school day, with support services provided by a special or regular education teacher within the regular classroom.

c. A regular class for most of the school day, with special education programs or services provided for part of the day. The services can be provided either in or out of the class by an "itinerant" teacher who serves many different special education students.

d. A regular class for most of the day, with special education or related services provided in a "resource room" for part of the day.

e. A special education "part-time class" for most of the school day, with some instruction in a regular classroom for part of the day.

f. A "full-time" special education class for the entire day, with some opportunities to spend non-academic time with regular education students.

9. _What if the child's needs cannot be met by a school district?_

If the child's educational needs can be met in a public school placement operated by the school district, such a placement must be provided. If not, placement for the child is accomplished by the intermediate unit which works with the school district to implement the child's Individualized Educational Program. If neither the school district nor the intermediate unit can meet the child's educational needs, the child must be placed, at public expense, in a private school or a school which specializes in meeting the educational and emotional needs of that student. Placement in a special school is called an Approved Private School (APS). This is a school which has specialized programs for children with certain learning disabilities (i.e. Autism). A placement in an Approved Private School can only be accomplished if the school district and parents agree on the placement, and there is no other educational program in the school district or the intermediate unit in which the child lives that is appropriate to accomplish the goals set forth in the Individualized Educational Program.

10. *Can parents' income be evaluated in determining special education benefits?*

Special education benefits and placement in an approved private school, if necessary, must be provided without evaluating parental income. The educational services provided by the school district must be free to all individuals who are qualified for special education benefits.

11. *Can special education benefits continue during the summer?*

Special education benefits must be individualized, i.e. there must be a specific individual plan set up to meet the needs of the handicapped child. The idea that a special education plan must be individualized has been interpreted to require a school district to provide an extended school year, beyond the 180 day school year normally provided for the non-handicapped child. To be eligible, parents must be able to demonstrate with medical documentation that significant regression will occur if there is a break in the child's educational program and that the child has a limited ability to regain these lost skills after the normal school year begins. The right to an extended school year can require that a school district provide special education benefits during weekends, summer months, or both.

12. *Can special education benefits continue after graduation?*

Special education will not continue if your child graduates. You should not allow your child to graduate if they still need special education benefits. Special education benefits can continue until your child is 21 years of age.

13. *Who has access to your children's school records?*

A local school district must comply, within thirty days, with a written request from parents or guardians for access to a child's special education records. Access includes the right of parents to inspect the records, receive an explanation of the records, obtain copies of any and all parts of the records, and designate a representative, example: doctor, attorney, etc., to examine or copy records. Parents may not be charged for the cost of locating records, but may be charged a reasonable copying charge.

14.   *What is mainstreaming?*

Mainstreaming occurs when a child who has been receiving special education benefits can return to school with students who are not in special education classes.

15.   *What are the special education due process procedures if parents disagree with the school district's IEP?*

The rights that parents have to initiate the due process procedures are as follows:

a.   Pre-Hearing Conference - A parent can request, in writing, a pre-hearing conference, at which time an informal conference is held to try and settle or resolve any disagreement.

b.   Due-Process Hearing - If the disagreement is not resolved at the pre-hearing conference, the parent has a right to a due process hearing. This due process hearing takes place before an impartial hearing officer assigned by the Pennsylvania Department of Education. At any step in the process, the parents may be represented by a lawyer or other person. They should be prepared to present evidence by way of reports, to document their position that their child needs a certain specialized program that the school district is not willing to provide.

c.   Appeal - The hearing officer's decision may be appealed by either party, the parent or the school district, to the Secretary of the Department of Education or the courts of the Commonwealth of Pennsylvania or the Federal District Court.

It is important to remember that during the time that it takes to obtain a decision through the due process procedures, the child's public school program remains the same as it did prior to the determination of the IEP. It is advisable that parents be prepared at the pre-hearing conference with all the documentation and reports they want the school district to consider so that an effort can be made to resolve differences and decide upon an IEP as early as possible.

Finally, it is important that parents realize they must monitor the school district to insure that they comply with the services specified on the child's IEP. If the parents believe the school district has failed to provide a specified program, then the parents may file a complaint with the Division of Regional Review of the Bureau of Special Education in Harrisburg.

16. *Can the school district be ordered to pay my attorney fees and expenses?*

Yes, a parent or guardian who brings an action for special education benefits against a school district and prevails may be awarded attorney fees and expert witness costs.

17. *Trends - special education not trivial*

A Federal Appeals court ruled that an educational program for a disabled student must provide more than "trivial" progress to comply with the **United States Education of the Handicapped Act**. In this case, the school district was providing special education benefits which they argued met the provisions of the law because the student was receiving some benefits from his education. The child's parents filed suit, claiming that his educational program was not appropriate because it was not individually tailored to their child's specific needs, and that the law called for more than a trivial educational benefit for their child. The court agreed, and ruled that when the Legislators drafted the **United States Education of the Handicapped Act**, they envisioned that "significant learning" would take place in a special education classroom.

Even though the courts are expanding special education benefits, a recent study showed that the number of the children receiving "appropriate" special education benefits is very small. Many parents are not even aware that special education benefits exist, nor are they aware of the type of benefits available or how to apply for these benefits.

B. **OTHER FEDERAL LAWS AFFECTING CHILDREN WITH SPECIAL NEEDS.**

1. **Americans with Disabilities Act of 1990** *(Pub. L.101-336) - (ADA)*

This Act extends civil rights protection to individuals with special needs/disabilities. The Act, which will be discussed in greater detail in Section XX, protects children and adults.

2. **The Developmental Disabilities Bill of Rights Act Amendments of 1987 (Pub. L.100-146; Reauthorized in 1990 and 1994)**

The purpose of this Act is to provide opportunities (such as grants), to enable individuals with special needs and disabilities to achieve their maximum potential. This law covers individuals who have a severe and chronic disability that:

(1)   is attributable to a mental or physical impairment, or a combination of mental and/or physical impairments;

(2)   is manifested before age 22;

(3)   is likely to continue indefinitely; and

(4)   causes substantial functional limitations in three or more of the following areas of major life activities:

- Self-care;

- Receptive and expressive language;

- Self-direction;

- Capacity for independent living or economic sufficiency; and

- Learning mobility.

3.   *The Rehabilitation Act of 1973, §504, (Pub. L.93-112)*

Section 504 of the Rehabilitation Act extends civil rights protection to individuals with disabilities or special needs. Children's advocates have been using §504 with increasing frequency to secure support services for children with disabilities who require special services in school. Even when these children do not meet criteria for special education under the *Individuals With Disabilities Education Act* (IDEA), they may be entitled to benefits under §504.

C.   *SUCCESSFULLY LITIGATED SPECIAL EDUCATION CASES*

1.   *Special Education Benefits - Coordination of Benefits - Traumatic Brain Injury*

A minor suffered a catastrophic head injury in an automobile accident. The parents' health care policy had a $1 million lifetime maximum. By creatively using the coordination of benefits clause, we were able to maximize the benefits to which the minor was entitled from the health care policy and from the school district for special education benefits. **SUGGESTION:** Obtaining medical and special education benefits for a catastrophically injured minor should not be pursued without a detailed plan which analyzes all available sources of funding.

2.   *Special Education Benefits - Approved Private School*

A minor suffered a catastrophic injury in a recreational accident. The parents' health insurance policy had a $2 million lifetime maximum. The school district was not able to provide for the educational needs for the child, either in the local school district, or in the intermediate unit (county-wide system). A claim was successfully filed against the school district, forcing the school district to pay for an approved private school (APS), which allowed the minor to receive specialized educational services in another state. **SUGGESTION:** Families should be very aggressive in advocating for the special education needs of their children. As soon as the needs of the child are identified, parents or their attorney need to actively pressure the school district to meet these needs without delays. Delay in the allocation of funding for the short-term and long-term educational needs of the child can be detrimental to that child.

3.   *Special Education Benefits - IEP - Computers*

A minor was catastrophically injured at birth. The full extent of the minor's cognitive difficulties did not become known to the parents until the child was approximately five years of age. The diagnosis was developmental delay with cognitive deficits. The health care providers and the family believed that the minor could benefit from a computer, along with a remedial cognitive training program. The school district denied this benefit. We filed a claim for the parents, and were able to convince the school district to include the computerized program in a written IEP for the minor. **SUGGESTION:** Today, local school districts are either refusing to pay for special education benefits, or attempting to limit the amount they are going to have to pay for children who are catastrophically ill or injured. It is vital that all family members and health care providers explore more creative ways to obtain computers and other assistive technology aids.

4.   *Special Education Benefits - Attorney's Fees - Due Process Hearing*

A minor was diagnosed with cerebral palsy, and had orthopedic and cognitive difficulties. It was the parents' contention that the school district was not providing an appropriate IEP. I filed for a due process hearing, and immediately prior to the hearing, the school district agreed to pay for the requested special education benefits. The hearing officer issued an award requiring the school district to pay for the fees and costs that the family incurred in hiring counsel. **SUGGESTION:** The **Handicapped Children's Protection Act of 1986** (Pub. L.99-372) makes the school district liable for reasonable attorney's fees and costs incurred to parents or guardians who prevail in due process hearings where there is a dispute with the school system over special education benefits and related services.

X. INTRODUCTION TO BENEFITS

Finding adequate health coverage for a catastrophically ill or injured minor or adult is a monumental task. Governmental and private insurance have enacted legal, contractual, and practical obstacles which make it very difficult, if not next-to-impossible, to find adequate health benefits for the timely transfer of an individual from a hospital into a rehabilitation facility or skilled nursing facility. To overcome these problems and other obstacles requires knowledge of the myriad regulations concerning reimbursement. It is often necessary to assemble a team of doctors, other health care professionals, attorneys, hospital administrators, insurance representatives, and legislators. Even with a team approach, it is necessary for family members and professionals to adopt a "Can Do" attitude. Unfortunately, short-term and long-term benefits for the catastrophically ill and injured will not be "voluntarily given to needed individuals"—-You have to fight for the benefits to which you and your family members are entitled.

A. *AUTOMOBILE INSURANCE BENEFITS*

1. *Motor Vehicle Injuries - Trauma Facts*

According to the American Trauma Society, motor vehicle incidents are the leading cause of accidental death in the United States, and cost Americans more than $170.6 billion. Persons aged 25 - 34 are more frequently involved in motor vehicle accidents than any other age group, and males are involved in more incidents than females.

In 1996, the overall fatality rate for death due to motor vehicle incidents was 43,300 deaths and 2.6 million injuries. Motor vehicle deaths occurred more frequently in places classified as rural. In rural areas the victims were mostly occupants of motor vehicles, while in urban areas more than half of the victims were pedestrians. Half of motor vehicle deaths occurred at night, and most within 25 miles of the victim's home.

Drinking is a factor in 41% of all fatal motor vehicle accidents. The most frequently reported environmental factor in all incidents is slippery surfaces.

Children under the age of four not protected by a child safety seat are eleven times more likely to be killed in a motor vehicle collision than children protected by a child safety seat.

Motor vehicle incidents in 1995 cost Americans more than $810 billion.

2.   *Pedestrian Injuries - Trauma Facts*

According to the National Safety Council, 6,100 pedestrians died in traffic collisions in 1996. People between the ages of 25 to 44 have the highest pedestrian death rate in traffic collisions, but about 41% of all traffic-related deaths are children ages one to nine who are pedestrians. 69% of pedestrian deaths are males.

More than half of all pedestrian deaths and injuries occur when pedestrians cross or enter streets, with about one-third occurring between intersections. Two out of three pedestrian deaths occur in rural areas. The ratio of deaths to injuries is high in rural areas, probably due to higher speed limits on rural roads. The most serious pedestrian injuries result from striking the hood, windshield, or top of the vehicle, not from subsequent impact with the road, or being run over.

More than half of the adult pedestrians killed in nighttime crashes with motor vehicles had blood alcohol concentrations of .10% or more.

3.   *The most common auto insurance problems*

Many family members do not have proper auto insurance coverage. Unfortunately, consumers do not realize that they do not have proper coverage until after an accident occurs. The most common auto insurance problems are:

a.   Wrongful denial of a claim.

It is a good practice to request that your insurance company explain in writing why they have denied your claim. You should request that the company provide you with a complete copy of your insurance policy so that it can be discussed immediately with your attorney.

b.   Slow payment of claims.

You have the right to have your insurance company promptly pay your medical bills. The insurance company that does not promptly honor your claim may be guilty of bad faith. See Section XI, Bad Faith: Winning Weapon in the Health Insurance Battle. You and your attorney must aggressively pressure your insurance company for prompt payment so that the care and medical treatment needed for the injured person is not jeopardized.

c.   Not being able to afford adequate insurance if your driving record is less than perfect.

If you have a poor driving record, you should contact several insurance companies, and possibly an insurance broker, to find the most affordable coverage for you and your family. Before you purchase coverage, it is good practice to review with your family attorney the type of auto insurance coverage you need.

d.   Assuming that companies will automatically give you the "proper coverage" for your family.

e.   Signing away rights before the full extent of injuries are known.

Never sign a release or any documents giving up your rights until you have reviewed the release with your attorney. Once you sign a release, it is too late to argue that you didn't understand what you were signing. It is assumed that if you sign a release you have read it, understood it, and have signed it knowingly, intelligently, and voluntarily. The burden will be on you or your family member to prove otherwise.

4.   *Insurance Coverage*

In all states, individuals with automobile insurance coverage carry the following benefits:

- Medical payments;

- Property damage;

- Liability coverage;

- Uninsured motorist coverage;

- Underinsured motorist coverage;

- Death and funeral benefit.

States vary as to how much minimum coverage each registered driver is required to carry; for example, State A may require individuals to carry $5,000 in medical coverage and $15,000 liability coverage, whereas State B will require $100,000 in medical coverage and $250,000 in liability coverage. In an interesting case, a Pennsylvania resident who was rendered a quadriplegic following an accident in New Jersey, has been awarded coverage for medical expenses from a New Jersey insurance company. The Pennsylvania court had awarded only $10,000 in medical expenses, the automobile medical insurance coverage available under Pennsylvania law. The appellate court applied New Jersey insurance law instead of Pennsylvania law, because the foreign state, i.e. New Jersey, offered greater protection for the injured person. This case illustrates the importance of carefully examining which jurisdiction will provide the maximum level of benefits for the catastrophically injured. An automobile accident must be thoroughly investigated by your attorney, no matter in which state the accident happened. Families should make sure that the attorney they hire to investigate an accident is thorough and examines every potential source of benefits in the pursuit of identifying adequate funding sources for both the short-term acute care and for long-term medical and rehabilitation needs.

71

5.   *Overview of Pennsylvania Automobile Insurance Benefits*

The following is an overview of the 1990 Pennsylvania auto legislation. It is not intended to substitute for a careful reading of the Act. The major provisions of the Act are followed by a commentary. To determine what insurance is appropriate for you and your family members, you should discuss the act in detail with your attorney.

a.   Automobile insurance coverages

(1)   The Act reduces the mandated amount of medical coverages from $10,000 to $5,000;

(2)   The purchase of wage loss, funeral benefit, uninsured and underinsured coverage became optional;

(3)   Allows the insured to choose a limited tort insurance policy in which a driver could waive the right to sue for damages for pain and suffering unless the injury was serious. Serious is defined as "death, serious impairment of body function or permanent serious disfigurement.";

(4)   Allows the insured to purchase optional first party coverage in the following amounts:

(a)   Medical up to $1.1 million;

(b)   Income up to $50,000 ($2,500 per month);

(c)   Accidental death up to $25,000, and funeral benefits $2,500.

b.   Election of limited tort options.

Unless the injury sustained in the auto accident is serious, the person who chooses the limited tort alternative would not be allowed to sue for pain and suffering (non-economic loss). If you do not choose the limited tort alternative, you retain your rights to bring a lawsuit for any damages: non-economic losses (pain and suffering), and economic losses (wage loss).

Even if an individual unwisely chooses to give up the right to sue for non-serious injuries, he or she will still retain the right to bring a lawsuit for damages suffered in a motor vehicle accident if the person at fault:

(1)   Is convicted or accepts accelerated rehabilitative disposition (ARD) for driving under the influence of a controlled substance in that accident;

(2)   Is operating a motor vehicle in another state;

(3)   Intends to injure himself or another person in the accident.

The limited tort option should not be chosen, since you lose your right to sue for non-serious injuries. The limited tort option also eliminates claims for pain and suffering unless serious injury results. Importantly, even if you choose the limited tort option, you <u>can still be sued</u> for injuries caused by your negligence for both serious and non-serious injuries.

c.   Choosing auto insurance coverage.

The 1990 auto insurance law requires insurers to disclose premium charges for policy renewals (both by mail and over the telephone). The savings in premium, if any, are to be placed clearly on the written forms to be signed by the insureds, if they want to reduce any insurance coverages.

All drivers should discuss with their attorneys maintaining the following coverages:

(1)   Property damage;

(2)   Wage loss - up to $50,000 ($2,500 per month);

(3)   Liability coverage - to protect you if you are at fault and injure someone in an accident;

(4)   Underinsured motorist coverage - should be chosen in the same amounts as the liability coverage to protect you if you are injured by someone who has insufficient liability coverage to pay for your wage loss and pain and suffering damages;

(5)   Uninsured motorist coverage - should be chosen in the same amounts as the liability coverage to protect you for your wage loss, pain and suffering if you are injured by someone who is uninsured. Uninsured motorist coverage will pay you for your unreimbursed wage loss and pain and suffering damages;

(6)   Waiver - **The 1990 Pennsylvania Financial Responsibility law** mandates that insurance companies offer certain amounts of medical, liability, uninsured motorist, and underinsured motorist coverage. You may elect to waive or give up your right to purchase higher limits of insurance. You should never waive any medical, liability, uninsured or underinsured motorist coverages without discussing this in detail with your insurance agent and your attorney.

(7)   Medical coverage of $1.1 million;

(8)   Funeral benefits.

Individuals should not reduce their auto insurance coverages without first examining any other family health insurance coverages and discussing the implications of any changes in their auto insurance coverage with their attorneys.

d.   Extraordinary Medical Benefits (EMB) coverage.

All drivers must determine whether or not they want to purchase extraordinary medical expense benefits coverage to protect them from catastrophic injuries. The following are important guidelines to remember:

(1)   Purchase of EMB coverage is optional;

(2)   EMB coverage can be purchased through non-automobile insurers. For example, through HMO's, etc.;

(3)   All automobile insurers must offer EMB;

(4)   EMB coverage will pay for necessary and reasonable accident related medical and rehabilitative expenses;

(5)   EMB coverage can be bought in $100,000 increments;

(6)   EMB coverage will not pay any of the first $100,000 in medical bills;

(7)   EMB coverage will pay medical expenses between $100,000 and a lifetime maximum of $1 million.

Extraordinary medical benefits coverages should be purchased by every driver in Pennsylvania. It costs about $50 per car to receive $1 million in medical coverage.

All drivers should carefully examine their insurance policies to determine if they have proper coverage to protect themselves and their family members. Once an accident occurs, it is too late to change your insurance coverage. Your coverage should be reviewed with your attorney after an accident - even if you have the proper coverage - to obtain your benefits as quickly as possible.

e.   Uninsured motorist - payment of medical expenses - Vehicle ownership not terminated.

The ramifications of ownership of an uninsured motor vehicle under Pennsylvania law are complex, and affect the ability of healthcare providers to have their medical bills reimbursed. Generally, owners of currently registered motor vehicles that are uninsured cannot recover payment for medical bills from their automobile insurance.

If an uninsured vehicle becomes inoperable prior to an accident, medical benefits will still not be available if the vehicle's registration was not properly terminated or transferred. For instance, even if the vehicle has been taken to a junkyard before the accident, the owner cannot receive medical benefits if the vehicle's registration has been maintained. If an automobile's registration is simply permitted to lapse, the owner can argue that he is no longer "an owner of a currently registered motor vehicle" and therefore he should not be precluded from recovering medical benefits from available insurance. Although the clear trend is toward denying a claim for medical benefits made by individuals who own uninsured automobiles, it is still prudent for you to consult with counsel to determine whether or not medical benefits can be paid under the particular facts and circumstances of your case.

6.   *When is a motor vehicle not a motor vehicle?*

Under the **Pennsylvania Financial Responsibility Law,** effective October 1, 1984, insurance policies must cover and pay medical expenses for any motor vehicle of the type required to be registered and operated in the Commonwealth of Pennsylvania.

Issues constantly arise as to whether or not motorcycles, mopeds, dirt bikes, all-terrain vehicles (ATV's), bicycles or snowmobiles are motor vehicles under the **Financial Responsibility Law** and whether catastrophic medical rehabilitation expenses will be paid.

a.   Motorcycles

According to the National Safety Council, motorcycle deaths and injuries have increased during the last decade, even though the total number of motorcycle registrations has decreased. Deaths of cyclists now represent 6% of all motor vehicle deaths. 75% of all motorcyclists' deaths occur among men ages 16 to 34. In 1996, there were 2,300 motorcycle deaths. More than 56,000 riders and passengers were injured, 57% due to collisions with other vehicles, 21% from non-collision incidents, and 15% with fixed objects. Over half of all motorcyclists killed in single vehicle crashes have very high blood alcohol concentrations (.10% or more).

Operators or passengers of motorcycles are specifically excluded and therefore not eligible for medical benefits under the **Financial Responsibility Law**. This does not mean that the accident should not be

investigated. Substantial medical benefits have been recovered from manufacturers of defective motorcycles and helmets. This source of benefits
should be investigated.

b.   Dirt Bikes

Courts have ruled that dirt bikes are not motor vehicles, since
they are designed for recreational use and not for use on public highways.
Dirt bikes do not have headlights, taillights, horns, turn signals, mirrors or
speedometers, and essentially because they lack these features they cannot be licensed under the motor vehicle code in Pennsylvania. Therefore,
the operator or passenger on a dirt bike cannot recover medical benefits
under the Financial Responsibility Law.

c.   Mopeds

The Superior Court in Pennsylvania has affirmed a ruling that a
moped is a motorcycle under Pennsylvania law, and therefore an operator
or passenger of a moped is not entitled to recover medical benefits under
the Financial Responsibility Law.

It is interesting that the court distinguished a dirt bike from a
moped, since a moped can be licensed as a vehicle for highway use, and
is a vehicle intended for highway use. The court decided, however, that a
moped is a motorized pedacycle, and that under the definition of motorcycle, a motorized pedacycle is considered a motorcycle, and therefore a
moped is a motorcycle, which is not eligible for Pennsylvania no-fault benefits.

It should again be stressed that even though riders are not eligible for benefits under the *Financial Responsibility Law*, medical benefits
have been recovered from manufacturers of improperly designed dirt
bikes, mopeds and helmets. This is especially important if a moped or dirt
bike was designed for minor children.

d.   Dune Buggies

Dune buggies are designed for recreational use and not for use
on public highways, and therefore are not motor vehicles. Individuals
injured on dune buggies are not entitled to medical benefits under the
Financial Responsibility Law.

e.   All-Terrain Vehicles (ATV's)

All-terrain vehicles are three-wheeled or four-wheeled vehicles,
usually manufactured by Yamaha, Honda, Suzuki and others, and are
specifically intended to be used for recreation and not for use on public
highways.   They are not motor vehicles within the meaning of the
Financial Responsibility Law, and if you are an operator or passenger of

an ATV, you are not entitled to benefits through the *Financial Responsibility Law.*

The Consumer Products Safety Commission in Washington, DC has held extensive hearings on the inherent dangers of All-terrain vehicles (ATV's) and All-terrain cycles (ATC's) for children. Catastrophic medical benefits have been obtained from manufacturers, insurance companies or helmet manufacturers in dune buggy and ATV cases, and should always be considered a source of first party medical benefits.

        f.   Bicycles

According to the Bicycle Federation of America, in 1997 at least 761 Americans died while riding bicycles, one of the the deadliest recreational activities in the nation. Experts blame biking hazards on increased aggressive driving, poor road design, and a public which is largely uneducated about the dangers of two-wheeled travel. Bicycle victims are of all ages. Last year, at least 248 children age 15 or younger died while riding bicycles, and 42 other victims were 72 years or older. About 40% of bicyclists admitted to hospitals have head injuries. Bicyclists who go to hospitals with head injuries are 20 times more likely to die if they were not wearing helmets at the time of the accident. There is no federal law requiring bicyclists to wear helmets, but approximately 15 states and many municipalities across the country have adopted helmet laws since 1987.

There are many cases where adults or children riding bicycles are injured as a result of a collision with a truck or automobile, giving rise to the issue of whether or not the injured person is entitled to medical benefits under the *Financial Responsibility Law*. Bicycle accidents should be promptly investigated to determine the correct source of first party medical benefits.

An example of an unusual circumstance for which medical benefits were allowed is as follows: A 15-year-old boy was injured when his trail bike collided with a truck on a public highway. Even though the boy was operating a trail bike, which is not a motor vehicle, the court ruled that the truck with which he collided was a motor vehicle, and therefore his injuries arose "out of the maintenance and use of a motor vehicle."

This phrase has been interpreted and benefits have been paid to individuals who were:

•   Drivers of motor vehicles;

•   Passengers in motor vehicles;

•   Pedestrians struck by insured vehicles;

•   Pedestrians struck by uninsured vehicles;

- Operator of a trail bike struck by a truck;

- Individual entering or alighting from a parked vehicle;

- Individual changing a tire of a vehicle along the side of the road.

If you are injured as a result of someone else's negligence while riding a bicycle, your accident should always be investigated. The most common sources of recovery in bicycle accidents are against the insurance company of the driver who caused the accident or the insurance company of the manufacturer of the bicycle. Also, claims can be pursued against helmet manufacturers if the helmet fails to meet government standards for head injury protection.

g.   Wheelchairs

A New Jersey court ruled that a motorized wheelchair is not a motor vehicle. The Judge ruled that although a strict literal interpretation of the motor vehicle code would include motorized wheelchairs as motor vehicles, the Judge did not believe that it was the intent of the legislature because, if it was, wheelchairs would have to be registered and insured.

h.   Horse and Buggy

I have successfully argued that an individual in Pennsylvania who was struck by an automobile while riding in a horse and buggy on the highway should receive his medical bills paid by the auto insurance of the driver who injured him.

I think you can see that the question "When is a motor vehicle not a motor vehicle?" is not an easy one to answer. The above list is not complete. The circumstances of each particular case must be examined to see if the facts meet the definition of "motor vehicle", and also to see if there were any other causes of the injury.

7.   *Most Common Highway Hazards*

Jury awards in the millions of dollars have been awarded to accident victims in lawsuits arising from accidents caused by hazards on the highway. The most common highway hazards fall into these categories:

a.   Failure to install proper lighting;

b.   Failure to install medial barriers;

c.   Poor maintenance practices.

These highway hazards are caused by state and local agencies, consulting engineers, construction contractors and utility companies who have failed to build, design and maintain safe highways, and have inadequately trained their maintenance personnel.

Other common highway hazards are:

   d.   Improper highway design: Improper highway design is a leading cause of accidents resulting in head trauma and other catastrophic injuries;

   e.   Improper location of telephone poles: Failure to place telephone poles in their proper place along the roadway is the second greatest cause of run-off-road fatalities;

   f.   Improper drainage of roadways leading to accumulation of water and ice;

   g.   Poorly designed on- and off- ramps;

   h.   Lack of warnings: Failure to install proper signs to warn of highway dangers, i.e. "Slippery When Wet", Reduce Speed", "High Accident Area".

   i.   Drop-off in highway shoulder.

Another major highway hazard is your automobile. Many catastrophic injuries could have been lessened or even avoided if the manufacturers of automobiles had properly designed and manufactured the vehicles with safety devices designed to eliminate or lessen injuries to operators and passengers. Some examples of design defects and improper equipment which have caused serious automobile accidents are: exploding gas tanks, improperly designed seat belts, and defective tires.

Manufacturers of automobiles have been forced to recall hundreds of thousands of vehicles because of defects in steering, braking, and other engineering mistakes. If you or a family member have suffered a serious injury in an auto accident, the vehicle should be examined by an engineer or accident reconstructionist. Often, in cases of serious injury, the driver is unable to describe the circumstances of the accident. It then takes an expert to determine whether or not the car itself caused or contributed to the accident. Too frequently, insurance companies will destroy the evidence by towing the automobile to a salvage yard and crushing it. If this occurs, it is almost impossible to reconstruct the defect in the vehicle that may have caused the accident or contributed to the injury. Persons who suffer catastrophic injuries should have all the circumstances of their accident investigated within days of the accident to determine if their accident was caused by a "highway hazard".

B. SUCCESSFULLY LITIGATED AUTOMOBILE CASES

1. *Automobile - Guardianship - Time Period - Loss of Benefits*

An individual was involved in an accident and suffered incapacitating head and spinal cord injuries. The spouse of the individual left the state and the treating hospital was not aware of any other family members or next of kin. The hospital had been treating the patient for almost a year when the spouse returned and questioned the hospital as to why they had not made an application for governmental benefits. The hospital admitted that there was a mistake, i.e. the hospital had never requested that a guardian be appointed for the incapacitated individual. Since there was no guardian with legal authority to apply for medical benefits, it was never done. The patient lost substantial medical benefits because a timely application was not made by the guardian. **SUGGESTION:** Guardianship must always be pursued, when appropriate, to ensure that deadlines to apply for Federal, State and contractual insurance benefits are met. For a more comprehensive discussion of guardianship, see Section IV, Guardianship.

2. *Automobile - Investigation - Traumatic Brain Injury*

My client was driving an automobile and was broadsided by another vehicle. As a result of the impact, the side door collapsed into the body of the car, causing major structural damage to the car, and traumatic brain injury to the driver. I hired an expert to evaluate the car, and he issued a report that the side door was defectively designed, in that it should have had reinforcement to prevent the inward collapse. **SUGGESTION:** This case further emphasizes that you should not permit your automobile insurance company to salvage or destroy your vehicle before an expert retained by you or your attorney has had an opportunity to inspect it.

3. *Automobile - Extra-Contractual Benefits - Third Party Recovery - Traumatic Brain Injury*

An individual was injured in an automobile accident, and exhausted the minimum automobile medical benefits available from insurance. We were able to convince a private health insurance carrier to provide benefits for the catastrophically injured client and wait to receive payment until after the trial against the negligent driver. At the conclusion of the case, the private health insurance carrier was reimbursed in full for all medical services rendered and a trust was set up to meet the client's lifetime medical needs. **SUGGESTION:** Today, federal and state governmental insurance plans are either refusing to pay the cost for catastrophic care or reimbursing at such a low rate that they are essentially not paying. It is vital that all health care providers explore more creative ways to provide their services and also get paid.

4. *Tractor-trailer - Bad Driving Record - Traumatic Brain Injury*

The minor plaintiff suffered a catastrophic brain injury when a tractor-trailer jackknifed on ice and snow and struck the vehicle in which he was riding. My investigation revealed that the truck driver was hired by the trucking company despite his long history of motor vehicle violations. A thorough search of the driver's background was very helpful in successfully resolving this claim. **SUGGESTION:** A careful background check of the parties involved in a serious accident can produce pivotal information which can be beneficial in pressuring the insurance company to settle or resolve your claim.

5. *Bicycle - Self-insured - Traumatic Brain Injury*

My client received a traumatic brain injury while riding on a bicycle path which was improperly maintained. He was thrown from the bicycle when the front wheel struck a hole on the bicycle path, and he suffered a catastrophic head injury. Investigation revealed that the city, which maintained the bicycle path, had knowledge of the defect prior to the accident. The claim was successful against the city even though the city did not have liability insurance and was self-insured. **SUGGESTION:** The fact that an entity, company or individual, does not have liability insurance should not deter you from filing a valid claim, because they may either be self-insured, or have sufficient assets to satisfy a judgment or award.

6. *Automobile - Underinsured Motorist Coverage - Traumatic Brain Injury*

A minor passenger was catastrophically injured when the driver of a vehicle negligently caused an accident. The parents recovered the full amount of liability insurance from their own insurance carrier. Since the limits of the driver's liability insurance were inadequate to pay for the lifetime medical needs of the minor passenger, a claim was made for underinsured motorist benefits against the parents' car insurance company. **SUGGESTION:** Underinsured motorist coverage is insurance coverage that you pay for, on your automobile, to protect you if you are injured by a driver who has insufficient liability insurance coverage to pay your wage loss, pain and suffering and future medical bills. Underinsured motorist coverage should be chosen in the same amounts as your liability coverage.

7. *Automobile - Uninsured Motorist Coverage - Pedestrian - Traumatic Brain Injury*

My client was a pedestrian who was struck by an automobile and sustained a traumatic brain injury. The negligent driver did not have automobile liability insurance and therefore the pedestrian was injured by an uninsured motorist. Our claim was successful against the pedestrian's own automobile insurance company for uninsured motorist benefits. Because there were five insured automobiles in the household, the injured person was then able to accumulate, or "stack", all the uninsured motorist coverages on the five vehicles. **SUGGESTION**: Uninsured motorist coverage is insurance coverage that you pay for, on your automobile, to protect you if you are injured by a driver who has no automobile liability insurance to pay your wage loss, pain and suffering, and future medical bills. Uninsured motorist coverage should be chosen in the same amounts as your liability coverage.

XI. BAD FAITH: WINNING WEAPON IN THE HEALTH INSURANCE BATTLE

Effective July 1, 1990, Pennsylvania law permits action against insurance companies that act in bad faith toward their insured. Not only automobile insurance claims, but every contractual claim arising under any policy of insurance will be subject to the provisions of the *bad faith law.*

Traditionally, bad faith has been defined as "the opposite of good faith, generally implying or involving actual or constructive fraud, or a design to mislead or deceive another, or a neglect or refusal to fulfill some duty or some contractual obligation, not prompted by an honest mistake as to one's rights or duties, but by some interested or sinister motive".

Essentially, insurers have a good faith duty not to withhold or deny insurance benefits maliciously or without reasonable cause. Examples of unreasonable claim settlement practices are:

A. *MISREPRESENTING PERTINENT FACTS OR POLICY OR CONTRACT PROVISIONS RELATING TO COVERAGE*

B. *DELAY IN RESPONDING TO A CLAIM*

C. *FAILURE TO ADOPT AND IMPLEMENT PROMPT INVESTIGATION OF CLAIMS*

D. *REFUSAL TO PAY A CLAIM WITHOUT ADEQUATE INVESTIGATION*

E. *FAILURE TO AFFIRM OR DENY COVERAGE IN A REASONABLE TIME*

F. *DELAYING THE INVESTIGATION OF CLAIMS OR THE PAYMENT OF BENEFITS BY REQUIRING SUBMISSION OF SEVERAL FORMS WHICH CONTAIN ESSENTIALLY THE SAME INFORMATION*

G. *EXPLOITATION OF AN INSURED'S VULNERABLE POSITION*

H. *ABUSE OF SUBROGATION RIGHTS*

I. *UNFAIR IMPOSITION OF INCREASES IN PREMIUMS FOR THE FILING OF CLAIMS*

J. *OPPRESSIVE DEMANDS*

K. *NOT ATTEMPTING IN GOOD FAITH TO EFFECTUATE PROMPT, FAIR, AND EQUITABLE SETTLEMENTS ON CLAIMS IN WHICH IT IS REASONABLY CLEAR THAT THE COMPANY IS LIABLE*

In an action arising under an insurance policy, if the court finds that the insurer has acted in bad faith toward the insured, the court may take any or all of the following actions:

1.   Award interest on the amount of the claim from the date the claim was made by the insured in an amount equal to the prime rate of interest plus 3%;

2.   Award punitive damages against the insurer;

3.   Assess court costs and attorney's fees against the insurer.

Similar bad faith actions have been permitted in California for many years and have resulted in significant awards. A two-year survey of 44 California verdicts for insurance company bad faith showed total punitive damages were $165 million. The THREAT of punitive damages, attorney's fees, interest and court costs should be a very effective tool to convince insurers to deal in good faith.

It is crucial that *all* persons who are seriously injured, and their families, understand their rights under the **bad faith law.**

This law should be used by your attorney to force insurance companies to pay claims promptly, fairly, and efficiently. See ***Pennsylvania Bad Faith Law,*** 42 Pa. C.S.A. §8371.

XII. WORKERS' COMPENSATION BENEFITS AND PROCEDURES

A. WORKERS' COMPENSATION INJURIES - TRAUMA FACTS - OVERVIEW

According to the American Trauma Society, in 1996, there were approximately 6,100 deaths as a result of work injuries. 3.9 million workers received disabling injuries in 1996. More than 40% of accidental work deaths in 1996 occurred to those between 25 and 44. 40% of these deaths involved motor vehicle incidents, and the second highest fatality rate, 20%, was due to violence. An additional 10% was due to falls. The highest disabling work injuries result from overexertion (31%), and the second highest result from being struck by, or struck against, an object (24%). The three parts of the body most frequently injured in work incidents occurred to the back, legs, and then the fingers. The total time lost for all workplace injuries in 1995 equalled 120 million days of productivity.

Worker's compensation and occupational disease laws provide benefits to workers who are injured on the job or contract an occupational disease. Worker's compensation provides (1) hospital, surgical, and medical expenses; (2) a percentage of lost wages as weekly compensation to the disabled worker; and (3) death benefits and burial expenses to a deceased worker's dependents. The detailed description of worker's compensation benefits and procedures below is based upon prevailing Pennsylvania law; however, the worker's compensation laws of New Jersey, Delaware and Maryland are similar in most respects to that of Pennsylvania.

Employers must provide for payment of worker's compensation to virtually any employee who is unable to work because of a work-related injury. Almost all typical employment situations are covered by worker's compensation law, and an employer must provide for worker's compensation even if he only employs one individual. However, some "casual workers" and domestic service workers may be excluded. The law applies to all injuries and many occupational diseases which arise in the course of employment. Moreover, the right to compensation exists as long as the injury or disease occurred in Pennsylvania, regardless of where the worker was hired, and may cover injuries or occupational diseases occurring outside Pennsylvania under certain circumstances. Finally, since the law requires employers to be responsible for a worker's injuries without regard to the employee's carelessness, the law also provides that employees may generally not recover damages from the employer in a legal action other than worker's compensation.

Compensation is generally paid beginning with the eighth day of disability, and compensation will be paid for the first seven days if the disability lasts fourteen or more days. The first payment of compensation must begin no later than the 21st day after the employer became aware of the injury. The amount of compensation will depend on the nature and duration of the disability in question.

B.   *WORKERS' COMPENSATION QUESTIONS MOST OFTEN ASKED*

Individuals who have been seriously injured in worker's compensation accidents have many questions concerning the benefits to which they are entitled under the law. Worker's compensation statutes were passed in all states requiring employers to provide certain wage and medical benefits for individuals who are injured in work-related accidents. I have answered below the most commonly asked questions concerning worker's compensation benefits:

1.   *Can I sue my employer if I am injured in a work-related accident?*

Employers are immune from suit - you cannot sue your employer but can only recover worker's compensation benefits, either from your employer if he is self-insured, or your employer's worker's compensation insurance company.

2.   *What does a Worker's Compensation insurance company have to pay for?*

Worker's compensation insurance companies must pay all your medical bills for treatments related to your worker's compensation injury for the rest of your life. In addition, the insurance company must pay a percentage of your wage loss for as long as you are disabled.

3.   *Does the amount a person receives for Worker's Compensation wage loss increase each year?*

Unlike Social Security Disability and some private pension benefits, worker's compensation wage disability benefits do not increase each year. The amount of wage benefits to which you are entitled are determined as of the day you are injured, and remain that way for as long as you are disabled.

4.   *Does Worker's Compensation pay for pain and suffering damages?*

Worker's compensation insurance companies only pay reasonable and necessary medical expenses and a percentage of your wage loss.

5.   *Does Worker's Compensation pay if I lose a hand in a product liability accident?*

By statute a worker's compensation carrier must pay if you have had an amputation or, for all practical purposes, you have lost the use of a specific part of your body. These benefits are called specific loss benefits and depend upon what part of your body has been injured and whether or not the injury is permanent in nature.

6.   *If I have been injured in a job-related accident, who can I sue for scarring and pain and suffering?*

Since you are not permitted under the law to sue your employer if you are injured in a work-related accident, the only party you can sue for pain and suffering damages is a third party who is responsible for your injury.

Example: A gas tank that you are cleaning at work explodes because it has a defective valve which was manufactured by company "X". You would receive your worker's compensation benefits, i.e. payment of your medical bills and a percentage of wages from your employer's worker's compensation insurance company, and you could also bring a lawsuit against the manufacturer of the defective valve.

7.   *How can I prove my work-related injury was caused by someone other than my employer?*

It is crucial that there be a prompt and thorough investigation of the circumstances surrounding your work-related injury. This investigation should be accomplished by trained attorneys, investigators, experts and engineers whose job it is to determine exactly what caused your accident. Photographs, witness statements and evidence must be secured as quickly as possible after a serious work-related injury occurs.

8.   *If I can prove a third party caused my injury, what can I claim in damages?*

Unlike a worker's compensation case where you can only recover a percentage of your wage loss and your medical bills, in a third party claim, you can recover lost wages not reimbursed by worker's compensation, damages for scarring, for pain and suffering, loss of companionship, emotional distress, loss of enjoyment of life, etc.

87

9. *Can my spouse bring a claim for any damages if I am in a work-related accident?*

A spouse can bring a claim against a third party for damages—for example, against the manufacturer of the defective valve—but a spouse cannot bring a claim against the worker's compensation insurance company or your employer.

10. *Does my employer have a right to be reimbursed for the wages and medicals they paid if I prove a third party caused my accident?*

By statute in most states, an employer, if self-insured, or a worker's compensation insurance company has the right to be reimbursed a certain percentage of the money expended if you and your attorneys prove that a third party caused your injury. The rationale for reimbursing the employer or worker's compensation insurance company is that you receive your worker's compensation benefits even if the employer is not at fault, therefore, if you prove that someone other than the employer is at fault, i.e. a third party, it is only fair to reimburse the insurance company or your employer for the benefits they have paid. It is important to remember that your employer or the worker's compensation carrier is very interested in determining whether a third party is responsible, since their rights to be reimbursed (subrogation rights) would be protected if you succeed with your lawsuit against a third party.

11. *Must I attend a medical exam scheduled by my employer or Worker's Compensation insurance company?*

In most states, you must attend a medical exam scheduled by your employer or your worker's insurance company to determine whether or not you are still disabled as a result of your work-related injury. You should always have your attorney or representative attend with you. Legally, you are entitled to a copy of the doctor's report after it is sent to the insurance company.

12. *Can I sue my employer if he intentionally injures me?*

In most states, you cannot bring a claim against your employer even if he intentionally injures you or is guilty of gross negligence. Some states are attempting to change the laws to allow an employee to bring a claim against an employer who is guilty of intentional misconduct, or gross negligence. The argument is that employers should lose their immunity if they are guilty of serious misconduct.

13. *If I am receiving Worker's Compensation benefits, can I also receive Social Security Disability?*

You can collect both, but Social Security Disability will receive some type of credit for the amount of worker's compensation benefits you are collecting. If you are injured and are unable to be gainfully employed for a year, you should apply for Social Security Disability Benefits.

C.   *PENNSYLVANIA'S WORKERS' COMPENSATION LAW - ACT 57*

Act 57 became effective on August 23, 1996. The major provisions of Act 57 are:

- Requires that workers must stay under the care of an employer-designated doctor for 90 days. The old workers' compensation law set the period at 30 days;

- Requires employees who have received total disability for 104 weeks to submit to a physical examination for a determination of disability under the American Medical Association (AMA) guidelines;

- Requires claimants to demonstrate 50% impairment rating to remain on total disability after 104 weeks;

- 50% impairment rating is based on the AMA guidelines. (NOTE: This is a very difficult standard for injured claimants to meet);

- "Impairment Rating" shall mean the percentage of permanent impairment of the whole body resulting from the compensable injury. The percentage rating for impairment under this clause shall represent only that impairment that is the result of the compensable injury and not for any pre-existing work-related or non-work-related impairment;

- Degree of impairment shall be determined based upon an evaluation by a physician who is licensed in Pennsylvania, who is certified by an American Board of Medical Specialties or its osteopathic equivalent, and who is active in clinical practice for at least 20 hours per week;

- If the claimant is determined to have an impairment rating of 50% or greater, total disability benefits will continue. If the claimant's level of impairment is less than 50%, the claimant will receive benefits under partial disability. Partial disability benefits under current law are limited to a maximum of 500 weeks. Partial disability shall apply if the employee is able to perform his previous work or can, considering the employee's residual productive skill, education, age and work experience, engage in any other kind of substantial, gainful employment which exists in the usual employment area in which the employee lives within Pennsylvania. Pre-existing work-related or non-work-related impairments shall not be included in determining total impairment;

- "Earning Power" shall be determined by the work the employee is capable of performing, and shall be based upon expert opinion and evidence which includes: job listings with agencies of the department, private job placement agencies, and advertisement in the usual employment area.

- Act 57 changes the procedure for calculating an individual's average weekly wage—the average weekly wage serves as the basis for an employee's workers' compensation rate. Compensation benefits will be calculated according to a worker's three highest quarters out of the last four. Previously, benefits were calculated on the highest single quarter;

- The employer may require the employee to submit to an expert interview to determine earning power and employability;

- Calculates earning power based on a person's age, abilities, and availability of real, existing jobs within a reasonable commuting distance—not hypothetical employment;

- Raises the penalty for delay of payments to employees from 20% to 50%;

- Workers' compensation wage loss benefits are offset by 50% of Social Security "old age" benefits and by the employer's share of pension and severance benefits. The Social Security offset is not applicable if an individual was collecting these benefits prior to the injury. The Social Security offset does not apply to hearing loss, disfigurement, and specific loss benefits (loss of limbs, etc.). The pension and severance offset is only applicable to contributions made by the employer who is liable for the compensable injury. Pension and severance benefits are full 100% offsets. None of the offsets are retroactive;

- Requires all employees to submit to two independent medical exams per year;

- Provides for an insurer-paid second opinion when invasive surgery is recommended by the physician designated by the employer;

- Requires an employee, if he chooses to follow the second opinion treatment, to receive the treatment from a designated physician for the first 90 days;

- If the insurer receives medical evidence that the employee is able to return to work in any capacity, then the employer must provide prompt written notice to the employee which states:

    (1) The nature of the employee's physical condition or change of condition;

    (2) The employee's obligation to look for available employment. Proof of available employment opportunities may jeopardize the employee's right to receive ongoing benefits;

    (3) That the employee has the right to consult with an attorney in order to obtain evidence to challenge the insurer's contentions.

- If the employer requests a supersedeas (an interim suspension of workers' compensation payments) based on medical evidence, the employee may establish his position by "a preponderance of the evidence", rather than "clear and convincing evidence", increasing the likelihood of prevailing on the merits of his defense. The workers' compensation judge's supersedeas decision shall not be appealable.

- An employee filing a petition seeking workers' compensation benefits or receiving benefits has the responsibility to report to the insurer the following:

    (1)   Employment or self-employment in any capacity;

    (2)   Wages from employment or self-employment;

    (3)   Employer's name and address;

    (4)   The amount of wages from employment or self-employment;

    (5)   The dates of such employment or self-employment;

    (6)   The nature and scope of such employment or self-employment;

    (7)   Any other information relevant in determining eligibility for, or amount of, benefits.

    This report to the insurer must be made within 30 days of employment or self-employment;

- Utilization review of all treatment rendered by a healthcare provider shall be performed by a provider licensed in the same profession and being of the same or similar specialty as that of the provider of the treatment under review;

- Requires insurers to pay providers partial payments when portions of a bill are disputed;

- If an employee files a Petition for workers' compensation, the parties, by joint agreement, may file a notice requesting an informal conference before a workers' compensation judge or hearing officer. This conference shall be scheduled within thirty-five days of the filing of the request to see if the parties can resolve their disputes. The results of the conference are binding only if mutually agreed to. The results of informal conferences, as well as any testimony, witnesses or evidence presented, shall not be admissible at subsequent proceedings on the claim;

- Incorporates the State Workers' Insurance Fund (SWIF) into the Workers' Compensation Act and requires all new workers' compensation judges to be:

  (1)   Attorneys;

  (2)   Have five years of workers' compensation experience;

  (3)   Complete and pass the training course and examination;

  (4)   Meet the 20 hour continuing education requirement, and;

  (5)   Meet such other requirements established by the Secretary. The Act grandfathers all current existing workers' compensation judges and hearing officers into the system.

- A person, including, but not limited to, the employer, the employee, the healthcare provider, the attorney, the insurer, the State Workers' Insurance Fund and self-insureds, commits an offense if the person knowingly, and with intent to defraud, does any of the following:

  (1)   Presents or causes to be presented to any insurer any statement forming a part of, or in support of, a workers' compensation insurance claim that contains any false, incomplete or misleading information concerning any fact material to the workers' compensation insurance claim;

(2)   Receives total disability benefits under this Act while employed or receiving wages;

(3)   Receives partial disability benefits in excess of the amounts permitted.

Civil penalties are set at $5,000.00 for a first offense; $10,000.00 for a second offense; $15,000.00 for subsequent violations.

- The statute of limitations on fraud cases is established at 5 years.

D.   *SUCCESSFULLY LITIGATED WORKERS' COMPENSATION CASES*

1.   *Workplace Accident - Ladder - Third Party Recovery*

A workman suffered a spinal cord injury as the result of a fall that occurred when he was working on a ladder at a job site. Our claim was successfully prosecuted, based on the theory that another workman, not his co-employee, improperly secured the ladder, and this led to the fall and resulting paraplegia. **SUGGESTION:** All construction site accidents should be thoroughly investigated to determine whether or not there is a contractor, subcontractor, or third party company, other than worker's compensation, against whom a claim can be made for damages.

2.   *Workplace Accident - Fork Lift - Third Party Recovery*

An employee was seriously injured when he was struck by a fork lift operated by a co-employee at his employer's place of business. A third party claim was brought against the manufacturer of the fork lift, since it was defectively designed and did not allow the operator of the fork lift to see the worker who was walking at the plant. **SUGGESTION:** Any time a product is involved in a serious or catastrophic accident, an outside expert should be retained to examine the product and determine whether the product was safe for its intended use.

3.   *Workplace Accident - Self-Insured Subrogation - Burns - Third Party Recovery*

An individual working in a steel plant suffered catastrophic burns when a furnace malfunctioned. Exhaustive investigation revealed that the foreign manufacturer of the furnace used an inferior/defective product in the manufacture of the furnace which caused the malfunction. The worker's compensation carrier was the self-insured employer. As a result of the successful product liability recovery, the self-insured employer received repayment of the medical bills and wages (subrogation) that they had paid the injured employee. **SUGGESTION:** All worker's compensation carriers and self-insured employers should aggressively investigate all serious injuries and illnesses to protect their subrogation rights.

[1] This will be better explained in the Managed Care Section.

XIII. GOVERNMENTAL BENEFITS

A.   *ELIGIBILITY ISSUES*

Many individuals who seek medical attention at an acute care facility or rehabilitation facility do not have private health insurance, such as Blue Cross/Blue Shield, Major Medical, or HMO. Often, an investigation reveals that the only available insurance is either Medical Assistance (Medicaid) or Medicare. Government insurance raises difficult issues for the health care community and for the patient when a personal injury claim is pursued. Eligibility requirements differ if a claimant seeks benefits arising out of a motor vehicle accident or workers' compensation accident.

1.   *Motor Vehicle Accidents*

If the person who is involved in a motor vehicle accident has automobile insurance, his or her auto insurance is primary, and must be exhausted, along with any other private insurance benefits, such as Blue Cross and Blue Shield, before that person becomes eligible for Medical Assistance benefits.

2.   *Workers' Compensation*

Under the Workers' Compensation Act, workers' compensation insurance is primary if a motor vehicle accident occurs within the scope of the person's employment. Medical Assistance should never be billed when a claim is being made for Workers' Compensation benefits.

3.   *Reimbursement Agreements*

Usually, persons who request governmental benefits will be asked whether or not they are contemplating a lawsuit or have actually filed a lawsuit as a result of their injury or accident. If an individual, or his or her guardian, advises Medical Assistance that a personal injury claim will be pursued, Medical Assistance will require that a reimbursement agreement be signed as a condition of eligibility. The reimbursement agreement will state that Medical Assistance will be reimbursed from the proceeds of any recovery.

B.   *SOCIAL SECURITY.*

There are two basic federal programs under Social Security providing direct and continuing financial assistance to disabled persons:

1.   *Social Security Disability Insurance Benefits (SSD)*

Social Security Disability insurance benefits will be paid to a disabled worker and his or her family if earnings are lost or reduced due to

96

the worker's disability and if the worker has earned credit for a certain number of pay periods under Social Security standards. (The amount of work credit needed depends upon the worker's age.) Persons are considered disabled if they have a physical or mental impairment which (1) prevents them from working, and (2) is expected to last for at least 12 months or to result in death.

If you are on worker's compensation, your Social Security Disability payment will be reduced. You may live with either your parents, spouse, children, or live by yourself, and still collect the full amount of Social Security Disability.

Even when there is a catastrophic injury, the Social Security Administration usually rejects a person's application for benefits. This rejection is sometimes based on insufficient medical documentation to determine a person's injury, insufficient work credits, etc. If you have suffered a catastrophic injury, you should appeal your denial of Social Security Disability benefits. It is very important that you obtain all the relevant medical information so that it can be presented to the Social Security Administration at the time you appeal the denial of benefits and file your application for reconsideration. In addition to presenting additional medical evidence, you should ask that your application be given priority, and request an immediate hearing, since you have suffered a catastrophic injury.

If you contact your Congressional district office, the Congressman's aide will make calls to the Social Security Department to check on the progress of your application and try to obtain an expedited hearing.

The Social Security Administration will require that you attend an independent medical exam (IME). There is nothing independent about this medical exam, since (1) Social Security picks the doctor, (2) Social Security pays the doctor for the examination, and (3) Social Security receives a copy of the report. You should always have your attorney or your representative attend the medical exam as your advocate. In addition, you should request, and follow up to receive, a copy of the report that the examining doctor will send to Social Security.

2.   *Supplemental Security Income (SSI)*

Supplemental Security Income (SSI) payments are made monthly to disabled persons who have limited income and assets. In order to qualify for SSI, a family must be considered financially needy and (if for a child) the child must be found disabled or blind by Social Security. You are entitled to appeal an unfavorable decision. Many decisions are reversed during the appeals process. It is recommended that you seek legal assistance when you appeal, because this process can become quite complicated.

3.   *New Regulation for Children's Social Security Income Disability Benefits*

In the 1990 **Zebley** Decision, the Supreme Court required the Social Security Administration to use an evaluation process for children comparable to the one it uses for adults claiming disability benefits. However, effective April 14, 1997, the Social Security Administration will implement new provisions affecting Supplemental Security Income (SSI) Benefits for Children.

On August 22, 1996, the **Personal Responsibility and Work Opportunity Reconciliation Act of 1996** changed the definition of disability for children under the SSI program. Under the new provisions, in order for children to qualify for SSI Disability Benefits, they must have a physical or mental condition that can be medically proven and which results in "marked and severe functional limitations" of substantial duration. This new law also requires that the medically proven physical or mental condition or conditions must last for a continuous period not less than 12 months or be expected to result in death. The child may not be considered disabled if he or she is working at a job that is considered to be "substantial work". The new standard also requires that a child's condition meet a specific physical or mental disability as found in the Social Security Administration's (SSA) "List of Impairments". The new regulation sets a higher standard of severity than the previous laws.

Using the new standards, the SSA will evaluate children in five (5) areas of development or functioning:

1.   Cognition and Communication
2.   Motor Skills
3.   Social
4.   Personal (Self-Care)
5.   Concentration, Persistence and Pace

Very young children will be evaluated on their "responsiveness to stimuli" in place of numbers 4 and 5.

The largest group effected by the new standard of review are children with serious mental, emotional and behavioral disorders. Among all children who previously qualified for SSI benefits, forty-two (42%) percent had mental disorders, and an additional thirty-two (32%) percent had mental retardation. Now these children must meet a new, higher standard of disability to remain eligible.

Also, under the new SSA Regulations, children will be required to have their cases reviewed more frequently and with a new "treatment requirement".

- Children will have their cases reviewed every three (3) years unless their condition is not expected to improve.

- Children who qualify for SSI due to low birth weight will be reviewed one (1) year after birth.

- Children who turn eighteen (18) years of age will be reviewed using the same eligibility criteria for adults. They will be reviewed within one (1) year after their eighteenth birthday.

- At this review, the child's parents must show evidence that the child is receiving treatment that is "medically necessary". (The treatment will improve or restore the child's functioning, if such treatment is available.)

Because SSI is tied to Medicaid coverage in most states, another major impact of the new regulations is that children who no longer "qualify" for SSI benefits may also lose their medical assistance. Children who lose their SSI benefits will continue to receive Medicaid only if they remain eligible on other grounds, i.e., their age or their families' low income.

Parents should be aware that if they are told that their child no longer qualifies for SSI under the new standards, they may appeal the decision. This is very important since, in most cases, their benefits will continue throughout the appeal process. Children are also entitled to receive Medicaid during their SSI appeal. Unfortunately, families should also be aware that if the final decision supports the denial, they may have to return the benefits paid during the appeal process.

Advocates for children should become familiar with the new disability regulations so that they can continue to assist families who are entitled to receive SSI benefits. They should stress to the parents the importance of documenting as much medical and other evidence about how the child's disability limits what he or she can do at home and in school. Functional limitation evaluation is still an important part of the benefits decision. When the case is being reviewed, the family should compile as much information as possible from doctors, nurses, therapists and teachers.

The changes in SSI benefits for disabled children will be profound and its impact is frightening. The new disability laws are being applied retroactively. Many children who previously met the eligibility requirements will be reevaluated and will have their benefits terminated when the new criteria are applied. Also, it is feared that many families may not apply for benefits when they hear that other children's benefits are being terminated.

Substantial Gainful Activity means work that involves significant physical or mental duties done for pay or profit.

Residual functional capacity is your remaining physical and/or mental capacity to perform work.

Disability means any physical or mental condition that is severe enough to limit a worker's performance of work.

Partial Disability is when you cannot perform some or all of the work you could have performed before your impairment.

Impairment is a mental or physical condition that lessens or prevents your ability to work.

Listing of Impairments means specific symptoms, signs, laboratory findings that are presumed to be severe enough to prevent you from working a year or longer.

Representative Payee is someone appointed by the Social Security Administration to assist people receiving benefits who are "unable to manage" their money.

C.   *MEDICARE*

The Medicare Act was signed into law in 1965. It is a federal government program which provides benefits for elderly patients. Initially under Medicare, all doctors were paid on the basis of "usual and customary" fees for a given service. In 1984, Medicare created financial incentives for hospitals to discharge patients as soon as possible, and not to admit them at all unless absolutely necessary. The incentives worked: In two years, the average number of in-patient days per Medicare recipient fell 22%. Unfortunately, under the strict Medicare guidelines many seriously ill and injured patients do not receive all of the needed care and rehabilitation they require.

Most people over 65 are entitled to Medicare Part A (hospital benefits) because they are eligible for Social Security retirement benefits. Individuals are also entitled to Medicare Part A if they are eligible for Railroad Retirement benefits. When you enroll for Medicare Part A, you are automatically signed up for Medicare Part B (medical insurance), for which you have to pay a monthly premium. If you choose, you can refuse Medicare Part B coverage. You are also entitled to receive Medicare Part A benefits if you are under 65 and have been eligible for Social Security Disability benefits for at least 24 months. This is critically important coverage for individuals who have suffered a catastrophic injury or illness.

If you are under age 65, and have a kidney impairment that "appears irreversible and permanent and requires a regular course of dialysis or kidney transplantation to maintain life", and you or your spouse qualify for Social Security or Railroad Retirement benefits, you are entitled to Medicare Part A. For dialysis patients, Medicare coverage begins either one or three months after treatment begins, depending on whether the treatment occurs at home or in an institution.

If you are over 65 and not entitled to Medicare Part A, you can still receive Part A coverage by enrolling in Medicare and paying a monthly premium.

The only long-term care services Medicare will pay for are: care in a Medicare-certified skilled nursing facility, part-time or intermittent home health services, and hospice care. You cannot rely on Medicare to meet either nursing home or home health expenses for the catastrophically ill or injured on a long-term basis.

D.   *MEDICAID*

Medicaid is also known as Medical Assistance and is a joint federal and state program. The federal government and the states share the cost of the Medicaid programs. Under Medicaid, persons who meet the eligibility requirements can obtain medical care from any doctor, hospital or health care provider that participates in the Medicaid program. In Pennsylvania, the Department of Public Welfare handles the Medicaid program, and applications for Medicaid eligibility can be made in your local county offices.

Eligibility for Medicaid is based on the income and other financial resources of the person or family applying. There are two levels of eligibility for Medicaid: (1) categorically needy, and (2) medically needy.

To be categorically needy, individuals or families are receiving some type of governmental benefits such as: Supplemental Security Income (SSI), Aid for Families with Dependent Children (AFDC), general medical assistance, etc.

1.   *Medicaid and Nursing Home Care*

According to one study, after only 13 weeks in a nursing home, nearly half of all elderly people living alone are poor enough for Medicaid. The process of depleting your resources until you qualify for Medicaid is called "spending down". To qualify for Medicaid, your assets and income must be extremely small. If you are in a nursing home, you must first "spend down" your assets, bank accounts, IRA's, second homes, stocks, bonds, essentially all your assets, down to a few thousand dollars. You are allowed to keep your primary residence, a car, personal clothing and household items. If you are in a nursing home, you must contribute all of your monthly income except for a small allowance for you and your spouse or other dependent for your nursing home expenses. **The Kennedy-Kasselbaum Act of 1997** significantly limits the use of "spending down."

2. _Medicaid and Children_

A child or family whose income requirements do not meet the eligibility standards for categorically needy may be considered medically needy and be eligible for Medicaid services. The specific criteria for determining whether or not a child or family is eligible for services under the medically necessary standards can be discussed with you at your local county assistance office.

Parental income is disregarded if:

• The child is under 21 years of age, and;

• Has an impairment severe enough to meet the disability standard under SSI. It does not matter if the child was turned down for SSI due to excess parental income.

Medicare and Medicaid are rapidly switching their insureds to a "managed care" concept. It is predicted that within five years, 75% of all Medicare and Medicaid subscribers will be covered in whole or in part by some type of health maintenance organization (HMO). This is not good news for the catastrophically ill and injured, since managed care insurers have traditionally limited payments for short-term and long-term rehabilitation needs.

E. **OFFICE OF VOCATIONAL REHABILITATION (OVR).**

1. _Purpose_

The Office of Vocational Rehabilitation (OVR) is an agency within the Pennsylvania Department of Labor and Industry whose purpose is to provide vocational rehabilitation services for the disabled. OVR will provide services for disabled children and adults, age 17 or older.

Funding for OVR is through the state legislature. If OVR services cannot be provided at the time that application is made, due to depletion of their budget, be sure to reapply at the beginning of the next fiscal year, beginning in July.

2. *Eligibility - application process.*

To be eligible for the services provided by OVR and vocational rehabilitation services, a person must: (1) have a physical or mental disability which creates an impediment to employment; and (2) be reasonably expected to become more employable as a result of vocational rehabilitation services. Employability is the ability to get a job, be a homemaker, or participate in some other type of work. The Office of Vocational Rehabilitation's central office is located in Harrisburg but individuals can apply at the sixteen (16) district OVR offices located throughout Pennsylvania.

Allentown	**800-922-9536**	**Reading**	**800-442-0949**
Altoona	**800-442-6343**	**Rosemont**	**800-221-1042**
DuBois	**800-922-4017**	**Washington**	**800-442-6367**
Erie	**800-541-0721**	**Wilkes-Barre**	**800-634-2060**
Harrisburg	**800-442-6352**	**Williamsport**	**800-442-6359**
Johnstown	**800-762-4223**	**York**	**800-762-6306**
New Castle	**800-442-6379**	**Hiram G. Andrews Center**	
Philadelphia	**800-442-6381**	**Johnstown**	**800-762-4211**
Pittsburgh	**800-442-6371**		

3. *Services provided.*

Vocational rehabilitation services include any goods or services necessary to render a handicapped individual employable.

a. Physical and Mental Restoration Services

Physical and mental restoration services include: (1) medical and corrective surgery and therapeutic treatment services; (2) necessary hospitalization in connection with surgery or treatment; (3) prosthetic and assistive devices; (4) eyeglasses and visual services; (5) special services (including transportation and dialysis); (6) diagnosis and treatment for mental and emotional disorders by a physician or licensed psychologist; and (7) physical, occupational, speech or hearing therapy.

b. Communication Services

Communication services include: (1) interpreter services for deaf individuals and reader and note-taking services for blind individuals; and (2) telecommunications, sensory, and other technological aids and devices.

c. Vocational Training

Vocational training includes: (1) orientation and mobility services for the blind; (2) recruitment and training services for handicapped individuals to provide them with new employment opportunities; (3) training designed to enhance personal and vocational adjustment; (4) books and other training materials; and (5) services to families of eligible persons which are necessary to enhance the adjustment or rehabilitation of the eligible handicapped person.

d.   Financial Support

OVR can assist with the estimated costs of subsistence during the individual's rehabilitation.

e.   Transportation

Transportation to assist in obtaining vocational rehabilitation services is available in some situations.

F.   *COBRA - CONTINUANCE OF EMPLOYER-SPONSORED MEDICAL BENEFITS.*

Families of catastrophically injured or ill individuals often overlook COBRA, (The **Comprehensive Omnibus Budget Reconciliation Act of April, 1986**), a federal law that can provide significant health insurance benefits for short-term and long-term rehabilitation needs.

1.   *What is COBRA?*

COBRA **(Consolidated Omnibus Budget Reconciliation Act)** is a federal law passed in 1986 that requires an employer to continue an employee's medical coverage and that of the employee's spouse and dependent children in certain situations.

2.   *Who is eligible for COBRA coverage?*

Persons who are eligible for COBRA benefits are called **"qualified beneficiaries"**. **"Qualified beneficiaries"** include the spouses and dependent children of covered employees. To be a **"qualified beneficiary"**, an individual must have been covered under a group health plan maintained by the employer on the day before a **"qualifying event"**, even if the person was covered for only one day.

A **"qualifying event"** can be

- The death of a covered employee;

- The termination of an employee (not through his gross misconduct);

- The reduction in hours of a covered employee's work week;

- A divorce or legal separation of a covered employee;

- An employee's entitlement to Medicare coverage;

- A dependent child's loss of dependency status due to reaching a certain age;

- An employee's retirement;

- Voluntary resignation;

- Strike or walk-out;

- Lay-off of a covered employee.

3. *Who must comply with this law?*

If an employer offers a group health plan to its employees, and has 20 or more full- and/or part-time employees (during at least 50% of the working days the previous year) it must comply with COBRA. Firms with fewer than 20 employees, including those who purchase group health insurance through trade associations or other similar arrangements, are not subject to COBRA requirements. There are some exceptions to the general COBRA requirements if the employer purchases health insurance through a multi-employer plan.

COBRA has two basic parts:

a. Employer provides coverage through its group health plan, offers it to the qualified beneficiary, and charges the qualified beneficiary for the coverage; and

b. Qualified beneficiary purchases the coverage at the price it costs the employer, plus a two percent surcharge.

4. *How long can a qualified beneficiary receive COBRA coverage?*

18 Month Coverage:

Employees and family members covered at the time of a qualifying event are entitled to 18 months of continued COBRA coverage when they would lose their coverage because of:

- The reduction in hours of a covered employee's work week;

- Retirement;

- Voluntary resignation;

- Strike or walk-out;

- Lay-off;

- Other employment termination for any reason other than gross misconduct.

36 Month Coverage:

Spouses and dependents of covered employees are entitled to 36 months of coverage if they would lose their coverage as a result of:

- The death of a covered employee;

- A divorce or legal separation of a covered employee;

- A dependent child's loss of dependency status due to reaching a certain age, under the Plan's terms;

- The covered employee's entitlement to Medicare coverage.

29 Month Coverage:

Qualified beneficiaries (such as a spouse or dependent child) who are disabled when the covered employee is terminated or when the covered employee's hours of work are reduced may have their 18 month COBRA eligibility extended by an additional 11 months, to 29 months. They may be charged up to 150% of the applicable premium for those additional 11 months. See page 111 section 9 for additional COBRA information.

5. <u>*What is the advantage to having access to COBRA?*</u>

Individual health insurance is usually more expensive than group insurance. In addition, individual health insurance is sometimes difficult to obtain if someone has a pre-existing health problem (such as a catastrophic illness or injury). Under COBRA, there is no medical screening pre-certification done prior to acceptance into the COBRA plan.

6. <u>*How long does a qualified beneficiary have to apply for COBRA insurance coverage?*</u>

A qualified beneficiary has sixty (60) days after the employer group coverage expires to decide whether or not to purchase COBRA.

7. *Can multiple family members be treated separately?*

Family members who are qualified beneficiaries may choose coverage options that are different from those chosen by a covered employee. These options can only be elected during the employer's open enrollment period, and the family members may then be charged premiums as if they were electing individual, and not family coverage.

8. *Can a qualified beneficiary change coverage?*

A qualified beneficiary must be permitted the same opportunities to change coverage as an active employee (although this may result in additional COBRA premiums). They may add a new spouse, add dependents, etc., even outside of open enrollment periods. If the employer offers more than one group health plan or option to employees in similar situations, with open enrollment periods, the employer must permit the qualified beneficiary the open enrollment options.

9. *What happens when the initial period of extension of benefits (Eighteen Months) under the COBRA coverage has lapsed, and the qualified beneficiary still wishes to be insured?*

An individual who has had an additional eighteen (18) months of COBRA coverage and still wishes continued coverage should inquire whether or not the employer or the insurance company offers conversion coverage. If the plan under which the person has been covered offers conversion coverage (an option to continue coverage under the plan at the present rate), a qualified person must be offered an option to enroll in the conversion coverage within one hundred eighty (180) days before the continuation coverage ends. Even though the insurance company cannot exclude a qualified person because of a new medical condition, the qualified person will probably have to pay much higher premiums—perhaps several times what was being paid before—usually for fewer benefits.

10. *Could a qualified beneficiary lose COBRA coverage?*

There are several instances in which a qualified beneficiary could lose COBRA coverage. Coverage would be lost if:

- The qualified person fails to pay his premium on time (A 30-day grace period);

- The qualified person becomes covered under another group health plan as an employee;

- The qualified person becomes entitled to Medicare benefits (not just eligible, but entitled);

- The sponsoring employer terminates **ALL** of its group health plans.

COBRA coverage can be continued if the group health plan under which a qualified person becomes covered contains any exclusion or limitation with respect to a pre-existing condition.

11.   *What are the responsibilities of the employees or other covered beneficiaries?*

An employer must be notified within 60 days of any qualifying event known only to the employee or qualified beneficiary, such as divorce or legal separation.

A qualified beneficiary who is eligible for 29 months of COBRA coverage because of a disability must notify the employer within 60 days of a final disability determination under the Social Security Act prior to the end of the standard 18-month COBRA coverage period.

12.   *What are the responsibilities of the employer to notify the employee or qualified beneficiary?*

In addition to including a general notice of COBRA rights in any summary plan description, employers must also inform new employees and their spouses of their rights and responsibilities, and advise them who the plan administrator is, if any. In cases of divorce or separation, both the covered employee and the spouse must be separately notified.

Specific time periods must be included in every COBRA notice, and the notice should contain all the information necessary to allow qualified beneficiaries to make an informed choice. Qualified beneficiaries should be reminded that if they want coverage they have 45 days from the date of their election to pay the premium. Employers must also inform covered beneficiaries during the last 180 days of their COBRA coverage of their rights to convert to individual coverage, when applicable.

Employers must also inform covered beneficiaries of any available options or changes in their coverage, either because of plan termination, modification of the existing plan, termination of all health coverage, or because the covered beneficiary has chosen to terminate coverage.

13.   *Will an Employer be Penalized for Not Complying with COBRA's Requirements?*

The most severe penalty for failure to comply is the employer's loss of all tax deductions associated with all of its health plans. The IRS can levy excise taxes of $100 a day, or $200 if more than one qualified beneficiary is affected by the same qualifying event. ERISA penalties of $100 per day can be levied against plan administrators who fail to follow notification procedures. Fines up to $500,000 per year may be imposed. In addition, any qualified beneficiary who has wrongfully been denied COBRA coverage can sue to recover all damages, including attorney's fees.

14. *What should be done by a person who is not eligible for COBRA, but who is in need of benefits for himself or for a family member who is catastrophically ill or injured?*

Persons who are not eligible for COBRA should check to see if there are any regulations or laws in their state which require the employer to continue employment-based health insurance coverage at group rates.

G. CONVERSION.

Conversion is a process by which a policy holder attempts to shift his or her health insurance. Prior to July 1, 1997, the effective date of the *Health Insurance Portability and Accountability Act*, individuals who were catastrophically ill and injured routinely faced conversion problems as insurance companies would attempt to "shift" them to another insurance company because of the illness or injury. Unfortunately, the *Health insurance Portability and Accountability Act* has not solved all conversion problems for the catastrophically ill and injured. In addition, it may be advantageous for family members, in certain situations, to convert from one health insurance policy to another, since the new policy may have additional short-term and long-term rehabilitation benefits. When attempting to convert a health insurance policy, you should do the following:

- **Obtain a copy of the entire health insurance policy presently in effect;**

- **Obtain a copy of the complete health insurance policy to which you are considering a change;**

- **Have both health insurance policies carefully reviewed by your insurance agent, or your attorney;**

- **Make sure your new policy will not create a lapse in health insurance coverage;**

- **Make sure there are no pre-existing condition clauses, or exclusions of coverage, that will limit your health insurance coverage in the event of a catastrophic injury or illness.**

H.   *QUESTIONS AND ANSWERS ON THE HEALTH INSURANCE PORTABILITY AND ACCOUNTABILITY ACT.*

The **Health Insurance Portability and Accountability Act** was signed into law by President Clinton in August 1996 and became effective July 1, 1997. The new law applies to both group and self-insured medical insurance plans. The purpose of the Act is to help curb runaway health care costs.

> 1.   *How does this law affect me and my family if I am applying for **group health insurance** for the first time?*

Persons applying for group health insurance for the first time cannot be denied coverage or charged a higher premium for either themselves, or their family members, because of their past or present medical problems. A waiting period for coverage of a pre-existing condition can be imposed.

> 2.   *What is a pre-existing condition?*

A pre-existing condition is defined as a condition for which medical advice, diagnosis or treatment was recommended or received within the previous six (6) months.

> 3.   *Can coverage be denied because of health-related factors?*

Coverage cannot be denied, nor can the setting of premiums be based on:

    a.   Health status;

    b.   Medical condition (physical and mental);

    c.   Claims experience;

    d.   Receipt of health care;

    e.   Medical history;

    f.   Genetic information;

    g.   Evidence of insurability;

    h.   Disability.

> 4.   *How is the birth of a child treated under this Act?*

If you give birth or adopt a child while covered by a group insurance plan, the child should be added to the plan within thirty (30) days.

5.   *Will the child be covered for a pre-existing condition?*

Yes, the child is covered as long as there is continuous coverage.

6.   *What happens if you CHANGE group insurance plans?*

If you **change** group insurance plans, you or your family cannot be denied coverage or charged a higher premium than the rest of the group because of a medical problem, past or present.

7.   *If you change plans, can you be denied coverage for a pre-existing condition?*

You cannot be denied coverage for a pre-existing condition as long as you have had continuous medical coverage (including Medicaid) for the past twelve (12) months.

8.   *What happens if I lose my group health insurance and have to look for **individual coverage**?*

Persons who lose their group insurance are guaranteed individual coverage regardless of their past or present medical condition. The person must have had prior coverage for the last eighteen (18) months and must be financially able to pay the premiums.

9.   *Has COBRA been affected by this new law?*

This law qualifies families for twenty-nine (29) months of COBRA coverage, if the individual becomes disabled during the first sixty (60) days of COBRA coverage. Currently, to obtain twenty-nine (29) months of COBRA coverage, the individual must have been disabled at the time of termination of employment or reduction in hours.

10.   *Can a person transfer assets in order to become financially eligible for Medicaid?*

The Kennedy-Kassebaum Health Bill, which goes into effect on January 1, 1997, makes it a crime for individuals to gift property to children if the donor plans to apply for Medicaid and is attempting to circumvent Medicaid regulations. Both the donor and the donor's lawyers can be given a $10,000 fine and 1 year imprisonment. Some experts estimate that persons who have used up or transferred assets to qualify for governmental programs have cost taxpayers approximately $4.3 billion a year.

11.   *What is a medical savings account (MSA)?*

The Medical Savings Account is a test program designed for small businesses (from 2 to 50 employees) that will allow for the sale of 750,000 MSA policies.

12.   *How does this law work?*

The Act allows employers to set up tax-free accounts for each employee, with almost any insurance carrier or bank, for as much as $3,375. Employees would then utilize these funds to cover medical expenses. Costs at a pre-arranged deductible amount are then paid for from the so-called Catastrophic Coverage Insurance Plan that the company buys.

13.   *Are there any portions of the Act that apply to persons who are self-insured?*

For those who are self-employed, an insurance tax deduction will be phased in. In 1997, 40% of the premium costs will be tax deductible, increasing to 80% in the year 2006.

14.   *Are there any tax savings if you purchase your own health insurance?*

Individuals who are buying a policy on their own will be able to deduct part of the cost of the premium from their federal taxes, if the total cost of medical and long-term care exceeds 7.5% of income. People 51-60 years old can deduct $750 of their premiums from their taxes; those over 60 years of age - up to $2,000; and those persons over 70 years of age - up to $2,500.

The **Health Insurance Portability and Accountability Act of 1996** can be of great benefit to those who are catastrophically ill or who have sustained catastrophic injuries. Families in this position should contact an attorney to be sure that all benefits are utilized.

XIV. SUBROGATION RIGHTS

A. SUBROGATION RIGHTS: AN EXPLANATION

Subrogation rights are the right of an insurance company, a state public assistance agency, or self-insured employer who pays your medical bills to be repaid for the cost of medical care they provided from any money you receive in a lawsuit or any settlement from a third party. Subrogation rights, the right to be repaid, are provided either by contract or by statute.

B. SUBROGATION - WORKER'S COMPENSATION LIENS

An example of a statutory subrogation right is Worker's Compensation. In a usual Worker's Compensation case, your employer's worker's compensation insurance carrier will pay all your medical bills and a percentage of your wage loss if you are injured. If your injury was caused by a third party — for example, a defective machine — and you recover a settlement from the manufacturer of the defective machine, the worker's compensation insurance carrier _by statute_ has a right to be reimbursed for the amount of the medical bills and wage loss they paid you.

C. SUBROGATION - PRIVATE HEALTH INSURANCE

A private insurance company will issue you an insurance booklet that has, by contract, language which gives the insurance company a subrogation right, or the right to be repaid the amount of their benefits. An illustration of subrogation language which usually appears in a private insurance contract is as follows:

> "When a covered person incurs medical expenses which are payable under contract, Worker's Compensation or any other similar statute, or payable because legal action is brought against any third party to recover damages for an injury or illness...

> "The Company is entitled to reimbursement for any payment which a covered person or covered dependent may receive from a third party..."

To illustrate: You are injured when a scaffold on which you are working collapses because it was defectively designed. It was manufactured and designed by Company X. You receive worker's compensation benefits, i.e. payment of your medical bills and a percentage of your wages, from your employer's compensation insurance company, and you bring a lawsuit against Company X, the manufacturer and designer of the scaffold. If you win your lawsuit against Company X, your employer's worker's compensation company would be reimbursed a percentage of the wages and the medicals they provided from any money you receive in settlement from Company X.

D.   *FEDERAL LIENS*

Federal law requires repayment of a percentage of monies expended by the government for medical care for an injured person if that person later receives monies from a third party action settlement or verdict.

E.   *PUBLIC ASSISTANCE LIENS*

Most states, including Pennsylvania, require persons who receive public assistance to sign a subrogation form, agreeing to repay their public assistance lien out of any settlement or verdict from a personal injury action. Usually, the state governmental agency is willing to compromise, or reduce, the amount of their lien, depending upon the lifetime medical needs of the recipient and the amount of monies recovered in the settlement or verdict.

F.   *LEVERAGE - PAYMENT OF MEDICAL BILLS: INADEQUATE INSURANCE*

Leverage can be most useful when the following three factors exist: (1) catastrophically injured person; (2) facility equipped to meet the individual's needs; and (3) no insurance or inadequate insurance.

The best way to explain the concept of leverage is to use an example. Johnny is catastrophically injured in a hotel swimming pool accident where no lifequard was present. Johnny and his family have no insurance to pay for his medical bills and, though there is a facility which believes they could successfully rehabilitate Johnny from his head injury and spinal cord injury, they are unwilling to accept him without insurance. An attorney representing Johnny files a lawsuit against the hotel claiming that Johnny's injury was due in part because of a defective swimming pool and a lack of a lifeguard at the pool. In the usual leverage situation, the medical facility agrees to treat Johnny with the understanding that they would get paid back the cost of their medical services from the money Johnny receives in his lawsuit.

1.   *Can the concept of Leverage be used only when there is no insurance?*

No, the concept of leverage can also be used when there is inadequate insurance to pay for the medical program needed.

2.   *Most common examples where the concept of leverage can be helpful:*

a.   Where no insurance is involved;

114

b.   Where there is a private insurance company involved, such as HMO, Blue Cross/Blue Shield;

c.   When there is a governmental agency involved, such as Medical Assistance or Medicare;

d.   When you have quasi-governmental benefits set up by statute, but the benefits are paid by an insurance company. Example: worker's compensation.

3.   *No insurance company*

a.   The most common example: a motorcycle accident involving the use of a helmet.

In this situation all elements are present: (1) catastrophically injured person - usually head injury; (2) facility equipped to meet individual's medical needs; (3) no insurance.

In the overwhelming number of motorcycle accidents, there is no medical insurance. The injured person, his guardian or attorney agrees to pay back the hospital out of the proceeds of a lawsuit for the medical care provided by the hospital. This is usually done by a Letter of Protection signed by the injured individual, the court-appointed guardian, the parents and the attorney.

4.   *Private Insurance - Example: ATV—All Terrain Vehicle case*

In the private insurance case there are usually the following factors involved:

Blue Cross, HMO, Blue Shield policy, etc.;

Subrogation clause in the contract - a subrogation clause in the contract states that the insurance company has the contractual right to be reimbursed for the monies they paid for medical and rehabilitation costs.

Where there is private insurance in a catastrophic injury, it is important that the attorney contact the insurance company immediately after a catastrophic injury or accident occurs so that the insurance company is aware that someone is investigating this accident. Since the insurance company has a right of subrogation, they will be interested in assisting in the investigation of the ATV accident. The insurance company will benefit if the injured individual recovers damages from the third party.

If you have explained to your insurance company that you are bringing a lawsuit against the responsible party, they may be willing to extend medical and rehabilitation benefits under their policy. If the insurance company extends these benefits, the insurance company will recover all or part of their money at the end of the lawsuit. The lawsuit against the responsible party is your leverage.

5.   *Governmental Leverage - Medical Assistance (Medicaid) and Medicare*

Medical Assistance (Medicaid) and Medicare have a statutory right of subrogation. This means that the legislature has determined that they have a right to be repaid for the cost of medical care if you recover any money in a lawsuit from a third party. Medical Assistance and Medicare will only pay for certain therapies, rehabilitation programs and services for the catastrophically ill and injured. You should attempt to have Medicare or Medical Assistance pay extra-contractual benefits for your injured family member. Since the governmental agency has a statutory right to be repaid if you collect any money, they are interested in you bringing this lawsuit and your leverage is that you will bring the lawsuit, keep them advised and work with Medical Assistance or and Medicare if they pay additional medical benefits for your family member. Using the concept of leverage with a governmental agency is much more difficult than with a private insurance company but I predict its use will be expanded in the future.

6.   *Government and the private insurance company: Worker's Compensation*

All states require certain worker's compensation benefits that an individual must receive if he is injured at work. Worker's compensation benefits are really a partnership, since the benefits are set up by the legislature in a statute, and a private insurance company actually pays the benefits to the injured individual. All employers are required by statute to purchase worker's compensation insurance and they usually purchase this coverage from private insurance companies.

In the worker's compensation situation, a private insurance company has a statutory right to subrogation, therefore, they have a lien on any recovery the injured individual obtains from a third party.

The usual types of worker's compensation cases where leverage can be used are construction accidents, scaffolding accidents, automobile accidents, etc.

Normally, a worker's compensation insurance company will have a subrogation division whose sole purpose is to recover monies expended by the insurance company for catastrophically injured claimants. An attorney and family member should contact the insurance company immediately after an injury or accident occurs because, obviously, it is in the interest of the worker's compensation insurance company to help you thoroughly investigate, preserve evidence and pursue a claim against a responsible third party, since the worker's compensation insurance company has a lien on any recovery and will get their money back.

Using the concept of leverage to assist in the placement of the catastrophically ill or injured in a facility equipped to meet the individuals' needs is not easy. Often, the hospital or rehabilitation facility will be reluctant to work with an attorney that they do not know and who has not successfully used the concept of leverage in the past. You should be represented by an experienced attorney who can convince the insurance company, governmental agency, medical or rehabilitation facility, that it is in their interest, as well as the catastrophically ill or injured person's interest, to cooperate and work together.

XV. MANAGED CARE: BENEFITS AND PROCEDURES

A. MANAGED CARE - AN OVERVIEW

Managed care was created by the health insurance industry to allow them to control costs by limiting the consumer's access to services. In the traditional form of health insurance, a consumer pays the bill for each visit. This type of insurance is called "indemnity insurance". In a managed care insurance plan, the purchaser (patient or employer) pays a set fee, and the managed care organization takes responsibility for providing whatever health services may be needed, regardless of cost. Managed care patients are not permitted to go to a hospital or to see a specialist unless they first receive a referral from the primary care doctor. The primary care doctor acts as a "gatekeeper" and is responsible for monitoring the total medical care of each patient assigned to him or her under the plan.

Managed care advocates argue that aggressive preventive medicine will result in lower medical costs. Many doctors and healthcare advocates have concerns about the quality of care a managed care organization provides. In a managed care system, many have argued that patients have become "covered lives", and healthcare services have suffered. Physicians and other healthcare professionals are joining with consumer groups, healthcare advocates, and attorneys for the catastrophically ill and injured, in calling for a "fairer system", which would be cost effective and still provide for the short-term and long-term medical needs of the individual.

B. MOST COMMONLY ASKED MANAGED CARE QUESTIONS

1. _What are the most commonly heard complaints about the managed care concept?_

- It takes too long to find out what my healthcare coverage is;

- The system of referral from primary-care physicians to specialists is too slow and cumbersome;

- When there is a disagreement with an HMO, the patient can speak only with a clerk and not a doctor;

- Managed care organizations rarely inform the patient that they have the right to appeal a denial;

- Physicians complain that they are not able to give superior quality of care under a managed healthcare system.

118

2. *What is a health maintenance organization (HMO)?*

Most health maintenance organizations have the following elements in common:

- Subscribers receive a comprehensive set of hospital and medical services for a set pre-paid premium. **Pre-paid** means the individual or employer pays for the services before receiving them;

- The services are provided by a group of medical professionals who receive a fixed monthly payment per individual, regardless of the services used by that individual. This is often called a **capitated fee**;

- Individuals can only use the physicians, hospitals and other healthcare professionals approved by the HMO.

3. *What is a preferred provider organization? (PPO)?*

A preferred provider organization or PPO is a group of medical-care professionals who agree to provide health-care services to employees of selected companies in return for a guaranteed volume of patients at a guaranteed per patient fee. You can go outside the PPO and use other physicians and hospitals, but you will have to pay considerably more in deductibles and co-payments.

4. *How does the HMO pre-paid concept differ from the traditional fee-for-service system?*

The major difference is in the way the HMO providers are paid. Under a fee-for-service system, the healthcare providers are paid for the service they render. Under the HMO system, the physicians and hospitals must live within a budget. The physician or hospital is paid a monthly or quarterly fee per patient regardless of the medical and hospital services provided.

5. *Can I change my primary care physician?*

Yes, but check the language of your insurance contract carefully, since some plans will only allow primary care physicians to be changed at specific times.

6. *What is economic credentialing?*

Economic credentialing is a process by which insurance companies determine which doctors cost managed care insurers the most money. Doctors may be dropped from a preferred provider list or have their hospital privileges limited if their treating patterns are not cost effective.

7. *Do physicians receive bonuses at the end of the year based on the managed care plan's financial performance?*

Yes, some plans award physicians and other healthcare professionals a bonus if the cost of referrals and hospitalizations is below the plan's targeted budget.

8. *In an HMO, does a primary-care physician receive a fixed monthly payment for each member regardless of how often the member sees the doctor?*

Yes, HMO's set up a "capitated fee" to cover the expected average cost of treating a member.

9. *What is case management?*

The HMO designates an individual as a case manager or rehabilitation nurse, who has the job of coordinating care, discharge planning, and arranging for attendant and home care, etc. Case managers are not patient advocates in the traditional sense, since they are hired by the managed care agency or insurer. Primarily, their job is to provide quality services while also reducing costs. Many healthcare advocates have argued that case managers cannot effectively advocate for the short-term and long-term needs of the catastrophically ill and injured while at the same time, reduce costs for the entity that hired them.

10. *Will an HMO pay all my medical bills if I am catastrophically ill or injured?*

Most individuals who are covered by a managed care plan, such as an HMO, have one million dollars lifetime maximum coverage per individual. The lifetime maximum carries over from year to year. For example, if you have an appendectomy which cost the managed care insurer $100,000.00 in one year then you would have $900,000.00 left on your lifetime maximum. Since $1 million dollars is usually insufficient to cover the lifetime needs of a person who is catastrophically ill and injured, careful planning and allocation of resources is necessary after the acute and subacute hospitalizations.

11. *If I want a referral to a specialist, but my primary care physician will not approve it, what should I do?*

If you believe it is urgent that you be seen by a specialist, and your primary care doctor disagrees, ask him/her to explain in writing why your condition does not require prompt medical attention. Because you must obtain a referral before you can go to a specialist in an HMO system, the process sometimes seems to take forever. This delay in referral to a specialist can result in a delay in diagnosis and a delay in receiving prompt medical intervention, especially when there is a catastrophic injury or illness. If you want to challenge your primary care doctor's decision, a written opinion from your doctor will be helpful in filing an appeal. Requesting the primary care doctor to put his/her views in writing may also cause the doctor to change his or her opinion and allow your referral.

12. *What is the usual procedure people use to find out what their health insurance coverage is?*

- Contact the insurance company - call a toll free number;

- Call the employee personnel department or your union shop steward;

- Read the brochure which was provided by the employer or the insurance company.

13. *How do I obtain a copy of my insurance plan?*

Your health insurer is required to provide you, upon your request, a copy of the insurance policy including any addendum, riders or endorsements. As soon as a catastrophic injury or illness occurs, you should request, by telephone and in writing, a copy of the complete insurance contract. Failure by the insurance company to promptly provide the requested documentation may subject the health insurer to an allegation that they are acting in bad faith.

14. *Do health maintenance organizations make mistakes when it comes to providing information concerning your coverage?*

Yes. Many studies have shown that health insurers provide information with regard to coverage that is inaccurate, misleading, incomplete and outdated. If you do not force your health insurer to provide you with prompt, complete, and understandable information regarding coverage — they will not do so. Individuals and family members of the catastrophically ill and injured must realized that obtaining benefits from an HMO in a managed care system is an adversarial process.

15. *What steps should I take if I want to file an appeal with a managed care health insurer?*

- **Get letters from doctors.**
  Whatever approach you decide to follow, you will need one or more doctors to support your position in writing. You should request a letter to support your position from your primary care provider and also obtain one or two outside opinions from doctors who are not associated with your insurance plan;

- **Obtain the plan's denial of care or coverage in writing;**

- **Ask your employer to write a letter in support of your position;**

- **Pursue the plan's appeal process;**

- **Hire a personal healthcare advocate, ombudsman, or attorney;**

- **File a complaint with your State's health insurance department or health insurance commissioner;**

- **Contact the media.**

16. *What are some examples of a health insurer acting in bad faith?*

- Misrepresenting pertinent facts, policy, or contract provisions relating to coverage;

- Delay in responding to a claim;

- Failure to adopt and implement prompt investigation of claims;

- Refusal to pay a claim without adequate investigation;

- Failure to affirm or deny coverage in a reasonable manner;

- Delay in the investigation of claims or the payment of benefits by requiring submission of several forms which contain essentially the same information;

- Oppressive demands;

- Not attempting in good faith to effectuate prompt, fair, and equitable resolution of a health insurance claim when it is reasonably clear that the health insurer is liable.

17. *Will my doctor get be penalized if he criticizes the health maintenance organization?*

Many HMO contracts contain clauses which have been described as "loyalty oaths" or "gag rules". These contractual clauses forbid your doctor from criticizing the health maintenance organization. You should ask your primary care provider if there is such a "loyalty oath" or "gag rule" in your contract. Consumer groups and the American Medical Association have argued that "loyalty oaths" and "gag rules" inhibit medical providers from properly advocating for, and treating, their patients.

18. *Who has access to my medical records in a managed care system?*

According to a 1993 poll by Harris and Associates, 85% of the public believe that protecting the confidentiality of health records is absolutely essential. Computer technology has compounded the problem of confidentiality of records. In the pre-certification process, a clerk or physician approves or denies the treatment after reviewing "records" that were obtained from "somewhere" without ever seeing the patient. The web of primary care physicians, pre-certification personnel, health insurance administrators, case managers and rehabilitation nurses, as well as trade associations, like the Medical Information Bureau (MIB), creates many new and troubling problems in protecting and enforcing patient confidentiality.

"Information is power" and I urge families of the catastrophically ill and injured not to release any health insurance information to anyone unless they specifically know **WHO, WHAT** and **WHERE**.

WHO - who is requesting the information? Do not send a copy of your information to just anyone;

WHAT - what information does the person need to review? You should not send the complete medical chart if the person only needs a copy of the CAT Scan;

WHERE - specifically, where are you sending this information? If you can send requested information to a specific doctor, mark it to his or her personal attention. This approach is a better alternative than sending a full copy of the medical records to the hospital department or to the medical records department.

Once the medical records are in the hands of someone other than the person you want specifically to review it, you have no control over where that person is going to send your records.

19. *Do managed care insurers usually pay for pre-existing conditions?*

It depends on the language of the insurance policy. Devices that can be used to force managed care insurers to pay for pre-existing conditions are: **COBRA; the Healthcare Portability Act; the ADA; and the Bad Faith Law** that pertains to health insurance coverage.

20. *Will the HMO provide funding for treatment at a facility that is not on the approved list of treating facilities?*

Yes, but this will not be readily provided.

C. *FUTURE TRENDS AND ACCOUNTABILITY*

A 1996 survey made by the Kaiser Family Foundation and the Harvard School of Public Health[1] found that 54% of the respondents said that, "The government needs to protect consumers from being treated unfairly by managed care providers and not getting the care they should from managed care plans."

Managed care health insurers have avoided responsibility for the wrongful denial of treatment for years. Their "immunity" from responsibility has been based on the fact that they have not been considered a "medical care provider" even though, in reality, they have been practicing medicine for years.

They have also been able to establish immunity under ERISA (The **Federal Employee Retirement Income Security Act**), which covers all employee benefit plans.

Several states have recently passed legislation holding managed care insurers responsible for their conduct.

In June 1997, Missouri House Bill 335 was signed into law. This bill adds health maintenance organizations to the definition of "health care provider". Texas recently enacted legislation requiring managed care providers to exercise ordinary care in making treatment decisions. If a provider is found to have breached that duty, the patient may sue in state court.

In August 1997, New Jersey passed the **Health Care Quality Act** which guarantees consumers the right to appeal when a request for care has been denied. The bill also requires anyone making treatment decisions to be a licensed physician and prohibits managed care providers from providing financial incentives to deny medically necessary care.

According to the authors of the study, many more states are following suit and enacting laws requiring HMO's to be accountable for their treatment decisions. Consumers are tired of the poor treatment and the bureaucracy that managed care insurers are known for.

D. **RECOMMENDATIONS FOR PATIENTS AND PATIENT ADVOCATES**

1. Obtain and carefully read the health insurance policy which defines your health insurance coverage;

2. Provide the health insurance company with the requested medical records, but do not give the health insurer or the managed care agency unlimited access to your medical records;

3. Verify health insurance coverage in writing — do not rely on telephone conversations with clerks;

4. Ask the physician if he or she has a financial incentive under a contract with the managed care insurer;

5. Work with the rehab nurse assigned by the managed care insurer, but remember, he or she represents the insurance company, and is also trying to represent you;

6. Be aware of roadblocks erected by the managed care health insurer to deny benefits for the catastrophically ill and injured. These roadblocks are: The pre-certification process, peer review, exclusions, limitations, definitions, and experimental clauses in the insurance policy;

7. Just because a health insurer requests a medical examination, it doesn't mean they are legally or contractually entitled to it;

8. Never go to an "independent medical exam" (IME) for your health insurer, workers' compensation carrier or the Social Security Administration without having an advocate, attorney, or family member with you;

9. Be aware that obtaining health insurance benefits from a managed care insurer is an adversarial process;

10.   If a loved one or family member is catastrophically ill or injured, hire a health care intermediary, a personal medical advocate, or an attorney.

CONCLUSION

As I indicated in the introduction of this book, *"The laws assist those who are vigilant, not those who sleep on their rights."* This legal maxim could never be truer than in today's world, when the health insurance industry is arbitrarily denying needed medical and rehabilitation benefits. You must contact an attorney or advocate to fight for the benefits to which you are entitled.

E.   *SUITS vs. MANAGED CARE - NEW HORIZONS*

The 1974 Federal Law, the **Employee Retirement Income Security Act** (ERISA) has been used by HMO's as a shield to protect them against medical malpractice lawsuits. Because of ERISA, HMO's attempt to claim that they are merely extensions of employee benefit plans, and thus are protected from state laws that have anything to do with health insurance. The law also makes it futile to attempt to sue managed care health insurance companies in either state or federal court. Consumer groups, healthcare organizations, doctors, and lawyers are requesting that state and federal legislatures change ERISA to allow families to sue managed care insurers. In the past two years, four federal appeals courts, in Denver, New York City, Philadelphia and Chicago, have ruled that HMO's and other managed care plans can and should, in some circumstances, be held liable for medical negligence. The Pennsylvania Supreme Court heard arguments in a recent 1997 case against U.S. Healthcare, an HMO based in Blue Bell, Pennsylvania. The Pennsylvania Supreme Court is expected to rule soon. Experts predict that the Pennsylvania case and other similar cases could ultimately be appealed to the United States Supreme Court.

F.   *SUCCESSFULLY LITIGATED MANAGED CARE CASES*

1.   *ATV - Exclusions - Health insurance benefits - Managed care - Traumatic brain injury and spinal cord injury*

The parents purchased an insurance policy containing a clause stating that children will receive 24 hour coverage if ill or injured. Their child was riding an ATV (three-wheeled All-Terrain Vehicle) when the ATV turned over and the minor suffered head and spinal cord injuries. The parents made a request to the health insurance company that the child's medical bills be paid, but the insurance company denied the claim. Their basis for the denial was that the health care policy excluded injuries v occurred on an ATV. Essentially, the insurance company told the fan "We accepted your premiums but you didn't read the fine p **SUGGESTION:** Certain exclusions are invalid and void as against public policy. All exclusions which attempt to deny payment for needed medical expenses should be challenged and discussed with your attorney as soon as possible after a catastrophic injury or illness.

2. *Misleading coverage information - Catastrophic illness - HMO - Bad faith*

The parents had a child born with cerebral palsy. The parents called their HMO and were told that they had a $1 million dollar lifetime maximum plan covering the child and "not to worry, they had good coverage". The hospital was also told that the parents had "good coverage". After the initial hospitalization stay, when it was time for the child to be discharged, the parents and the hospital learned from the HMO that home care, attendant care, rehabilitation care and long term nursing care would not be covered, since the policy specifically excluded children whose care, in the opinion of the HMO, was "custodial in nature". I accepted this case and I successfully argued that the HMO was "acting in bad faith", since they initially told the family in the hospital that there was coverage and were now attempting to deny needed care. **SUGGESTION:** Some studies show that over 40% of the time, the coverage information provided by health insurers to parents and healthcare providers is wrong, outdated, incomplete, and misleading. It is critical that you have a trained person read the language of your health insurance policy to determine what short term and long term benefits you are entitled to from your health insurer.

3. *Medical necessity - Home modification - Durable medical equipment - Spinal cord injury*

An individual suffered a spinal cord injury (quadriplegia) in a diving accident. The rehabilitation facility and the person's treating doctor wrote reports indicating that home modifications were necessary due to the patient's limitations. Initially, the managed care insurer denied the requested benefits. They also denied a "specialized wheelchair" on the basis that the policy indicated that they only had to pay for a non-motorized wheelchair. **SUGGESTION:** I obtained the insurance policy from the managed care insurer and discussed with the treating doctors how the policy language defined "medical necessity" and "durable medical equipment". After the treating doctors and I reviewed the policy language, they re-wrote their reports indicating why home modifications were medically necessary and why, in their opinion, a motorized wheelchair met the definition of durable medical equipment. On appeal, the managed care agency reversed their decision and agreed to pay for both the home modifications and the specialized wheelchair.

4. *Extracontractual benefits - Third party recovery - Subrogation*

An individual was riding his motorcycle and was wearing a motorcycle helmet. An automobile forced the motorcycle operator off the road and the driver who caused the accident was never identified. The driver of the motorcycle was thrown to the ground and the helmet that he was wearing cracked. The HMO paid for the acute care hospitalization but denied all short-term and long-term rehabilitation care, since it was their position that these benefits were not covered under the policy. An exhaustive investigation revealed that the foreign manufacturer of the helmet had used an inferior/defective lining in the manufacture of the helmet, which caused the helmet to crack on impact. I successfully argued to the HMO that they should pay "extracontractual benefits". The HMO agreed to pay extracontractual benefits because they would receive repayment for the medical bills (subrogation) they paid for the insured, out of the successful product liability suit against the manufacturer of the helmet. **SUGGESTION:** All catastrophic injuries and illnesses should be aggressively investigated to determine whether or not the concept of **extracontractual benefits** and subrogation can be used to obtain additional short-term and long-term rehabilitation benefits.

5. *Coma awareness/coma stimulation programs - HMO's - Policy language*

An individual I represented suffered anoxia, but the HMO refused to pay for a coma stimulation/coma awareness program. The HMO's decision was based on the fact that the policy language specifically indicated that the policy did not pay for a coma stimulation/coma awareness program, and also that the medical director of the HMO believed that such programs were "experimental". **SUGGESTION:** I was able to successfully argue that an insured should be given the opportunity of a coma stimulation/ coma awareness program to show whether or not they have the cognitive capacity to be rehabilitated. Coma awareness/coma stimulation programs are controversial, and most managed care insurers will not agree to pay for such programs unless they are forced to.

6. *Suits against HMO's - Improper care*

Parents argued that their daughter suffered brain damage as a result of the negligence of one of the HMO's treating physicians. The family sued the doctor as well as the HMO. The HMO argued that it does not make "medical decisions" and that they are protected from lawsuits by a 1974 federal law that regulates employee benefits (ERISA). **SUGGESTION:** Many courts are not accepting the argument that HMO's are setting guidelines for care but should not have any legal liability. Most courts have held that consumers should be able to sue their health insurance plan. Careful consideration should be given as to whether or not to sue an HMO, given the specific facts and circumstances of your case.

7. *Spinal cord injury - Vacation - Exclusion*

An individual, while on vacation, suffered a spinal cord injury. The person's family called the health insurer, who indicated that they did not have to pay to fly the individual back to the United States for treatment, since the language of the policy excluded any injury or accident that occurred outside the territorial United States. I argued that relying on this exclusion was acting in bad faith and the exclusion was "unfair" and should be void as against public policy. The health insurer reversed its decision and paid for the short term and long term care for the spinal cord injured individual. **SUGGESTION:** If you are catastrophically ill or injured, <u>never</u> accept a denial of coverage from your insurance company without first examining the policy and fighting to determine whether or not the initial decision can be overturned. The amount of treatment, the kind of treatment, whether or not you can receive your long-term care at home, in a transitional living unit, in a group home, or in a nursing home, will depend upon whether or not you can successfully win your appeal.

8. *Pre-certification - Gatekeeper - Managed care insurers*

An individual had a traumatic brain injury. The treating doctor recommended a long-term rehabilitation stay to improve cognitive functioning. The managed care health insurer would not pre-certify the hospital stay, basically reasoning that it did not believe the individual could benefit from an in-patient rehabilitation. The individual with the traumatic brain injury had never had a prior in-patient brain injury rehabilitation program. After the family hired counsel, the managed care organization agreed to pay for the in-patient hospitalization stay. **SUGGESTION:** Many health care advocates believe that the pre-certification process used by managed care insurers is unfair, adversarial, and abusive. In the pre-certification process, the health insurer has all the decision-making power. The health insurer has the policy; they know what information is contained in the policy; they wrote the policy; and they pick the pre-certifying doctor, who must give permission for treatment. This pre-certification process is an adversarial process and family members of the catastrophically ill and injured should adopt the following approach:

- Ask for a curriculum vitae (CV) or resume of the pre-certifying doctor;

- Ask about prior decisions by the pre-certifying or reviewing doctor, i.e. how many times has the doctor pre-certified before on this issue and how many times did he rule in favor of the insurer versus the patient;

- Ask, specifically, how long it will take for the pre-certification decision to be made, and how you will be notified of the pre-certification decision;

- Demand a written copy of the pre-certification decision;

- Ask for the information on the appeal procedure, in writing, before the pre-certification decision is made;

- Start preparing documentation to appeal the pre-certification decision. (Statistically, it is very likely that the pre-certification decision will not be in your favor if you are catastrophically ill or injured.)

G. GLOSSARY OF MANAGED CARE TERMS

ACUTE ILLNESS: An illness that has occurred suddenly and may be serious.

ADMITTING PRIVILEGES: The authorization a hospital gives to a medical doctor or other healthcare provider to admit and treat a patient in that facility.

ALLOWABLE COSTS: Medical charges that are covered by a particular insurance plan.

ASSISTED LIVING FACILITY: A living facility in which aides or attendants help a disabled person do ordinary chores, routines, and other activities of daily living.

ATTENDING PHYSICIAN: A doctor who is primarily responsible for the care of a patient in a hospital.

CAPITATION: A payment system in which the insurer provides a set fee per patient to cover all medical services the person receives from the healthcare provider. The healthcare provider usually receives a monthly capitation fee per patient.

CASE MANAGEMENT: The process whereby the health insurer coordinates the treatment plan of the catastrophically ill and injured individual. In a case management system, the treatment plan is usually coordinated by the treating physician or the rehabilitation nurse.

CATASTROPHIC INJURY OR ILLNESS: A medical condition that may last a lifetime, or result in the need for long-term care.

COINSURANCE: The percentage an insured person pays for a visit to a physician or other healthcare provider. The percentage varies from plan to plan.

CONVERSION: Process by which a subscriber or insured changes his or her health insurance coverage.

CO-PAYMENT: Fixed dollar amount the patient pays for health care services at the time of receiving the service.

CUSTODIAL CARE: Care usually provided in an institution for an individual's basic physical needs. Custodial care is not paid for under many HMO plans. According to insurance company guidelines, custodial care is necessary when a patient is no longer making rehabilitative gains.

DEDUCTIBLE: The amount of money that an individual must pay out-of-pocket in a calendar year before the insurance company begins paying medical bills.

DISCHARGE PLANNING: Planning process that begins before a patient is discharged from an acute care hospital, rehabilitation facility, or nursing facility. Family members should be involved in the discharge planning process.

DURABLE MEDICAL EQUIPMENT (DME): Medical equipment such as walkers, wheelchairs, ventilators, etc. Durable medical equipment is defined differently under each health insurance policy.

ENROLLMENT: Number of persons included in a particular health plan. The "enrollees" are often referred to as "covered lives" in the plan.

EMERGENCY: An injury, illness, or acute medical condition likely to cause death, disability, or serious illness if not treated immediately. The term "emergency" is defined differently under each health insurance policy.

EXCLUSIONS: Illnesses or injuries that an insurance policy specifically will not cover.

FEE-FOR-SERVICE PLAN: Traditional system of payment by insurance companies to doctors. Doctors would charge the insurance company what they consider a reasonable, customary price, and the insurance company would pay. The system whereby an insurer reimburses a hospital or physician each time a policyholder receives care is often called an "indemnity plan".

GATEKEEPER: The primary-care physician responsible for coordinating your healthcare and providing a referral to a specialist.

GROUP INSURANCE: Coverage purchased for an individual through a group - usually an employer, union or self-insured trade group.

HEALTH MAINTENANCE ORGANIZATION (HMO): An organization that provides health insurance coverage for a specified number of individuals for an agreed-upon fixed sum.

LIFETIME MAXIMUM: The total amount of benefits an insurance company will pay out for an individual during the individual's lifetime.

LONG-TERM CARE: Care provided to individuals who have a catastrophic injury or illness who can not take care of themselves without assistance.

PRE-CERTIFICATION: A process required by the managed care health insurer before they will agree to pay for the requested surgery or medical treatment.

PRE-EXISTING CONDITION: A health condition, for example, diabetes, that a patient had before he or she purchased a health insurance policy. Pre-existing conditions are usually excluded from coverage.

PREMIUM: The regular charge, usually monthly, that a health insurer receives.

PEER REVIEW ORGANIZATION (PRO): A physician's group responsible for assuring that patients are getting services they need according to minimum professional standards.

PROGNOSIS: A prediction by a health-care provider to a patient, and to the health insurer, concerning the likely course of an illness or injury. In terms of prognosis, a health insurer is interested in "how long" and "how much" a particular illness or injury is going to cost them in dollars.

REHABILITATION: This term is defined differently under each health insurance policy. A patient must be improving medically for a health insurer to continue to pay ongoing medical bills.

SELF-INSURANCE: Self-insurance is a practice whereby a group of individuals, a company, or a group of companies set aside funds to pay for their own healthcare services.

UTILIZATION REVIEW: A term used by the health insurance industry to make sure that treatment received by patients is necessary and appropriate. Utilization review decisions are often criticized by healthcare advocates as being "one-sided" in favor of the health insurer.

H.   *HMO - LIABILITY FOR NEGLIGENT CARE.*

A growing number of courts have recognized that HMO's should be held responsible for the quality of care given to their patients. Many arguments have been made in support of holding HMO's liable under a corporate negligence theory if they result in the denial of proper care. Litigation can be expected to increase in many states as the courts follow the trend toward expanding corporate liability and rule that HMO's are liable for corporate negligence and are vicariously liable for the negligence of their healthcare providers.

1.   *Wickline Theory of Liability: Recognized that the duty of care exists with respect to utilization review decisions and patients*

a.   *WICKLINE vs. STATE OF CALIFORNIA*, 192 Cal. App. 3rd 1630, 228 Cal. Rptr. 661 (2nd Dist. 1986). Physician recommended surgery, and the California Med-Cal Program, which conducts utilization review, approved the surgery and a ten-day post-operative length of stay. Prior to discharge, the physician requested an eight-day extension due to post-surgical complications. The Med-Cal physician consultant authorized only a four-day extension. The patient was discharged after the four-day period without further protest from the attending physician to extend the hospitalization. Nine days after leaving the hospital, Wickline was re-admitted under emergency conditions, and her right leg required amputation. She sued Med-Cal, the company that completed the utilization review, claiming that it was negligent in failing to grant the eight-day extension as originally requested by her physicians, causing premature discharge and injury.

The court in Wickline held:

"Third party payors performing utilization review may be held legally accountable when medically inappropriate decisions result from defects in the design or implementation of cost-containment mechanisms."

For example, the court said,

"Utilization review company could be responsible when appeals made on a patient's behalf for medical care are arbitrarily ignored or unreasonably disregarded or overridden."

2. *How Do Families Prove "Wickline" Liability - That a Health Insurer Has Breached The Duty Of Care That They Owe To Patients?*

a. The health insurer or utilization review organization (URO), does not have detailed selection criteria, minimum qualifications, and training procedures for its personnel who make the decisions concerning whether or not you are approved for the requested healthcare;

b. The URO or health insurer fails to review all available medical records before pre-certification or the requested health care benefit is denied;

c. The URO or health insurer fails to communicate with the attending physician before denying the requested benefit;

d. All of the health insurer or URO's written and verbal communications (i.e., policies, contract, consent forms, manuals, marketing materials, appeal procedures, etc.) should reflect that the patient's physician alone governs the particulars and the duration of the requested medical care;

e. Emergency admissions should always be exempt from pre-admission certification requirements;

f. Insureds, family members, and the physicians involved in the plan should be fully informed of the appeal mechanisms available to them;

g. Both the attending physician and the insured should have immediate rights to appeal a non-certification decision, i.e. a decision denying the requested medical and rehabilitation care.

CONCLUSION

The third-party payor system in this country was expressly structured to avoid interference with the doctor/patient relationship. Only a patient's treating doctor or health care professional could determine an individual's course of treatment. Today, with managed care, cost constraints are beginning to change the traditional relationship between patients, third-party payors, and health care providers. Managed care organizations are aggressively using utilization review companies, pre-certification procedures, auditing, case managers and rehabilitation nurses, and peer review, to limit their exposure. Managed care entities are requiring health care providers to sign preferred provider agreements or other contractual obligations, which places health care professionals in a position of conflict, i.e. a health care professional is in the unenviable position of having a contractual obligation to the managed care company to limit costs, while also having a moral and ethical obligation to treat the patient regardless of cost. The challenge for the medical community in a managed care setting will be to deliver appropriate care for the patient in a cost-effective manner. The challenge for the legal community is to secure all available health insurance benefits to meet the short-term and long-term medical and rehabilitation needs of the catastrophically ill and injured.

[1] David Strickland, Trial magazine, Sept, 1997 News & Trends

XVI. TRAUMATIC BRAIN INJURY

A.   *TRAUMATIC BRAIN INJURY - TRAUMA FACTS*

One brain injury occurs every 15 seconds in the United States, and is the leading cause of death and disability of young adults. According to statistics from the Brain Injury Association, each year in America over 2 million persons, half of which are young children, sustain head injuries. Of these injuries, 373,000 are serious enough to warrant hospitalization, and over 100,000 persons die from head trauma.

In the United States, the leading causes of traumatic brain injury are automobile accidents (50%), falls (21%), violence (12%), and sports and recreation (10%).

From 50,000 to 110,000 persons receive injuries classified as "moderate to severe". Moderate to severe brain injuries require extensive long-term rehabilitation services. Costs for long-term and short-term rehabilitation over a lifetime of caring for a person with a severe brain injury averages $5 million to $10 million. Injuries cost the nation $25 billion a year.

B.   *TYPES OF HEAD INJURY*

Generally, head injuries may be broadly classified as either **open head injury**, in which the skull is penetrated, or **closed head injury**, where no actual penetration has occurred. Skull fractures frequently occur with head injuries, and may be either **depressed** or **non-depressed**. Skull fractures can usually be visualized through the use of x-rays, CT scans, and MRI's. A fractured skull with an open wound or a gunshot wound to the head are examples of open head injuries. Closed head injury often occurs as the result of an acceleration or deceleration of the brain. This can occur as a whiplash or in a blow to the head, and may be experienced when the head strikes the windshield of a car in a crash, or when the head is thrown backward and forward in a rear-end collision. A **diffuse axonal injury** is the most common type of head injury, and is classified as a closed head injury. A person can suffer the following as the result of a head injury: **cerebral contusions**; **epidural hematomas**; **subdural hematomas**; **intra-cerebral hemorrhages**; and **concussions**.

Many factors contribute to the severity of the brain injury. These factors include whether or not the individual was unconscious or in a coma, and what part of the brain was injured:
- Frontal
- Temporal
- Occipital
- Parietal lobes
- Brain stem

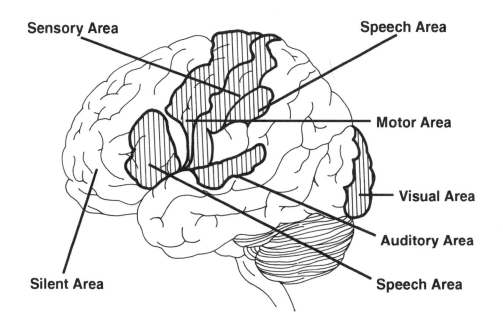

Sensory Area

Speech Area

Motor Area

Visual Area

Auditory Area

Silent Area

Speech Area

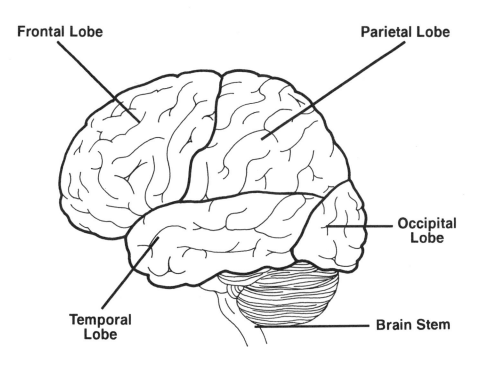

Frontal Lobe

Parietal Lobe

Occipital Lobe

Temporal Lobe

Brain Stem

C.   **CLASSIFICATION OF BRAIN INJURY**

    1.   Mild

    2.   Moderate

    3.   Severe

D.   **MILD TO MODERATE - POST-CONCUSSIVE SYNDROME**

Brain injury can be present in a person who has never lost consciousness. The alteration of consciousness caused by the blow to the head may instead have taken the form of a period of feeling dazed, confused, or agitated. Persons with mild to moderate brain injury are beset by residual problems that usually escape detection in ordinary medical examinations. Because these problems are undefined or improperly defined, they become more frightening and debilitating to the victim.

Doctors frequently treat patients who have complaints of disorientation, difficulty organizing their thoughts, short- and long-term memory problems, headaches, dizziness, double vision, hypersensitivity to light or sound, or fear and confusion when in crowds. The patient exhibits periods of feeling dazed, confused, or agitated and is having problems at home and difficulty on the job. Often, these symptoms lead to a diagnosis of "post-concussive syndrome."

Post-concussive syndrome is defined as

"a complex reaction that usually occurs subsequent to a head injury or other severe threat to the individual's life. The syndrome, which is most commonly encountered by psychiatrists, neurologist, and industrial physicians, may include headaches, dizziness, weakness and fatigue, anxiety, depression and emotional instability, difficulty in concentrating, forgetfulness, and general irritability. Although theses symptoms may gradually decrease over several months, they occasionally persist and result in permanent personality change. Severe and persistent nightmares are frequently associated with the post-traumatic syndrome."[1]

"According to Lishman, neurosis

"certainly represents the commonest of the psychiatric sequelae of head injury, in some series outnumbering all other forms of disability together. Included here are depressive reactions; anxiety states often with phobic symptomatology; neurasthenic reactions with fatigue, irritability and sensitivity to noise; conversion hysteria; obsessional neurosis; and, most common of all, a variety of somatic complaints, including headache and dizziness, which may become the subject of anxious introspection and hypochondriacal concern...the longer neurotic symptoms persist, the less likely they are to be the expression of brain damage.

"In the early stages of convalescence, however, such symptoms are probably founded on transient *physiological* disturbances in brain function."[2]

Proper planning for the treatment of a post-concussive disorder must begin with a thorough understanding of the complex medical and legal issues involved. Medical professionals must do a prompt, factually correct and thorough investigation of the manner in which the injury occurred. Treating professionals must document in detail their preliminary diagnosis, the nature of the brain injury, the cause of the injury, whether or not there are any pre-existing conditions that have been aggravated, and the final diagnosis. They must also project the long-term medical needs of the individual. A post-concussive injury that is neither recognized medically, nor proven legally, can produce devastating long-term results.

E.   *SEVERE HEAD INJURY - PERSISTENT VEGETATIVE STATE*

Dr. Fred Blum, creator of the term "persistent vegetative state", states: "Vegetative state describes a body which is functioning entirely in terms of its internal controls. It maintains temperature, heartbeat and pulmonary ventilation, maintains digestive activity, maintains reflex activity of muscles and nerves for low-level responses, but there is no behavioral evidence of either self-awareness or awareness of the surroundings in a learned manner." It has been estimated that there are approximately 10,000 to 25,000 persons in the country in a persistent vegetative state. I have represented numerous persons in a persistent vegetative state, whose conditions were caused by drowning, traumatic head injury, and anoxia (lack of oxygen to the brain). It is critical that all family members of someone who is in a persistent vegetative state discuss with a qualified attorney what medical benefits are obtainable under your available health insurance policy.

F.   *ACUTE CARE TREATMENT*

When someone has suffered a traumatic brain injury (TBI) in a motor vehicle accident, it is good practice for the emergency room physician to personally question the other occupants of the car. If there are no passengers to question, or the others are themselves injured, the physician can speak with the witnesses to the accident, other drivers, paramedics and police officers. They can describe to the doctor whether the damage to the vehicles involved was minor, moderate, or severe. Facts such as: Was the person ejected from the vehicle, and if so, how far was the person thrown; was there bleeding from the ears; was there a period of unconsciousness; was there evidence of drug or alcohol use; was the victim wearing a seat belt or seat belt and shoulder harness; was the air bag inflated; can all be determined at this time. Any details that can be obtained from witnesses to the accident, other occupants of the motor vehicle, investigating police officers, emergency medical technicians, first responders and paramedics, will provide crucial information in the earliest stages of treatment and diagnosis for a post-concussive injury.

A head injured patient is often unable to respond to questions concerning his medical background, or the information obtained is unreliable. A spouse, parent, family member or next of kin can provide necessary medical history, including family medical history.

A complete medical history for a person with a suspected post-concussive injury is imperative.

The questions that need to be answered are:

- Has there ever been a prior head, neck, or back injury?

- Is the patient currently undergoing treatment for any medical condition?

- Is the person taking any medication?

- Has there been prior psychological or psychiatric treatment?

- Has the person ever been treated for depression?

- Are there any significant medical problems in the individual's history?

Obtaining the complete medical history is essential. Doctors should not rely on their staff to obtain this information, but should themselves contact the family doctor and all other treating professionals to get an accurate assessment of the patient's prior health history.

Increasingly, insurance companies are reviewing medical charts and submitting cases for peer review before paying medical benefits. If the treating professional has underestimated the post-concussive injury, the difficulties in receiving medical reimbursement from an insurance company for future care and in proving the post-concussive injury at trial increase. It is important to note that health care insurance companies require information on the specific nature of the injury, an estimation of the costs and future length of treatment, and a prognosis, so that adequate monies can be reserved for future treatment.

G.   *DIAGNOSIS OF HEAD INJURIES - TYPES OF TESTS*

1.   *Objective vs. Subjective Testing*

Objective evidence of a head injury is generally shown by the use of computerized typography (CT) scans, x-rays, electroencephalogram, and magnetic resonance imaging (MRI). Some courts and insurance companies have accepted as objective evidence of a head injury, testimony based upon positive emission topography (PET) scans, evoked potentials, and brain electrical activity mapping (BEAM) tests, and SPECT scans.

The most common type of subjective testing offered as proof of a traumatic brain injury is neuropsychological testing. Neuropsychological testing will often demonstrate cognitive deficits of a patient, since more traditional testing methods, such as CT scans, X-rays, MRI's, do not document objective findings of organic impairment. One third of the patients who had been gainfully employed before their accident were still unemployed three months later, and were still suffering headaches and memory deficits.

The "objectivity" of neuropsychological testing as a barometer for documenting traumatic brain injury has been called into question by insurance companies and the courts. Evidence based on "subjective testing" will be viewed more favorably by the courts if there is additional evidence such as a positive MRI, EEG, etc. These "objective" tests give the trial attorney more leverage in trying to prove or disprove a post-concussive disorder. The courts will usually allow testimony concerning any medical testing if the scientific knowledge in that field is advanced enough to permit a reasonable opinion to be given by an expert.

2.   *Measures of Cognitive Functioning - Head Injury*

a.   **RANCHO SCALE**

The levels of cognitive functioning scale was developed by the head injury treatment team at the Rancho Los Amigos Hospital in California. This scale is useful for families and health care professionals since, by referring to level 1 through 8, family members and professionals can "speak the same language" and identify the level of cognitive functioning of an individual patient.

RANCHO SCALE

I   *NO RESPONSE.*

Patient appears to be in a deep sleep and is completely unresponsive to any stimuli presented to him/her.

II   *GENERALIZED RESPONSE.*

Patient reacts inconsistently and non-purposefully to stimuli in a nonspecific manner. Responses may be physiological changes, gross body movements and/or vocalization;

III   *LOCALIZED RESPONSE.*

Patient reacts specifically but inconsistently to stimuli. Responses are directly related to the type of stimulus presented. He/she may follow simple commands in an inconsistent, delayed manner;

IV   *CONFUSED, AGITATED.*

Patient is in a heightened state of activity with severely decreased ability to process information. He/she is detached from the present and responds primarily to his/her own internal confusion. Behavior is frequently bizarre and non-purposeful relative to his/her immediate environment. Verbalization is frequently incoherent and/or inappropriate to the moment;

V   *CONFUSED, INAPPROPRIATE, NON-AGITATED.*

Patient appears alert and is able to respond to simple commands fairly consistently. However, with increased complexity of commands or lack of external structure, responses are non-purposeful, random, or at best, fragmented toward any desired goal. He/she is aware of the environment, but is highly distractible and lacks the ability to focus attention to a specific task. Verbalization is often inappropriate; confabulation may be triggered by present events. Memory is severely impaired, with confusion of past and present;

VI   *CONFUSED, APPROPRIATE.*

Patient shows goal-oriented behavior, but is dependent on external input for direction. He/she follows simple directions consistently and shows carry-over for related tasks. Responses may be incorrect due to memory problems, but they are appropriate to the situation. Past memories show more depth and detail than recent memory;

VII   *AUTOMATIC - APPROPRIATE.*

Patient appears appropriate and oriented within hospital and home settings, goes through daily routine automatically, but frequently robot-like, with minimal or no confusion, but has shallow recall of recent events. He/she has superficial awareness of, but lacks insight into, his/her condition. Judgment and problem-solving abilities are decreased, realistic planning for the future is lacking. Pre-vocational or avocational evaluation and counseling may be indicated;

VIII   *PURPOSEFUL AND APPROPRIATE.*

Patient is alert and oriented, is able to recall and integrate past and recent events and is aware of and responsive to culture. He/she shows ability for new learning, accepts his/her life role, and needs no supervision once activities are learned. He/she may continue to show a decreased ability in abstract reasoning, tolerance for stress, judgment in emergencies or unusual circumstances. Social, emotional and intellectual capacities may continue to be at a decreased level but functional in society.

b.   **GLASGOW COMA SCALE**

The Glasgow Coma Scale, which is based upon eye opening, verbal and motor responses, is a practical means of monitoring changes in level of consciousness. If each response on the scale is given a number (high for normal and low for impaired responses), the responsiveness of the patient can be expressed by summation of the figures. The lowest score is 3, the highest is 15.

GLASGOW COMA SCALE

Eyes	Open	Spontaneously	4
		To verbal command	3
		To pain	2
		No response	1
Best motor response	To verbal command	Obeys	6
	To Painful stimulus*	Localizes pain	5
		Flexion-withdrawal	4
		Flexion-abnormal	3
		Extension	2
		No response	1
Best verbal response**		Oriented and converses	5
		Disoriented and converses	4
		Inappropriate words	3
		Incomprehensible sounds	2
		No response	1
		TOTAL	3-15

*Arouse patient with painful stimulus if necessary
** Apply knuckle to sternum - observe arms

3. *Misdiagnosis vs. Non-diagnosis*

Numerous studies have indicated that head injuries are consistently under-reported because of misdiagnosis and non-diagnosis. This is especially true in mild head injury cases, where the injured individual looks healthy, was never rendered unconscious, was never admitted to a hospital, but months and years later continues to suffer from "head injury symptoms". Misdiagnosis and non-diagnosis of traumatic brain injuries can lead to insurance and legal problems, since the attorney usually does not have the medical documentation necessary to prove the association between the injury or illness and the on-going medical problems. The problem of documenting mild TBI and post-concussive injuries is complicated when a managed care patient needs pre-certification for procedures, or when referral to a specialist is needed.

4. *Types of Impairments - Head Injuries*

Since I have represented clients with traumatic brain injuries for almost twenty years, I have found many of them have exhibited the following impairments after they have suffered a traumatic brain injury:

- **Short-term memory deficits**;

- **Long-term memory deficits**;

- **Memory gaps**;

- **Confusion**;

- **Difficulty in retrieving the proper word or phrase**;

- **Difficulty in doing mathematic calculations**;

- **Difficulty in word-finding**;

- **Slowness in processing information**;

- **Difficulty in comprehending written words**;

- **Attention and concentration**;

- **Seizures**;

- **Spatial reasoning - ability to recognize shapes of objects, judge distances accurately, etc.**;

- Depression;

- Psychological and psychiatric problems;

- Difficulties in goal-setting, planning;

- Anxiety;

- Withdrawal;

- Denial;

- Frustration;

- Anger;

- Irritability;

- Restlessness;

- Mood swings;

- Impulsiveness;

- Sexual dysfunction;

- Apathy;

- Aphasia;

- Fatigue;

- Balance problems;

- Impairments of the senses: vision, hearing, touch, taste, smell;

- incontinence of the bowel or bladder;

- Diminution of IQ;

- Loss of physical strength;

- Confabulation.

5.   _Aphasia_

Aphasia is a disorder caused by damage to the brain which affects an individual's communication skills. The most common difficulty of an individual who suffers from aphasia is the ability to express oneself when speaking. Persons who have aphasia may also have difficulty in reading, writing, comprehension, and understanding speech. It is estimated that more than 1.5 million persons in the United States have aphasia. According to studies, approximately one-third of the persons who sustain severe traumatic head injuries acquire aphasia.

6.   _Seizures_

Localized seizures that affect a specific area of the body or a single area of the central nervous system are called **focal** or **partial** seizures. **Petit mal** and **grand mal** seizures are types of generalized seizures which involve the entire brain and often lead to a loss of consciousness. There are many different definitions for a seizure. A generally accepted definition is that a seizure is an **episodic, involuntary, alteration in consciousness, behavior, sensation, or motor activity**. Individuals who have a traumatic brain injury are likely to suffer from a seizure disorder. Legally, it is important to document the frequency, length, type, and duration of a seizure in order to be able to prove that the seizure was caused by the accident or injury, and in order to prove to the health insurer the need for cognitive training and a seizure management program.

H.   OTHER TYPES OF BRAIN INJURY

1.   _Traumatic Brain Injury and Electrical Burns_

Major electrical injury can cause widespread tissue destruction, with resulting permanent auditory dysfunction and brain damage. Numerous studies have shown that electrical burns can cause intra-cranial/epidural hematomas, brain swelling, and long-term neurologic damage. I have represented many individuals who have suffered significant electrical burns. I have found that the head injury problem from which they suffer are often not documented properly, or are minimized. It is essential that health care providers carefully document any neurologic damage that has occurred, in order to access the funding from the health insurer.

2.   _Lead Poisoning - Developmental Delay_

Countless studies have found that lead poisoning can cause permanent brain damage, learning disabilities, and developmental delay injuries. Blood-lead levels as low as 10 ug/dl/m have been associated with behavioral, hearing, learning, and growth problems in children. Deteriorating paint in homes remains the leading cause of lead poisoning in children. Flaking lead paint and lead water pipes are often found in poor, aging homes.

The Consumer Product Safety Commission reports that some playground equipment may also pose a lead paint poisoning hazard for children ages 6 and under. Since the effects of ingesting lead are cumulative, exposure to lead paint on playground equipment may increase the risk of lead poisoning to children who have already been exposed to lead paint from home and other sources.

Lead poisoning has been identified as a developmental disability, since it may take many years before the learning difficulty, or other medical problems associated with lead poisoning, becomes apparent to parents, physicians, and teachers.

Cognitive dysfunction is the most common of the developmental disabilities. If you believe your child is "developmentally delayed" or "slow", you should have your child promptly evaluated to determine whether or not there are physical or cognitive impairments which may be slowing your child's development. It is important to document the areas of delay, and the cause of the problems. Prompt documentation of lead paint exposure in children showing developmental delay problems will make it easier to obtain special education benefits from the child's school, and rehabilitation benefits from the health insurer.

I.   *TYPES OF TREATMENT FOR BRAIN INJURY*

1.   <u>Coma Stimulation - Coma Awareness Programs</u>

Most health insurance companies refuse to pay for short-term and long-term care benefits for a person who is in a persistent vegetative state, suffering from locked-in syndrome, is in a coma, or has been diagnosed as a minimally responsive patient. Insurers argue that the impaired person is not able to be rehabilitated and is receiving custodial care. Recent studies have shown that many persons who have been diagnosed as vegetative or "minimally responsive" are, in fact, sporadically seeing, hearing, and thinking. Two studies from England have found that up to 60% of vegetative patients are misdiagnosed and do have some degree of consciousness. Coma stimulation and coma awareness programs chart the opening and closing of patients' eyes, and test whether patients can register sights and sounds. These programs take EEG's to monitor brain activity and experiment with lowering doses of sedatives, pain killers, and other drugs that can suppress signs of consciousness. A chart of the signs of awareness attempt to document patterns that might signal intermittent conscious awareness. The key is to attempt to develop a system of communication with the traumatically brain injured patient, whether it is blinking of the eyes, or jerking of the hand, or mumblings. Once communication has been established, argument can be made to the health insurer that the traumatically brain injured person can benefit from an in-patient rehabilitation program. Experts have found that delays in the commencement of a coma stimulation, coma awareness, or intensive rehabilitation program will lessen the chance that an individual will be able to regain lost skills and return to independent living.

I have been successful in obtaining funding from health insurers for coma stimulation and coma awareness programs. To be successful, an attorney must be contacted by the family as early as possible. The attorney needs to work closely with the treating doctors to document as much objective information as possible to use as evidence when health insurers challenge recommended rehabilitation programs.

Short-term and long-term rehabilitation for the traumatically brain injured can include the following:

- **Coma stimulation and coma awareness programs**;

- **Physical therapy**;

- **Occupational therapy**;

- **Speech therapy**;

- **Cognitive therapy**;

- **Psychological counseling**;

- **Psychiatric counseling**;

- **Attendant care**;

- **Nursing services**;

- **Counseling and peer counseling**;

- **Vocational services**;

- **Social and family services**;

- **Seizure management**;

- **Behavioral training services**;

- **Neuropsychiatric services**;

- **Medical services**;

- **Therapeutic recreation**;

- **Respite care**;

- **Group homes**;

- Sub-acute care;

- Transitional living services;

- Community re-entry services;

- Community skills program;

- Day-care program;

- Case management services;

- Special education services.

J.   *BRAIN INJURY LEGISLATION*

The ***Traumatic Brain Injury Act of 1996*** allocates $24.5 million over the next three years for research and state grants. The Act seeks to "provide moneys for increased basic, applied and outcomes research; expand the health-related data gathering systems to account properly for the incidence and costs of traumatic brain injury; provide grants for special projects and health and related research; develop innovative prevention programs; and expand the protection and advocacy systems already in place in this county to work with individuals who have experienced traumatic brain injury."

K.   *SUCCESSFULLY LITIGATED CASES*

1.   *Pool Case - Anoxia - Persistent Vegetative State*

I was co-counsel in a case which, at the time, resulted in the largest verdict in the history of Pennsylvania - $24,250,000. In this case, lifeguards hired by an apartment complex were inattentive, and inadequately administered CPR to a child. As a result, the minor child suffered an anoxic brain injury and lapsed into a persistent vegetative state.

2.   *Coma - Persistent Vegetative State - Coma Stimulation/Coma Awareness Program*

I was counsel in a case where my client was a Level 2 on the Rancho Scale. The family believed that the individual could benefit from an in-patient rehabilitation program. The health insurer, which was a managed care provider, argued that the individual could not benefit from the rehabilitation program, since her care was custodial in nature. I was successful in using the health insurance contract, a bad faith argument, and medical documentation from the treating doctors, to prove that my client could benefit from a coma stimulation/coma awareness program. **SUGGESTION:** A family should be aggressive in fighting a managed care

149

insurer when they are denied the recommended programs for the patient. Families need to recognize that obtaining health insurance benefits from a managed care insurer is an adversarial process.

3.   *Guardianship - Time Period - Loss of Benefits - Traumatic Brain Injury*

An individual was involved in an accident and suffered traumatic brain injuries. The spouse of the individual left the state and the treating hospital was not aware of any other family members. The hospital had been treating the patient for almost a year when the spouse returned and questioned why the hospital had not made an application for governmental benefits. The hospital admitted that they erred by not requesting that a guardian be appointed for the incapacitated individual. Since there was no guardian with legal authority to apply for medical benefits, application was never made, resulting in a substantial loss of medical benefits. **SUGGESTION:** Guardianship must always be pursued, when needed, to ensure that all deadlines for necessary benefits are met.

4.   *Special Education Benefits - Coordination of Benefits - Traumatic Brain Injury*

A child suffered a catastrophic head injury in an automobile accident. The parents' health care policy had a $2 million lifetime maximum. By creatively utilizing the coordination of benefits clause, we were able to maximize the health care and special education benefits for the child. **SUGGESTION:** Obtaining medical and special education benefits for a traumatically brain injured child should not be pursued without researching and analyzing all available sources of funding.

5.   *Birth Trauma - Statute of Limitations - Traumatic Brain Injury*

The parents contacted me approximately 9 years after the birth of their child. They had recently read an article in a magazine which discussed a lawsuit that was filed based on facts which appeared to be similar to the facts concerning the birth of their child. The hospital and the hospital's insurer argued that, although the hospital and the doctors may have been negligent and caused the child's injury at birth, the time limit for bringing an action on behalf of the child had lapsed, and they alleged that the parents should therefore be barred from bringing a claim at this time. I contended that since the parents did not immediately discover that the actions of the doctors and/or hospital had contributed to the cause of their child's condition, they should not be barred from bringing a claim at this time. This argument was successful. **SUGGESTION:** Claims involving minors should always be reviewed by an attorney, since in many states, minors are permitted to bring a claim up to 21 years after the injury.

6.   *Product Liability - Creative Investigations - Traumatic Brain Injury*

An individual was a passenger in a sport/utility vehicle which was involved in a motor vehicle accident. The vehicle rolled over three times, causing the driver to suffer catastrophic brain injuries. The insurance company totalled the truck and paid the family the "book value" for the vehicle. The family contacted me six months after the accident, and when we checked we found that the vehicle involved in the accident had a history of "rollover problems" and had been recalled in the past. When we attempted to locate the vehicle, we found that it had been moved three times and was in another state. Fortunately, the vehicle had not been crushed. **SUGGESTION:** Investigation of all serious accidents must be immediate and thorough. In most states, a product liability action cannot be instituted if the product is not available for inspection.

7.   *Automobile - Underinsured Motorist Coverage - Traumatic Brain Injury*

A spouse was catastrophically injured when the driver of a vehicle negligently caused an accident. The husband recovered the full amount of liability insurance from their own insurance carrier. Since the limits of the driver's liability insurance was inadequate to pay for the lifetime medical needs of the wife, a claim was made for underinsured motorist benefits against the family's car insurance company. **SUGGESTION:** Underinsured motorist coverage is insurance coverage that you pay for, on your automobile, to protect you if you are injured by a driver who has insufficient liability insurance coverage to pay your wage loss, pain and suffering and future medical bills. Underinsured motorist coverage should be chosen in the same amounts as your liability coverage.

8.   *Tractor-Trailer Accident - Investigation - Traumatic Brain Injury*

The minor plaintiff suffered a catastrophic brain injury when a tractor-trailer jackknifed and struck the vehicle in which he was riding. My investigation revealed that the truck driver was driving in an impaired condition (he had been driving for over 24 hours without sleep—in violation of company rules). The investigation also revealed that the driver of the tractor-trailer had a long history of motor vehicle violations. **SUGGESTION:** A careful background check of the parties involved in a serious accident can produce criminal information which can be beneficial in pressuring an insurance company to settle your claim.

9.   *Scaffold - Third Party Recovery - Traumatic Brain Injury*

A worker suffered a traumatic brain injury as the result of a fall that occurred when he was working on a scaffold at a job site. The claim was successfully resolved based on the theory that the scaffolding was defectively designed, and this lead to the fall and resulting injuries. **SUGGESTION:** All construction site accidents should be fully investigated to determine whether or not there is a contractor, subcontractor, engineer, architect, or other third party company, other than the worker's compensation carrier, against whom a claim can be made for damages.

10. *Slip and Fall - Statements - Traumatic Brain Injury*

An individual fell down steps and suffered a traumatic brain injury. Family members and witnesses to the fall gave detailed statements to the insurance company. The insurance company denied benefits based on incorrect information received in the statements. **SUGGESTION:** You should never give a statement to any insurance company investigator or adjuster, either orally or in writing, without first discussing your legal rights with an attorney.

11. *Helmet - Product Liability - Failure to Meet Governmental Safety Standards - Traumatic Brain Injury*

A helmeted individual was a passenger on a motorcycle. The driver lost control of the motorcycle and the rider was thrown off the motorcycle, striking his head on the roadway. The helmet cracked, and the individual suffered a fractured skull with resulting traumatic brain injury. A structural analysis of the helmet revealed that it was defective because it did not meet governmental safety standards. A lawsuit against the helmet manufacturer was successful and a structured settlement was awarded to pay for the client's lifetime medical bills. **SUGGESTION:** Any time a catastrophic injury occurs and a product is involved, the product should be carefully examined to determine whether or not it was defective. Many products must be manufactured to meet industry and governmental safety standards. The product involved in your accident should never be destroyed, altered, modified, or changed in any way until it has been examined by your attorney and an expert.

12. *Developmental Delay - Traumatic Brain Injury*

A minor suffered significant brain injury and learning disability as the result of ingestion of paint chips at a home which his parents were renting. The minor child's problems were not noticed by the parents until the child became school age. Testing revealed that the child had very high levels of lead in his blood, and that this was causing his developmental delay injuries. **SUGGESTION:** Any time a child is exhibiting difficulty with motor skills, speech, or cognitive skills, an evaluation should be done by competent professionals to determine whether or not the child is suffering from "a developmental delay injury".

CONCLUSION

In the twenty years that I have practiced law, I have represented over a thousand persons who have suffered traumatic brain injuries. I am finding it increasingly difficult to obtain both short-term medical and long-term rehabilitation benefits for my clients. Governmental restrictions and managed care insurers are constantly implementing new rules and regulations to limit and deny access to the needed benefits.

It has been shown that extensive rehabilitation is a very effective treatment for brain injury. Therefore, it is important to adopt an aggressive approach to funding. It should not be assumed that funding will be both available and accessible, when the reverse is true. You and your attorney must be prepared to fight and constantly advocate for the injured person.

[1]Blinder: Psychiatry and the Everyday Practice of Law, 2nd ed. 1982, p151.
[2]Lishman WA: The psychiatric sequelae of head injury. Psychological Medicine 3:304-318, 1973

L. ***BRAIN INJURY ORGANIZATIONS***

BRAIN INJURY ASSOCIATION
105 N. Alfred Street
Alexandria, Va. 22314
800-444-6443

BRAIN INJURY ASSOCIATION OF DELAWARE
302-537-5770

BRAIN INJURY ASSOCIATION OF NEW JERSEY
908-738-1002

BRAIN INJURY ASSOCIATION OF NEW YORK
518-459-7911

SOUTH CENTRAL PA BRAIN INJURY CHAPTER
610-286-9776

XVII. SPINAL CORD INJURY

A. SPINAL CORD INJURY - TRAUMA FACTS

According to the National Spinal Cord Injury Association[1], approximately 7,800 new spinal cord injuries (SCI) occur in the United States each year. It is estimated that another 4,860 persons have died before reaching an acute-care hospital. 82% of those who suffer spinal cord injuries are male. Most of the injured are between ages the ages of 16 and 30. Motor vehicle accidents are the leading cause of SCI (44%), followed by acts of violence (24%), falls (22%), and sports injuries (8%), and other causes (2%). Two-thirds of sports injuries are from diving accidents. More than 49% of all spinal cord injuries occur between May and September. Over 53% of all accidents occur on Fridays, Saturdays and Sundays.

The statistics vary, but there are approximately 200,000 to 500,000 persons already disabled by spinal cord injuries from years past. Combined medical costs for spinal cord injured individuals will surpass $2 billion annually. One study sponsored by the National Institutes of Disability and Rehabilitation Research, found: 34% of all spinal cord injury cases admitted to the spinal cord injury system arrived within 24 hours of injury. In 1992, the average length of stay for a spinal cord injured individual with quadriplegia was 95 days, and for a paraplegic, 67 days. The study also found the source of payment for acute care treatment breakdown was as follows: Private Insurance 53%, Medicaid 25%, Self-pay 1%, Office of Vocational Rehabilitation (OVR) 14%, Worker's Compensation 12%, Medicare 5%, Other 2%. Additionally, one-third to one-half of all persons with spinal cord injury are re-admitted each year to the hospital for injury-related treatment.

B. WHAT IS A SPINAL CORD INJURY?

The National Spinal Cord Injury Association describes a spinal cord injury as a lesion of the cord which results in paralysis of certain parts of the body and corresponding loss of sensation. Spinal cord injury can occur at various levels of the spinal cord - cervical, thoracic, or lumbar areas.

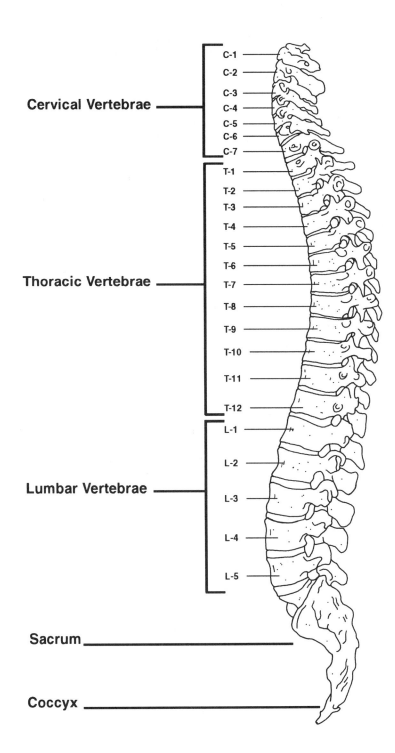

Cervical Vertebrae
- C-1
- C-2
- C-3
- C-4
- C-5
- C-6
- C-7

Thoracic Vertebrae
- T-1
- T-2
- T-3
- T-4
- T-5
- T-6
- T-7
- T-8
- T-9
- T-10
- T-11
- T-12

Lumbar Vertebrae
- L-1
- L-2
- L-3
- L-4
- L-5

Sacrum

Coccyx

C. INCOMPLETE VS. COMPLETE INJURY

A complete spinal cord injury occurs when all motor and sensory function is lost below the level of the injury. In an incomplete spinal cord injury, there is some motor and/or sensory function below the level of the injury. A complete spinal cord injury does not mean the spinal cord has been cut or severed.

FRANKEL SCALE FUNCTIONAL CLASSIFICATION [2]

A   COMPLETE
No preservation of motor or sensory function

B   INCOMPLETE—PRESERVED SENSATION ONLY
Preservation of any sensation below the level
of injury, except phantom sensations

C   INCOMPLETE—PRESERVED MOTOR NONFUNCTIONAL
Preserved motor function without useful
purpose; sensory function may or may not be
preserved

D   INCOMPLETE—PRESERVED MOTOR FUNCTIONAL
Preserved functional voluntary motor function
that is functionally useful

E   COMPLETE RECOVERY
Complete return of all motor and sensory
funtion, but may still have abnormal reflexes

D. IMPAIRMENTS: QUADRIPLEGIA - PARAPLEGIA - QUADRIPARESIS

Quadriplegia refers to paralysis of all four extremities—usually from approximately the neck down. *Quadriplegia* usually results when an injury occurs at or above the C-7 vertebra. *Paraplegia* refers to paralysis of the lower extremities—from approximately the waist down. *Paraplegia* happens when damage is done to the thoracic, lumbar, or sacral area of the spinal cord. *Hemiplegia* is a term used to refer to paralysis of one side of the body. *Quadriparesis*, *Paraparesis*, and *Hemiparesis* are terms used to refer to weakness, and not total paralysis.

E.   *MEDICAL PROBLEMS ASSOCIATED WITH SPINAL CORD INJURY*

- Urinary tract infections

- Reduced breathing capacity - Sometimes requiring the use of a ventilator

- Impairments of the circulatory system

- Dysfunction of the kidney, bladder, and bowels

- Spasticity - Muscles move or jerk involuntarily

- Muscle spasms

- Autonomic dysreflexia - A condition of dangerously high blood pressure, sweating, chills, headache, and facial flushing. Usually occurs in individuals with SCI above the 6th thoracic level

- Skin/pressure sores (decubitus ulcers)

- Chronic pain

- Heterotopic ossification - The formation of new bone deposits in the connective tissue surrounding the joint (primarily the hip and knee)

- Pressure ulcers

- Carpal tunnel syndrome - Overuse of the hands in transfers and propelling wheelchairs

- Sexual dysfunction

- Psychological and psychiatric coping difficulties

- **Contractures**

- **Reflux - The back-flow of urine from the bladder into the ureters and kidneys**

F. *TRENDS - MEDICAL TREATMENT - REIMBURSEMENT*

The trend in the medical community is toward aggressive treatment of spinal cord injury. The third National Acute Spinal Cord Injury Study began in 1982 at 14 centers in the United States and Canada. This large-scale trial, involving 500 patients, hopes to prove the effectiveness of two drugs in preventing loss of function. All patients will get a standard dose of methylprednisolone (MP). According to the National Spinal Cord Injury Association, two years ago NACIS II proved that this steroid reduces disability if given within a few hours of injury. Another group in the study was given a drug called tirilizade, also known as "lazeroid". Tirilizade acts similarly to MP by reducing the extensive nerve fiber destruction that follows the initial trauma. Researchers are very excited about recent "nerve regeneration" studies performed on laboratory animals. The Christopher Reeve Foundation and other spinal cord injury associations are leading the fight toward raising the necessary funds to expand spinal cord injury research in the next century.

G. *HOME MODIFICATIONS - ASSISTIVE TECHNOLOGY DEVICES AND SERVICES*

Assistive technology devices (See Section XX) are an essential part of the life of a spinal cord injury survivor. Thousand live day-to-day with the aid of a mechanical respirator. Many can be weaned from mechanical breathing devices, but some will require the use of a ventilator permanently. To improve the quality of life of spinal cord injured individuals, advocates have attempted to obtain funding for home modifications and assistive technology services from governmental agencies and private health insurers (including worker's compensation carriers). Generally, worker's compensation carriers, private health insurers, and governmental agencies will not pay for home modifications. Sometimes, the Office of Vocational Rehabilitation (OVR) will do some minimum home modifications such as ramping, widening of doorways, small revisions to bathrooms. Payment for extensive home modifications are rare.

H. *SUCCESSFULLY LITIGATED CASES*

1. *Above-ground Pool - Spinal Cord Injury*

An individual suffered spinal cord injury when he dove into an above-ground swimming pool. An investigation revealed that the pool was defectively designed, and countless numbers of individuals had been injured in a similar manner while using this type of pool. Insurance benefits were recovered from the manufacturer of the pool. These benefits were structured so the client receives monthly income for the rest of his life. **SUGGESTION:** All swimming pool accidents resulting in serious injury should be investigated. It is almost impossible to visually estimate a pool's depth. Everyone should be aware of the water's depth before diving in, and no one should ever dive into an above ground swimming pool.

2. *Exclusions - Health Insurance Benefits - Long-Term Coverage - Spinal Cord Injury*

Individuals purchased a health insurance policy containing a clause stating that they would receive 24-hour coverage if they were ill or injured. A family member suffered quadriplegia which required 24-hour attendant and nursing care. The family submitted the medical bills to the health insurance company, but the company denied the request for long-term coverage for attendant and nursing care. Their basis for denial was that the policy excluded payment for long-term care considered "custodial" in nature. I was successful in arguing that the exclusion was invalid and void as against public policy. **SUGGESTION:** All exclusions which attempt to deny payment for needed medical expenses should be discussed with your attorney as soon as the payment of the claim is denied.

3. *Automobile Accident- Crashworthiness - Airbag - Spinal Cord Injury*

My client was driving an automobile when he was struck head-on by another vehicle. The airbag did not deploy on impact, and the driver suffered quadriplegia. I hired an expert to evaluate the car, and he issued a report which stated that because of the defective design of the airbag, it did not deploy. **SUGGESTION:** When there has been a serious or catastrophic injury, you should not permit your automobile insurance company to salvage or destroy your vehicle before an expert, retained by you or your attorney, has had the opportunity to inspect it.

4. *Slip and Fall - Investigation - Spinal Cord Injury*

An individual fell down apartment steps and suffered a spinal cord injury (paraplegia). An investigation revealed that the stairway violated the local building code. Luckily, photographs were taken of the faulty stairway before the apartment owner renovated the stairway. **SUGGESTION:** Many homes, apartments, restaurants, and office buildings do not meet the architectural and other safety standards that apply. When an injury occurs, the structure in question should be carefully examined to be sure that all safety standards and building codes have been met.

5. *Health Insurance - Ventilators - Bad Faith*

An individual was involved in a swimming pool accident and suffered quadriplegia. The health care provider requested coverage information from the health insurer. The health insurer provided incorrect and misleading information as to the health insurance coverage. The health insurer denied the requested rehabilitation hospital stay, durable medical equipment (ventilators) and 24-hour nursing care recommended by the treating doctor. After reviewing the health insurance policy, I found that there was coverage for the requested services. **SUGGESTION:** I filed a bad faith claim against the health insurer for misleading the family and the health care provider concerning the "coverage information". Bad faith is a principle of law which applies in all states, and essentially can be a valuable weapon against health insurers if they are providing incorrect, incomplete, misleading, or outdated coverage information for the purpose of denying medical treatment or services for an individual.

6. *ATV - All-Terrain Vehicle - Warning - Traumatic Brain Injury and Spinal Cord Injury*

A minor was injured when a three-wheeled All-Terrain Vehicle (ATV) flipped over, causing catastrophic head and spinal cord injuries. We argued that the ATV was inherently dangerous and defective in design, since the ATV would tip over, roll over, and pin riders under the vehicle. The minor was awarded a medical trust fund which will pay lifetime medical and rehabilitation expenses. **SUGGESTION:** Explicit warnings should appear on any products, especially those that hold serious potential danger for children. Consumers need to be aware of the dangers and make sensible choices when purchasing products. Parents should not allow children to ride on ATV's because of the risk of injury. Children lack both the coordination and judgment skills that are needed to control the vehicle safely.

7. *Home Modifications - Spinal Cord Injury*

An individual was working on a scaffold at a construction site when the scaffold collapsed. Extensive investigation revealed that the scaffold, which was erected by the general contractor, not by the injured person's employer, was defectively designed. I requested that my client's employer's worker's compensation carrier pay for home modifications for my client, who was rendered quadriplegic. Worker's compensation carriers are not required to pay for home modification, and there are no state statues that require them to do so.

I was able to convince the worker's compensation carrier to pay for my client's home modifications, by agreeing to a re-payment of a percentage of the medical bills and wages from any settlement with the third party (subrogation). **SUGGESTION:** All worker's compensation carriers and self-insured employers should aggressively investigate all serious ill nesses and injuries, to protect their subrogation rights. All persons whose spinal cord injury occurred at work should investigate whether or not there is a third party claim, since this avenue may give them leverage to convince a worker's compensation carrier to pay for home modifications and assistive technology devices and services.

8. *Fork Lift - Third Party Recovery - Spinal Cord Injury*

An employee was seriously injured when he was struck by a fork lift operated by a co-employee. A third party claim was brought against the manufacturer of the fork lift, since the defective design did not give the operator of the fork lift an unobstructed view and he could not see the worker walking in the plant. **SUGGESTION:** Any time a product is involved in a serious or catastrophic accident, an outside expert should be retained to examine the product and determine whether the product design made it safe for its intended use.

9. *Laminectomy - Negligence - Quadriplegia*

The client's worker's compensation carrier paid for him to have a laminectomy - surgery on the discs in his back - following an injury he suffered at work. The doctor who performed the surgery was negligent and, as a result of this negligence, the client suffered quadriplegia and became totally disabled. The worker's compensation carrier paid my client's medical bills, which totalled millions of dollars, and a percentage of his lost wages. The lawsuit was successful, seeking lost earning capacity, pain and suffering damages, loss of enjoyment of life and societal pleasures, future medical coverage, and reimbursement of the worker's compensation carrier's lien. **SUGGESTION:** The medical records should always be reviewed when a medical procedure results in a serious injury.

10. *Durable Power of Attorney - Spinal Cord Injury*

An individual suffered quadriplegia and was ventilator-dependent as the result of an automobile accident. The family members were having difficulty in obtaining both health insurance benefits and Social Security disability benefits. There was concern that the person's medical condition would deteriorate and he would not be able to communicate his intentions for future care. I had a durable power of attorney executed by the individual, giving his spouse the authority to make these decisions if he was no longer able to do so. **SUGGESTION:** A durable power of attorney is a specific document in which a competent individual, prior to his or her incapacitation, names another person to act on his or her behalf at such time as that individual becomes unable to manage his or her own affairs. The person named in the durable power of attorney, in this case the spouse, would serve as the guardian of the individual without the necessity of petitioning the court to have the individual declared incapacitated in the event of medical disability. A durable power of attorney should be used when an individual suffers a catastrophic injury or illness and his or her future decision-making abilities are in question.

It is a difficult battle for me to obtain the much-needed devices and services for my spinal cord injured clients, but fortunately many cases have been successful. My strategy begins with a careful review of the language of the health insurance policy or governmental regulations and statutes. This necessary evidence, along with the reports from treating physicians and therapists; statistical and other surveys which document the improved quality of life and the medical necessity of the requested programs, services and devices along with the cost of projected lifetime care; help to present a compelling case to the payor.

I. *SPINAL CORD INJURY ORGANIZATIONS*

NATIONAL SPINAL CORD INJURY ASSOCIATION
8300 Colesville Road, Suite 551
Silver Spring MD 20910
800-962-9629 TOLL FREE
301-588-6959
WEBSITE: HTTP://www.spinalcord.org

AMERICAN ASSOCIATION OF SPINAL CORD INJURY NURSES
75-20 Astoria Blvd
Jackson Heights NY 11370
718-803-3782

AMERICAN PARAPLEGIA SOCIETY
75-20 Astoria Blvd
Jackson Heights NY 11370
718-803-3782

AMERICAN SPINAL INJURY ASSOCIATION
345 East Superior Street, Room 1436
Chicago IL 60611

AMERICAN PARALYSIS ASSOCIATION
500 Morris Avenue
Springfield NJ 07081
800-225-0292

EASTERN PARALYZED VETERANS ASSOCIATION
75-20 Astoria Blvd
Jackson Heights NY 11370
718-803-3782

NATIONAL PARAPLEGIA FOUNDATION
333 North Michigan Avenue
Chicago IL 60601

PARALYZED VETERANS OF AMERICA
801 Eighteenth Street NW
Washington DC 20006
202-USA-1300
800-424-8200

SPINAL CORD SOCIETY
Route 5, Box 22A
Fergus Falls MN 56537
218-739-5252

**AMERICAN ASSOCIATION OF SPINAL CORD INJURY
PSYCHOLOGISTS AND SOCIAL WORKERS**
75-20 Astoria Blvd
Jackson Heights NY 11370
718-803-3782

XVIII. BURN INJURIES

A.   BURN INJURY - TRAUMA FACTS

According to the Burn Foundation, there are approximately 5,500 deaths and 1.25 million injuries each year due to burns/fires. About 50,000 of these injuries require hospitalization, almost half of them in specialized burn centers. Children ages 0 to 4, and the elderly, 75 and older, are at the greatest risk for burn injuries. In fact, fire/burns are the second leading cause of unintentional deaths in children 1 to 4, and the third leading cause of injury and death for ages 1 to 18. More than 35% of all fire/burn injuries and deaths are to children.

About 75-80% of burn injuries occur in the home. The increased use of alternative heating devices, especially wood and coal burning stoves and kerosene heaters, has led to a surge in contact burns. Death rates are high in rural areas and in the poorest sections of large cities. Hot tap water and heated foods and beverages are major sources of burn injuries, especially to young children. Hot foods and liquids spilled in the kitchen are the largest single source of burns to children. Also, matches and cigarette lighters in the hands of very young children are a significant factor in fire deaths. Frequently, the elderly receive burn injuries from the ignition of clothing or bedding in cooking or smoking incidents.

B.   INTRODUCTION TO BURN INJURIES

The medical costs associated with severe burn injuries are astronomical. Acute care costs alone can exhaust the entire limit of a health insurance policy. Advancements in burn injury research and reconstructive techniques have given new hope to burn survivors, but finding payment sources for these procedures is a difficult process.

Extensive investigation into the cause of the accident is essential in order to identify liability issues and fund the payment of medical costs. A legal investigation of the accident should begin immediately, because fires can result in widespread destruction of evidence. At times there are numerous component parts that could have caused or contributed to the accident, i.e. in the case of a furnace explosion, the furnace has many different parts and the various manufacturers of each must be identified; in addition, photographs of the area where the fire or accident occurred should be taken before any alteration or clean-up is begun.

C.   TYPES OF BURNS

There are five basic types of burns:

1.   _Chemical burns_ - Caused by acids and other chemicals;

2.   *Thermal burns* - Caused by flames, hot surfaces, fires or explosions;

3.   *Scald burns* - Resulting from contact with hot liquids and steam;

4.   *Electrical burns* - Caused by contact with high voltage electricity, high tension wires, lightning, electrocution;

5.   *Radiation burns* - from exposure to sunlight, x-rays, or nuclear emissions or explosion.

Two factors determine the severity of a burn injury: The depth of the burn and the size of the burn.

- **First degree is the least serious (reddening of the skin)**;

- **Second degree burns result in the destruction of the outer layer of the skin**;

- **Third degree burns - all skin has been destroyed, skin grafting required**;

- **Fourth degree burns - all skin has been destroyed and there is injury to the organs, muscles, tissues, and burns beneath the skin.**

D.   *COMMON CAUSES OF BURN INJURIES*

1.   *Electric heaters/electrical heat tapes*

Most of the fires caused by portable electric heaters are because of design defects, tip-overs, proximity to combustible material, defective automatic thermostats, defective fan motors, use with inadequate extension cords, and other equipment problems.

There are about three million portable heating units sold each year at an average cost of about $30.00. Three manufacturers—Arvin, DeLonghi and Rival—account for more than half of the market. According to the Consumer Product Safety Commission, defective portable electric heaters have been involved in nearly 3,000 residential fires each year, causing hundreds of deaths and injuries. Property damage caused by defective electric heaters in each of the last two reported years exceeded $45 million. The Consumer Product Safety Commission has found that more deaths result from the use of portable electric heaters than from any other type of portable heaters. The commission also discovered that the heaters have a higher death rate per fire than any other group of electrical products and that internal failure of heaters—not consumer negligence—was the probable cause of most heater-related fires.

Lawsuits can be filed in portable electric heater cases but they require substantial analysis and testimony by experts, to prove the origin and cause of the fire. All three of the major manufacturers—Arvin, DeLonghi, and Rival—have been involved in litigation resulting from defective portable electric heaters.

Some of the improvements urged include the requirement that heaters carry permanent and uniform consumer warnings. These would specify the dangers of using extension cords with the heaters, using heaters in bathrooms and using them near combustibles such as furniture, draperies, and bedding. Consumers should be particularly warned to use smoke detectors if the heaters are used near children and the elderly or in any room where people sleep. Heaters should also be equipped with tip-over and overheating safety features, as well as a warning light and an audible warning alarm that is activated if the heater overturns or overheats.

The American Trial Lawyers Association, in a February 1992 public service announcement, issued important safety tips to consumers buying portable heaters. Included among them are the following:

- Shop for a heater with the safety features identified above, and purchase only a heater that satisfies the most recent Underwriters Laboratories (UL) standard;

- Install smoke detectors in any area heated by a space heater;

- Never place a heater on the edge of a bathtub or sink;

- Always keep heaters unplugged when not in use.

Electrical heat tapes are wrapped around pipes to keep them from freezing and bursting during cold weather. Although safe electrical heat tapes do exist, the United States Consumer Product Safety Commission estimates that 95% of all heat tapes purchased for consumer use in the United States do not conform to Underwriters' Laboratories or other voluntary product safety standards.

Faulty electrical heat tapes have been involved in some 3,300 residential fires annually. These fires result in approximately 20 deaths, 100 injuries and $25.4 million in property loss each year. Most deaths, injuries and property losses are caused by heat tapes that do not meet established safety standards. Safe electrical heat tapes typically use grounded 3-prong plugs, higher heat-rated PVC coating, and a metallic "grounding braid". This braid helps keep resistance wires separated, provides a path to the ground in case of a short circuit, and acts as a heat sink to dissipate heat and prevent it from building up to ignition temperatures if the consumer allows the tape to overlap. Safe heat tapes are manufactured to insure they meet minimum standards for fire resistance. The fire hazards associated with substandard materials in unsafe heat tapes are compounded by inadequate installation instructions and hazard warnings. Most packaging materials and product inserts make no direct reference to fire dangers. Instead, they give a vague warning indicating that overlapping may cause overheating and product failure.

Numerous consumer groups have urged the Consumer Product Safety Commission to establish mandatory national safety standards for heat tapes, since the voluntary standards have proven inadequate. These groups have requested that defective electrical heat tapes be identified, recalled, and destroyed. The Consumer Product Safety Commission staff has recommended regulatory action, but the Commissioners have declined to follow this recommendation, deciding instead to begin a limited study of heat tapes.

    2.   *Scalds*

    a.   Scalding tap water

300,000 scald injuries are treated in emergency departments each year, 100,000 of them to children. Scald injuries often result in permanent disfigurements and psychological damage, according to the Burn Foundation.

Water heaters are also a significant factor in many of the scald injuries that are treated. Domestic hot water heaters usually have three settings: warm, which heats water to 100°; normal, 120°; and hot, 140°. Comfortable bathing temperature is about 102°. Hot tubs are usually 104° to 106°. A person can sit in 125° water for a few minutes before getting burned, but at 140° a burn occurs in seconds. The Gas Appliance Manufacturer's Association has indicated that the industry changed the "normal" setting on water heaters from 140° to 120° in the mid-1980's because of the risk of burn injuries, but at the urging of detergent and dishwasher manufacturers, they continued to build heaters that could heat water to 140°. All water heaters should have warning labels on the outside of the tank. Nearly 90% of the deaths due to scalding tap water occur in bathtubs.

Attorneys have successfully litigated cases for plaintiffs who were injured while trying to escape from unexpected bursts of hot water at hotels, motels, hospitals, restaurants, etc. Water heater manufacturers have also been held liable for failing to include anti-scald devices and mixing valves on their heaters, or warn that their heaters produce water hot enough to cause severe burns. The price of anti-scald devices ranges from $20 for temperature-control valves, to $150 for combination valves.

b.   Scalding - Fast-food Chains

Complaints have been made against some fast-food chains because beverages have been served at extremely high temperatures, resulting in immediate serious scald injuries. Despite legal action against them, some fast food chains continue serving beverages at dangerous temperatures.

c.   Scalding - Explosions, Products

3.   *Smoke Detectors*

Despite the increased use of residential smoke detectors and fire-detection devices, occupants of many homes, apartment buildings and hotels have sustained injury or death as a result of fires. Often, the cause of the burns or death has been the defective design of the smoke detector or fire-detection devices, or the inadequate warnings supplied by the manufacturer of the residential smoke or heat detector.

The Federal government recommends that smoke detectors be installed in any room where portable electric heaters are utilized. The Consumer Product Safety Commission reports that half of the deaths and one-third of the injuries resulting from portable electric heater fires occur at night when the heater is operating. According to a 1980 "Residential Smoke Alarm Report", by the International Fire Chiefs Association, a vast majority of residential fires occur when people are asleep and most of these are the slow-smoldering type, which provide a great deal of smoke before there is a fire. This report also found that many manufacturers unconsciously over promote their fire detection devices, lulling the public into a false sense of security.

Families rely on a smoke detector to sound an alarm in a timely manner and escape time is critical. Recent studies have shown that many smoke detectors do not activate until smoke becomes quite dense. There are two different types of smoke detectors, an ionization and a photo-electric type. The ionization smoke detector is the most common. Studies have shown that the ionization type reacts quickly to flames, however, it takes twice as long to react in slow smoldering type fires. The photo-electric smoke detector works best in slow smoldering type fires. Experts recommend that families install a combination ionization/ photo-electric smoke detector.

4.   *Defective Products*

Medical advances in the treatment of burn and inhalation injuries have greatly reduced the mortality rate. Speed in obtaining competent medical care is critical, and this should be provided at a regional burn trauma center. The costs associated with treatment of severe burn injuries is beyond the means of the average family not insured by a substantial private health insurance policy. Burn cases have been litigated to provide the necessary long-term medical benefits for burn survivors and their families.

I am often faced with the dilemma of trying to obtain third party medical benefits for burn survivors in accidents where evidence has been destroyed. Investigations are often hampered due to delays and lack of evidence, and for this reason, a prompt investigation is a necessity.

Quite often, the successful identification of the cause of the fire will directly relate to the amount of benefits that are available for needed reconstructive surgeries, therapy and rehabilitation.

E. **TYPES OF BURN-RELATED INJURIES SUCCESSFULLY LITIGATED**

1. *Explosions, house fires*

a. *Gas Explosion - Negligent Installation - Failure to perform inspection.*

A family had a propane gas tank installed in their home. Shortly after installation, they left their house for several hours. When they returned, an explosion occurred, severely burning several family members. The family successfully sued the gas company, alleging that its employees had been negligent in installing the gas tank; failed to install the tank according to its own gas system installation manual; and failed to comply with industry standards. The injured parties proved that the gas company employees had failed to cap a gas line in one of the bedrooms, allowing the house to fill with propane gas.

b. *Clothes Dryer - Heating Coils located too close to drum.*

When clothes in an electric clothes dryer caught fire, the baby sitter tried to smother the fire with a pillow, which also caught fire. She threw the pillow, and it struck a minor child causing second and third degree burns on the minor's face, arms, and thighs. General Electric, the manufacturer of the dryer, settled the claim, since it was proven that the dryer's heating coils had been located too close to the clothes drum, which had caused lint to catch fire and ignite the clothing.

169

c.   *Lawn Mower - Gas fume ignition*.

An individual was operating a riding lawn mower when it ran out of gas and the engine stopped. The individual picked up a nearby gas can and was refueling the tank when an explosion occurred. The plaintiff successfully argued that the design of the mower was defective since its gas tank had been located too close to the muffler. Engineering tests demonstrated that after two minutes of operation, the engine's muffler reached high enough temperatures to be an ignition source for gas vapors.

d.   *Hair Product*.

A minor applied an over-the-counter dandruff medicine to her scalp. When her head later accidentally touched the flame of a candle, the over-the-counter medicine ignited. The minor suffered second and third degree burns to her scalp and face. The plaintiff's attorney successfully settled a suit against the manufacturer and distributor of the product, since the product was made up of 90% petroleum and was highly flammable. The manufacturer and the distributor failed to warn of the product's flammability.

e.   *Apartment Complex - Building owner liability*.

A family were guests at a pig roast hosted by the owner of an apartment complex. A 19-month-old child fell into a pit filled with hot coals and suffered severe burns. The parents successfully sued the owner of the complex since the pit had been located just 4-5 feet from the family recreation center where children were playing, and had been left open and unattended.

2.   *Gasoline spill*

An individual was pumping gasoline in a service station when the coupling which attached the nozzle to the gasoline hose separated. Gasoline spilled on the individual, and when she approached a service station employee, he directed her to a wash basin which had a portable electric space heater under it. As she approached the wash basin, her gasoline-soaked clothing ignited and she suffered second and third degree burns. The individual successfully showed that her injuries were due to the defective product (the hose coupling).

3.   *Chemical burns*

4.   *Flammable children's clothing*

A structured settlement was negotiated for a minor who suffered burns when the nightgown she was wearing ignited. The manufacturer had failed to treat the garment with a flame-retardant substance and warn of the danger of flammability.

Investigations revealed that manufacturers knew flammable children's clothing were dangerous products and that they could not pass federal safety tests. Lawsuits involving flammable fabrics used in making children's clothing have led to strengthening of the federal flammability standards;

5.   *Defective Bic Lighters*

Bic introduced its disposable butane lighters in 1972 and, unfortunately, since that time many people have been seriously burned, and some killed, by fires caused by defects in these disposable lighters. Until recently, the company has been quietly settling cases, and would typically require secrecy as one of the terms of the settlement. A court has ordered Bic Corporation to release hundreds of documents relating to the safety of its lighter, including the results of safety tests performed by the company, and complaints by consumers. When a 2-year old girl died in a fire started in her bedroom by a 4-year old with a Bic lighter, the parents filed a product liability claim against Bic Corporation, alleging that the lighter was defective and unreasonably dangerous because it lacked child-resistant features and adequate safety warnings. Bic Corporation agreed to redesign their lighter by 1991 so that it is child-resistant;

6.   *Improperly designed gasoline tanks - Motor vehicles*

a.   *Negligently placed pick-up truck fuel tank*

A settlement was obtained for a boy who was burned when a pick-up truck's fuel tank exploded during an automobile accident. The boy's mother argued that the truck had been defectively designed with an improperly placed fuel tank.

b.   *Gas tank explosion in rear-end collision*

A settlement was obtained for a man who was severely burned after his automobile was hit from behind and burst into flames. The plaintiff's attorneys successfully proved that the design defect in the gas tank had been the cause of the explosion, since it was in the immediate crush zone, and was unprotected by the frame of the automobile.

c.   *Motorcycle - Defective Fuel Cap*

A person was injured when the motorcycle he was riding struck a tree. Upon impact, the motorcycle's gas cap popped off the tank, soaking the driver's clothes with fuel. His clothes ignited and he suffered third-degree burns. A successful settlement was negotiated since it was proven that the fuel cap was defectively designed and should have been able to withstand the pressure of impact, without coming off the tank.

7.   *Work-related accidents*

a.   *Inadequately insulated electrical plug*

A successful verdict was reached for the estate a man who was electrocuted while he was working with an industrial power unit. I was able to prove that the wiring in the unit's plug lacked non-conduction insulated sleeves.

b.   *International Harvester tractors - Defective vent hole*

Gas tanks on International Harvester tractors had a defective vent hole which caused burning gasoline to spew onto its users. The manufacturer continued to market farm tractors with defective fuel caps and fuel tanks even after receiving notice of severe injuries to a number of farmers. Only after attorneys successfully sued and obtained jury awards for compensatory and punitive damages did the manufacturers change their defective design.

8.   *Electric burns*

a.   *Inadequately elevated power lines - Quadriplegia*

While inspecting the roof on a commercial building, a man sustained catastrophic injuries when he became tangled in high voltage power lines. He successfully sued the owner of the property, which also owned the power lines, arguing that it had failed to maintain an adequate clearance between the power lines and the building. He also successfully sued the utility company alleging that it had been negligent in failing to elevate and de-energize the lines.

9.   *Electric heaters*

10.   *Lack of smoke detectors*

A female was in a motel fire without smoke detectors. A claim was brought against the motel owner for their failure to provide operating smoke and heat detectors.

• A minor was killed in a house fire which was rented in violation of state law, because of the landlord's failure to provide a smoke detector. In addition, it was alleged that the source of the fire was a defective product and that the landlord failed to maintain the electrical system, i.e., loose electrical connections, aging circuit boxes and improper amperage of the circuits in the circuit breakers.

• The plaintiff lived in HUD (Housing and Urban Development) housing with two minor children. The apartments were not equipped with smoke detectors. The family had requested a smoke detector from the landlord, but he refused since they were moving to another apartment shortly. A claim was filed for the deaths of two children based on the fact of this landlord's failure to provide smoke and heat detectors. Negligence claims have also been brought against HUD for inadequate safety inspections of existing smoke alarms.

• Several family members were severely burned by a fire in their rented home. The home had not been equipped with smoke detectors. The family alleged by failing to install smoke detectors the defendants (the owners), had breached an implied warrant of habitability that required them to provide a safe dwelling to the occupants of the rented premises. It was also alleged that the failure to provide smoke detectors violated a County Fire Prevention Code.

• Multiple deaths and burn injuries occurred in an apartment building fire. The apartment building was not equipped with heat and smoke detectors or fire walls, and some of the deaths were caused by inhalation of toxic fumes. A suit was filed based on the following theories:

Failure to provide smoke detectors;

Failure to install fire walls; and

Improper ventilation.

11. *Failure of smoke detectors to work properly or give adequate warning*

Two persons died in a fire in an apartment complex when a smoke detector failed to warn them. The smoke detector did not have batteries at the time of the fire. A suit was filed against the apartment complex because of the failure to maintain an operating smoke detector and their failure to warn. Suit was also brought against the manufacturer for the negligent design of the smoke detector.

• A smoke detector in a mobile home failed to operate and a child died in the fire. The children were playing with a cigarette lighter near a foam mattress which caught fire. Counsel argued that smoke detectors which were wired into the electrical system of the trailer had no battery back-up. A products liability claim was brought against the manufacturer of the detector and the manufacturer of the flammable mattress.

• The tenants in a housing authority project had their electrical services terminated prior to the notice date on their late payment bill; they therefore used candles for lighting purposes. During the night, a candle ignited a curtain, causing the dwelling to be engulfed in flames. Smoke detectors in the housing authority project failed to operate. Claims were filed against the housing authority and the manufacturer of the defective smoke detector.

• The door to an apartment house did not have operable locks as required by State law. An arsonist entered the building and started a fire. The fire alarm system and fire protection system were inoperative and the claimants had to jump from the fourth story and suffered extensive injuries. Suit was filed against the landlord because of the defective smoke and heat detectors, for not maintaining the smoke and heat detectors, and for lack of security.

These cases are only a sample of the types of cases which have been successfully litigated to provide necessary long term medical benefits for burn survivors and their families. The particular facts and circumstances of your case should be discussed with your attorney as quickly as possible after a serious accident or injury so that the investigation can promptly begin.

F.   **COSMETIC VS. RECONSTRUCTIVE SURGERY -**
      REIMBURSEMENT OF MEDICAL BILLS

Insurance companies will usually pay for reconstructive surgery for a serious burn. Generally, an insurance company will not pay for surgery that they believe is cosmetic rather than reconstructive in nature. I strongly believe that ALL surgery for burn survivors is reconstructive in nature and should be honored by available insurance. There are two arguments you should make in attempting to prove to the insurance company or health care provider that your requested surgery is reconstructive in nature: (1) that there has been loss of tissue that must be reconstructed; and (2) that there has been a loss of function of the particular part of your body that has been burned.

G.   **BURN INJURY SUPPORT GROUPS**

PHOENIX SOCIETY FOR BURN SURVIVORS....800-888-BURN
ABOUT FACE 215-491-0602

XIX. CEREBRAL PALSY

The American Academy for Cerebral Palsy and Developmental Medicine defines cerebral palsy as "a persistent, but not unchanging, disorder of movement and posture appearing in the early years of life due to traumatic or inflammatory brain damage, or to a non-progressive disorder of the brain..." The United Cerebral Palsy Association (UCPA), the major national voluntary agency serving those with cerebral palsy, states that cerebral palsy is a condition caused by damage to the brain during pregnancy, labor, or shortly following birth. "Cerebral" refers to the brain, and "Palsy" to a disorder of movement or posture. It is neither progressive nor communicable. The UCPA estimates there are 1.5 million persons with cerebral palsy in this country.

There are three main types of cerebral palsy: spastic - stiff and difficult movement, athetoid - involuntary and uncontrolled movement, ataxic - disturbed sense of balance and depth perception. There may be a combination of these types for any one individual. Other types do occur, although infrequently.

Cerebral palsy is characterized by an inability to control motor function. Depending on which part of the brain has been damaged, and the degree of involvement of the central nervous system and other systems, one or more of the following may occur: increased or decreased muscle tone; spasms; involuntary movement; difficulties with gait and mobility; seizures; impairment of sight, hearing or speech; and mental retardation.

According to the UCPA,

"Any damage to the brain, whether caused by defective development, injury, or disease, may produce cerebral palsy. Among the causes is an insufficient amount of oxygen reaching the fetal or newborn brain. Other causes may be associated with premature birth, Rh or A-B-O blood type incompatibility between parents, the infection of the mother with German measles or other viral disease in early pregnancy, and micro-organisms that attack the newborn's central nervous system. Most causes of cerebral palsy are related to the childbearing process and, since the condition is not inherited, the condition is often called congenital cerebral palsy. A less common type is acquired cerebral palsy; head injury is the most frequent cause, usually the result of motor vehicle accidents, falls, or child abuse."

Generally, the causes of cerebral palsy are grouped into three major categories according to the period in which the potential problem may develop. These categories are:

A.   *Pre-Natal* - from the time of conception to the time of labor;

B.   *Natal* - from the onset of labor to the actual birth of the baby;

C.   *Post-Natal* - from the time of, and after, the birth of the child.

According to the UCPA, it is estimated that some 500,000-700,000 children and adults in the United States have one or more symptoms of cerebral palsy. It was roughly estimated that currently about 3,000 infants are born with cerebral palsy each year, and some 500 pre-school children acquire cerebral palsy annually.

The UCPA further states that cerebral palsy can be prevented.

"Measures of prevention are increasingly possible today. Pregnant women are tested routinely for the Rh factor and, if RH negative, they can be immunized within 72 hours after the pregnancy terminates and prevent adverse consequences of blood incompatibility in a subsequent pregnancy. If the woman has not been immunized, the consequences of blood incompatibility in the newborn can be prevented by exchange transfusion in the baby. If a newborn baby has jaundice, this can be treated effectively by phototherapy in the hospital nursery. The increased use of neonatal intensive care units, particularly for 'high risk' infants, has helped to decrease the occurrence of cerebral palsy. Other preventive programs are directed toward reducing exposure of pregnant women to virus and other infections, unnecessary exposure to X-rays, drugs and medications and the control of diabetes, anemia and other nutritional deficiencies. Of great importance are optimal well-being prior to conception, adequate prenatal care and protecting children from accidents or injury."

A 1997 study suggests that many hard-to-explain cases of cerebral palsy, a major cause of physical disability, may be caused by infection - not by oxygen deprivation during the birth process. Research studies estimate that infections in the mother's womb or urinary tract may account for at least 12% of cerebral palsy in normal-weight babies. According to the study, aside from oxygen deprivation, other causes of cerebral palsy include brain malformation and genetic defects. According to the Cerebral Palsy Association, each year about 5,000 babies in this country are diagnosed with cerebral palsy. Caring for the 5,000 who are affected costs $2.4 billion. It is anticipated that as a result of this study doctors will do cultures of amniotic fluid in increasing numbers, do more sampling of placentas, and give more antibiotics.

It is very important that families obtain the necessary health insurance, governmental insurance, and special education benefits available to pay for attendant care, continuing therapies, vocational training, living accommodations, counseling, transportation and other short-term and long-term rehabilitation needs. It is often necessary for families to file suit against their local school district for denial of needed special education benefits for a child with cerebral palsy. Also, claims are often filed by parents against hospitals, doctors, and health insurers. alleging that negligent care received in the pre-natal or birthing process was a substantial factor in causing cerebral palsy.

D.   ***SUPPORT ORGANIZATIONS***

UNITED CEREBRAL PALSY FOUNDATION....(800-USA-5UCP)

PENNSYLVANIA ELKS MAJOR PROJECTS, INC.
NURSES WHO ADVOCATE FOR CHILDREN WITH
CEREBRAL PALSY ....(814-926-4404)

XX. ASSISTIVE TECHNOLOGY AND PERSONAL ASSISTANCE

A.   *QUESTIONS AND ANSWERS: ASSISTIVE TECHNOLOGY*

1.   *What is Assistive Technology?*

Assistive technology refers to devices or services that enhance personal independence. Examples of assistive technology are:

- electric scooters

- wheelchairs

- communication devices

- medical equipment

- respirators/ventilators, and

- equipment that expands an individual's vocational options and positively affects their quality of life.

Assistive technology has also been called adaptive technology or rehabilitation technology.

2.   *What are Assistive Technology Devices?*

The ***Technology Related Assistance for Individuals with Disabilities Act of 1988***, defines assistive technology devices as "any item, piece of equipment, or product system, which acquired commercially off the shelf, modified, or customized, that is used to increase, maintain, or improve functional capabilities of individuals with disabilities". Assistive technology devices can include electronic readers, computers, control lights, duralogs, telephones, <u>anything</u> where a medical or legal argument can be made that the device will improve the life of the person with the disability or special need.

3.   *What are assistive technology services?*

The ***Technology Related Assistance for Individuals with Disabilities Act of 1988*** defines assistive technology service as "any service that directly assists an individual with a disability in the selection, acquisition, or use of an assistive technology device". Assistive technology services can include equipment, training, product adaptations, information and referral services.

4. *Does the* **Americans with Disabilities Act** *(ADA) cover assistive technology?*

The **American with Disabilities Act** (ADA), signed into law on July 26, 1990, protects individuals with disabilities from discrimination in employment, public services, transportation, public accommodations, and telecommunications. Each title of the Act specifically references assistive technology devices or equipment as a means to achieve access and equal opportunity.

5. *What is the ADA's definition of a "person with a disability"?*

A "person with a disability" is anyone with a physical or mental impairment that substantially limits one or more major life activities, such as caring for one's self, performing manual tasks, walking, seeing, hearing, speaking, breathing, learning, and working.

6. *Are assistive technology devices and services considered special education services?*

Assistive technology services and devices are considered special education services. Assistive technology devices and services should be considered when developing a child's IEP (individualized Education Program). The **Individuals with Disabilities Education Act** (IDEA) includes definitions of assistive technology devices and services.

7. *What type of assistive technology device or services will a school district pay for?*

School districts will pay for:

- Assessments
- Hearing tests and aides
- Occupational therapy
- Physical therapy
- Cognitive therapy
- Speech and language services
- Medical devices
- Vision services and transportation services

8. *How do parents obtain special education funding from the school district for assistive technology devices and services?*

The following is a good approach in attempting to obtain services:

* Be creative;

* Include all services and devices requested in an IEP (contractually enforceable document);

* Modify the IEP as the need for assistive technology devices and services change;

* Be aggressive. In requesting assistive technology from a school district, the process to obtain funding is an adversarial process;

* Use as leverage, the fact that a school district will not want to pay for an "approve private school";

* Request a due process hearing.

9. *What assistive technology devices and services does private insurance pay for?*

Private insurance usually pays for assistive technology devices and services that are "medically necessary" and meet the definition of "durable medical equipment". To receive reimbursement from a health insurer, the assistive technology device or service must be:

* Medically necessary under the language of the particular policy or statute;

* Covered under the Durable Medical Equipment language of the policy or statute;

* Cost effective;

* Not excluded under the specific language of the policy or statute;

* Not be for custodial care services.

10. *When is an assistive technology device or service considered medically necessary?*

"Medically necessary" means that the service or device is required to treat the condition, illness or disease. Health care professionals may disagree about whether or not a specific service or device is medically necessary and I recommend that a request for assistive technology services or devices be documented with studies, cost analyses, statistics and a second or third medical opinion.

180

11. *What is durable medical equipment?*

Most insurance plans define durable medical equipment as equipment which is:

- Used primarily for a medical purpose;

- Necessary for the diagnosis or the treatment of the illness, or disease;

- Designed to be able to withstand prolonged use, i.e. that the equipment is durable;

- Primarily used for the home.

12. *Is a computer considered an assistive technology device?*

School districts are more inclined to pay for computers because they are cost effective and compatible with other forms of adaptive technology. A 1996 study on computers found that school districts will spend an estimated $4.1 billion on school technology in 1996, up from $3.9 billion in 1995-1996. The key in obtaining computers as an assistive technology device from a school district is integrating the use of the computer into a "overall plan" which enhances the educational opportunities for your child.

13. *Is a motorized wheelchair an assistive technology device?*

Yes. In seeking funding for a motorized wheelchair versus a non-motorized wheelchair, it is helpful to argue that the requested device is medically necessary and reduces functional limitations.

14. *Is the commercial distribution of wheelchairs regulated?*

In the United States, the Food and Drug Administration (FDA) regulates the distribution of wheelchairs. Wheelchairs are also regulated by the Safe Medical Devices Act of 1990 and the Medical Device Amendments of 1976 and 1992.

15. *Have there been significant safety problems with wheelchairs?*

The most common types of safety problems associated with wheelchairs are:

- Defects in the wheelchair which cause vibration or involuntary acceleration;

- Wheelchair tipping caused by lack of tipper bars, or inadequate or poorly designed tipper bars, allowing the wheelchair to tip over and/or the user to fall out of the wheelchair;

- Poorly designed rollers or steel caster forks, which support a wheelchair, cause the wheelchairs to buckle under stress;

- Electrical wiring problems causing electrical short circuiting;

- Inadequately designed motor and gear box assemblies, which render a wheelchair inoperable;

- Backrest hinges with weld cracks;

- Turn-off switches which do not turn the wheelchair off. This problem can cause significant safety hazards.

16. *Are home modifications considered an assistive technology service?*

Most private insurance policies and governmental policies will not pay for home modifications.

17. *Is a van modification considered an assistive technology service?*

Insurance companies and OVR (Office of Vocational Rehabilitation) will sometimes pay for van modifications if you can show the following:

- If the requested expense is for the modification of the van, and not the purchase of the van;

- If the individual requesting the van modification has passed a driver's test at an approved rehabilitation facility;

- If the van modification is cost effective, and will enable the individual to be gainfully employed;

- If the van modification aids in transportation for doctor's visits and ongoing therapies.

18. *What is architectural accessibility?*

Architectural accessibility refers to a building that can be easily entered and used by persons with disabilities.

B. LAWS AFFECTING INDIVIDUALS WHO NEED ASSISTIVE TECHNOLOGY DEVICES AND SERVICES

1. ***Americans with Disabilities Act of 1990*** (Pub.L.101-336);

The Americans with Disabilities Act of 1990 (ADA) prohibits discrimination against persons with disabilities in employment, public services, transportation, public accommodations, and telecommunications services.

a. Employment

The ADA became effective for businesses with 25 or more employees on July 26, 1992. Employers with 15 or more workers must have complied by July 26, 1994. Exempted from the provisions of the Act are businesses with fewer than 15 employees, the Federal Government (not Congress) and private membership clubs.

All aspects of employment are covered, including the application process and hiring, on-the-job-training, advancement in wages, benefits, and employer-sponsored social activities.

Essentially, the ADA protects qualified disabled persons from job discrimination. To be considered a qualified disabled person, a job applicant or employee must be able to perform the essential functions of the job. Employers must accommodate employees known mental or physical disabilities unless that would impose an "undue hardship".

To determine undue hardship, the ADA allows employers to consider the cost and nature of the accommodation, budget, staff size, type and location of the facility. For example, a wheelchair user applies to be a secretary at a downtown consulting firm. The essential functions of the job are typing, shorthand and delivering mail. The applicant scores the highest on the skill test, but steps in the suite will prevent him or her from distributing mail to some offices. In this case, the firm could accommodate the disability by either installing a ramp or asking another employee to bring mail to the inaccessible offices (in exchange for one of a colleague's duties).

Employers must provide disabled employees with reasonable accommodations that are needed to perform the essential duties of the job. Examples of accommodations are: modifying work schedules, reassigning job duties, removing architectural barriers, and offering auxiliary aids, interpreters or taped text.

A qualified individual with a disability is a person who has a physical or mental impairment substantially limiting a major life activity, has a record of such impairment or is regarded as having an impairment. A disability can include a physiological disorder or condition, cosmetic disfigurement, anatomical loss, emotional disorder or condition. A disability also includes conditions, diseases, and infections. Examples of conditions are orthopedic, visual, speech and hearing impairments. Examples of diseases and infections are cerebral palsy, epilepsy, muscular dystrophy, cancer and HIV infection.

The ADA does not guarantee an individual with a disability the right to a job. The employer remains free to make decisions based on the particular skills or knowledge necessary for the job. The decision made by the employer regarding who to hire must be based on reasons unrelated to the existence or consequence of a disability. The employer is not required to give preference to an applicant with a disability over another applicant without a disability.

The first step an employer should take is to determine the essential functions of a job, those tasks that are necessary to perform the job. Written job descriptions prepared before a position is advertised are considered evidence of essential job functions. Employers cannot ask questions about disabilities on applications or interviews, nor can they use selection criteria that screen out disabled people, unless those questions or tests are job-related.

The responsibility not to discriminate under the ADA goes beyond an employer's own office. Employees may not enter into contracts or relationships with labor unions, employment agencies or other outside organizations that would indirectly cause discrimination against disabled employees. Training seminars, conferences and meetings must also be accessible. An employer cannot discriminate against a non-disabled applicant or employee just because he or she is related to or associated with someone who is disabled. As an example, an employer would violate the ADA if it did not hire a woman for fear that she would be absent often to care for her disabled husband. Also, an employer could not fire an employee because his partner is infected by HIV (the virus which causes AIDS).

b.   Medical Examinations

Generally, the ADA prohibits employers from requiring pre-employment medical examinations or inquiring about a disability at a job interview, but there are limited exceptions. Employers may ask about disabling conditions if they are job related (asking potential truck drivers if they have any visual impairments). Employers may offer a job conditioned on the results of a medical exam, but only if all entering employees in the position are given the pre-employment exams and all employee medical records are kept confidential.

Optional, employer-sponsored health activities, such as "wellness programs", exercise classes, fitness programs, cholesterol testing, are allowed under the ADA as long as they are voluntary and information about the test is kept confidential.

c.   Drug Testing

Employer drug testing is legal under the ADA. Testing for illegal drugs is not considered a medical exam under the ADA. The Act specifically provides that an individual currently using illegal drugs is not a "qualified individual with a disability".

The law does protect alcoholics and past drug users who have successfully completed rehabilitation treatment. Under the ADA, employers may hold legal drug users and alcoholics to the same performance standards as other employees, even if poor performance or other unsatisfactory behavior is due to drug or alcohol use. Employers may administer ongoing drugs tests to insure that individuals who formerly used illegal drugs are no longer using them. Employers must still comply with state laws and regulations governing medical exams and drug testing.

d.   Public Accommodations

Title II of the Act requires that disabled people have equal access to public accommodations, including shops, offices, and recreation areas. Public accommodations such as restaurants, hotels, theaters, doctors offices, pharmacies, retail stores, museums, libraries, parks, private schools, and day care centers may not discriminate on the basis of disability, effective January 26, 1992. Private clubs and religious organizations are exempt.

The purpose of the public accommodation section of the ADA is to prevent incidents of exclusion and discrimination from occurring. Public places must be physically accessible to disabled people. The ADA requires businesses to remove architectural and communication barriers which are "readily achievable". Readily achievable is defined as "easily accomplishable and able to be carried out without much difficulty or expense". A business can consider its overall size and budget, number of employees and the type of facility to determine if barrier removal is readily achievable.

New construction and renovation of facilities are also covered by the ADA. Effective January 26, 1993, all newly built commercial facilities must be accessible to disabled people.

e.   Public Transportation

Wheelchair lifts on buses, subway and train stations with elevators will be a common sight for commuters, in compliance with the ADA

185

regulations requiring public transportation systems to be accessible to disabled riders. Because air travel is addressed by the **Air Carriers Access Act,** airlines are not covered by the ADA, although it does apply to ground transportation between terminals and parking lots at airports. School bus transportation is also exempted from the ADA.

Effective August 26, 1990, transportation authorities can only purchase new buses that are accessible to persons in wheelchairs. Amtrak is subject to the ADA. New railroad cars must include a place to store wheelchairs, a place to secure a wheelchair as a seat, and an accessible rest room. Food services must also be accessible.

f.   Telecommunications

Title IV of the ADA required telephone companies to provide continuous telecommunications relay services for hearing impaired and speech impaired persons 24 hours a day.

g.   Penalties for violating the ADA

From the plaintiff's perspective, the scope of coverage under the ADA permits plaintiffs more opportunities to bring causes of action because more employers will be covered under the ADA than under prior acts. Title VII provides for remedies, including injunctions, reinstatement, back pay, promotion, hiring, and reasonable attorney's fees. The Act does not provide for compensatory or punitive damages. The ADA does provide that the prevailing party may receive reasonable attorney's fees, including litigation expenses and costs, in any action or administrative proceeding commenced pursuant to the ADA, at the discretion of the court. The ADA incorporates many of the remedies and procedures found in Title VII of the **Civil Rights Act of 1964.** An aggrieved individual has the right to file a law suit only after first filing a charge with the Equal Employment Opportunity Commission (EEOC). EEOC powers include the authority to receive and investigate charges of discrimination, as well as to bring civil actions in individual cases against employers that engage in "pattern and practice" discrimination.

2.   *Health Insurer may be Liable as "Employer" under ADA for Limiting Employee Benefits*

In the case of *Carparts Distribution Ctr. v. Automotive Wholesalers, Association*, the First Circuit Court of Appeals ruled that a trade association offering a self-funded medical reimbursement plan through its administering trust is subject to the **Americans with Disabilities Act** (ADA). The health insurer and trust could be liable for limiting benefits to $25,000 for AIDS-related illnesses, rather than the $1 million dollar lifetime benefits afforded other plan members.

The court observed that Title I of the ADA makes it unlawful for a covered entity to discriminate against a person on the basis of a disability in regard to fringe benefits available by virtue of employment. The trial court ruled that a health insurer is not a "covered entity" under the ADA, because the ADA defines a "covered entity" as "an employer, employment agency, labor organization, or joint labor-management committee."

However, the First Circuit Court of Appeals rejected the trial court's analysis, and identified three theories in which a health insurer could be considered an employer under the ADA.

- First, the guidelines of the ADA published by the Equal Employment Opportunity Commission establish that "employer" is to be given the same meaning under the ADA as under the *Civil Rights Act of 1964.* The court concluded that a defendant would be an employer if it exercised control over the employees' health care coverage, an important aspect of employment.

- Second, even if an employer retains the right of control over administering the plan, an insurer could be rendered an employer under agency principles if it acts on behalf of the employer in providing health benefits.

- Third, the court cited cases interpreting Title VII of the *Civil Rights Act of 1964* to apply to actions taken by a defendant (insurer) against someone who is not technically the insurer's employee. The plaintiff is protected if the defendant (insurer) significantly affects access to employment opportunities.

In *Carparts*, the court held that if an insurer's sole purpose is to enable an employer to delegate the responsibility of providing health insurance to employees, then the employer and insurer are so intertwined that the insurer will be considered an employer. The court identified two tests relevant to this inquiry:

    a.   Whether the insurer had authority to determine the level of benefits, and;

    b.   Whether employees had a choice of alternative health plans through their employer.

The implications of this decision for the catastrophically ill and injured are monumental. Persons who are catastrophically ill and injured should have their insurance policy/medical reimbursement plan examined by an attorney if they believe that because of their illness or injury they are receiving less benefits than other individuals covered by the plan.

187

3.   *Air Carrier Access Act of 1986*

Airlines were specifically excluded from the application of the ADA because Congress had already passed legislation, the *Air Carrier Access Act of 1986* (ACAA). This Act provides "no air carrier may discriminate against any otherwise qualified handicapped individual, by reason of such handicap, in the provision of air transportation." 49 U.S.C. Section 1374 (c) (1) (1988). In 1990, the Department of Transportation promulgated regulations interpreting the requirements of the *Air Access Act of 1986.* These regulations require that:

- Domestic airlines be equipped with folding armrests on half the aisles;

- Widebodied aircraft must have lavatories accessible to the handicapped;

- Planes with 100 or more seats must have priority space for storing a wheelchair in the cabin;

- Wheelchairs and other handicapped assistive devices, such as canes or crutches, have priority for in-cabin and baggage compartments over other passengers' baggage;

- Airlines cannot prohibit the handicapped from bringing their personal ventilators and respirators, as well as non-spillable batteries and seeing-eye dogs, aboard the aircraft;

- Planes with 60 or more seats with an accessible lavatory must have an on-board wheelchair in the cabin.

Discrimination in airports was addressed by Congress in the *Rehabilitation Act of 1973* and the *Developmental Disabilities Act of 1978*, which prohibit discrimination in any program or activity receiving federal financial assistance. Essentially, the Department of Transportation regulations require that airports make the necessary changes in their facilities to permit access by the handicapped. Ticketing, baggage check-in and retrieval, boarding, telephones, teletypewriters, vehicle loading and unloading, parking, waiting areas, airport terminal information, and other public services (example: drinking areas, eating areas, and rest rooms) all must be made accessible.

- In a reasonable accommodation with the airline industry, retrofitting existing aircraft is not required unless the airline replaces the entire cabin interior or lavatories.

- Airlines may not charge handicapped persons for the amenities required by the Department of Transportation regulations, but may impose a reasonable, non-discriminatory charge for optional services such as on-board oxygen, electrical hook-up for respirator, accommodation of stretchers, etc."

- Airlines may not require advance notice that a handicapped person will be traveling, although they may require up to 48 hours notice where an individual needs special accommodations, i.e. oxygen, a ventilator, special ventilator equipment, etc.

- Airlines which operate an aircraft of more than 19 seats are obliged to train their personnel in the requirements of the Department of Transportation regulations.

- Airline employees must provide assistance to the individual with special needs in enplaning and deplaning, and in making flight connections and providing transportation between gates.

4. ***The Rehabilitation Act of 1973, Section 504 (Pub. L.93-112)***

This Act extends basic civil rights protection to individuals with disabilities. Under this Act, institutions or organizations that engage in discriminatory practices may lose federal funding;

5. ***Technology-Related Assistance for Individuals with Disabilities Act of 1988*** (Pub. L. 100-407)

The purpose of this Act is to develop technology-related assistance programs and to extend assisted technology to individuals with disabilities and their families;

6. ***Architectural Barriers Act, (P.L. 90-489, 42 U.S.C. 451 et seq [1968]);***

7. ***Uniform System of Handicap Parking, 102 Stat. 3335***

A statute that provides uniform regulations requiring handicapped parking for individuals with special needs;

C.　　　***PERSONAL ASSISTANCE SERVICES***

Personal assistance services aid individuals with their daily living needs, i.e., personal maintenance, hygiene, child-rearing, shopping, work related activities and community integration activities. Many health insurers agree to pay for personal assistance services and attendant care services because it is less expensive than an LPN, RN, group home, or care in a residential facility.

1.　　　*Attendant Care*

Attendant care services are those tasks performed by a personal care attendant while assisting a person with a disability in daily or routine activities of survival. These activities include, but are not limited to, bathing, dressing, transportation, etc. Attendants will usually adjust their schedule to the daily living routine of the injured or ill individual.

LANDMARK VICTORY FOR HOME ATTENDANT CARE

On October 2, 1995, the United States Supreme Court agreed with the Federal Appeals Court that the Commonwealth of Pennsylvania must provide attendant care services in "the most integrated setting appropriate" to the individuals needs.

The facts of this case are as follows: A 43-year-old mother of two contracted meningitis, which resulted in paralysis from the waist down. Since 1989, she has been a patient at the Philadelphia Nursing Home. She is able to use a wheelchair and is able to cook and attend to her personal hygiene and grooming. Even though she is not capable of fully independent living, she does not require the custodial care of a nursing home.

There was testimony that she could receive the type of attendant care services she needs at home as effectively as in a nursing home. The cost of nursing home care, in her case, is approximately $44,000.00 annually. The Federal government pays approximately $24,000.00. The Commonwealth of Pennsylvania pays an additional $20,000.00. The cost to provide home care in her case is approximately $10,000.00.

The United States Supreme Court agreed with the Third Circuit Court of Appeals that the will of the United States Congress was for the "integration of persons with disabilities into the economic and social mainstream of American life". Additionally, the ADA requires that a "public entity shall administer services, programs, and activities in the most integrated setting appropriate to the needs of qualified individuals with disabilities".

The Commonwealth of Pennsylvania based its case on the fact that the state Legislature had not provided funding for home attendant care services. The federal courts held that the Department of Public Welfare could not rely on a funding mechanism of the General Assembly to justify administering its attendant care program in a manner that discriminated, and then argue that it would not comply with the ADA. The United States Supreme Court agreed with the Appeals Court finding that state funding mechanisms could not justify discrimination.

Consumer advocates have consistently pushed for more Personal Assistance Services (PAS), called **attendant care** in state law, for the many Pennsylvanians with disabilities who are on waiting lists. There may be as many as 5,000 individuals with disabilities in Pennsylvania who are waiting for Personal Assistance Services (attendant care services). Many of these individuals are in nursing homes and other institutions because they can not obtain Personal Assistance Services.

In order to be eligible for Attendant Care Service, a person must:

a. Be an adult (18 through 59).

b. Be a mentally alert individual with a physical disability, who meets all of the following requirements:

   (1) Experience any medically determinable physical impairment which can be expected to last for a continuous period of not less than twelve months;

   (2) Is capable of selecting, supervising and, if needed, terminating an attendant;

   (3) Is capable of managing his/her own financial and legal affairs; and

   (4) Because of physical impairment, requires assistance to complete functions of daily living, self care and mobility including, but not limited to the following:

   • routine bodily functions
   • dressing/undressing
   • preparation and consumption of food
   • bathing

(5)　　Be determined by The Center for Independent Living, following an attendant care intake interview and/or assessment, to need Attendant Care Services.

(6)　　Be a resident of the state from which attendant care services are being requested.

2.　　*Home Care*

For most families of catastrophically ill and injured individuals, home care is their first option. Unfortunately, most health insurance policies and governmental programs do not pay for attendant care, nursing care, physical therapy, speech therapy, and other care provided for in the patient's home. There are many ways you can obtain home care benefits. The following approaches should be explored:

- Examine the language of your health insurance policy carefully to determine whether or not home care as an option is specifically excluded;

- Examine the health insurance policy to determine whether or not home care options are limited;

- Examine the health insurance policy to determine whether or not the language which limits or excludes home care is too restrictive and amounts to bad faith;

- Enter into negotiation with the health insurer or self-insurer to determine whether or not they will pay extra-contractual benefits;

- Investigate the catastrophic injury or illness to determine whether or not the concept of "subrogation" or "leverage" can be used—this concept would allow the health insurer or self-insurer to be reimbursed for the sums they have expended for home care from funds collected from the liability insurance carrier of the person or entity that caused the catastrophic injury or illness.

D. **SUCCESSFULLY LITIGATED ASSISTIVE TECHNOLOGY AND PERSONAL ASSISTANCE CASES**

1. *Wheelchairs - Lack of Tipper Bars - Safety*

A partially disabled individual was provided a wheelchair that did not have "tipper bars". Tipper bars prevent a wheelchair from falling over when the user leans back in the chair. While using the wheelchair, my client suffered quadriplegia when the wheelchair tipped over. **SUGGESTION:** Your treating doctor, occupational therapist, physical therapist, and equipment vendor should work together to insure that the assistive technology device meets your specific medical and physical requirements.

2. *Computers - Special Education Benefits - Minors*

A family requested a computer from the school district for their child, who suffered from cerebral palsy. The school district declined to pay, taking the position that they were legally required to provide "education", not "the best education". By showing that the child's ability to be educated was compromised without a computer, we were successful in obtaining funding for the computer. **SUGGESTION:** Many school districts, like health insurers, will not pay for assistive technology devices and services unless they are forced to. The special education process is an adversarial process.

3. *Home Modifications - Assistive Technology - Purchase of New Home - Self-Insured*

An individual working in a boiler plant suffered a catastrophic injury (burns and quadriplegia) when a boiler malfunctioned. The investigation revealed that the manufacturer of the boiler used an inferior/defective product which caused the malfunction. The workers' compensation carrier was the self-insured employer. Most workers' compensation carriers and self-insured employers do not have to pay for home modifications or for the cost of purchasing a new home. As a result of the lawsuit that was filed against the manufacturer, I was able to convince the self-insured employer to pay for the purchase of a home to meet the needs of the quadriplegic. **SUGGESTION:** The repayment of medical benefits and wages paid by workers' compensation carriers, self-insured employers, and private health insurers can be important leverage in convincing them to pay for housing and other assistive technology devices and services.

4. *Ventilators - Personal Assistance Services - Assistive Technology*

An individual was injured in an automobile accident. The treating doctors wrote a prescription for a "state-of-the-art ventilator" and 16 hours of personal assistant services. The auto insurer would only pay for four (4) hours of assistant services and would not pay for the ventilator prescribed by the treating doctor. I argued that the ventilator and 16 hours of personal assistant services were medically necessary and that the denial of these requests constituted "bad faith". The day before a lawsuit was filed, the insurance company agreed to pay. **SUGGESTION:** Health insurers rely on the fact that because family members are overwhelmed by the injury or illness to their loved one, they will not appeal, fight, and advocate for the benefits to which they are entitled.

E. *REHABILITATION INFORMATION*

NATIONAL REHABILITATION INFORMATION CENTER
NATIONAL CLEARINGHOUSE FOR INFORMATION ON
DISABILITY NEEDS .... (800-346-2742)

XXI. REIMBURSEMENT ALTERNATIVES - NEW HORIZONS

A.   *VENTILATOR PATIENTS*

1.   *Statistics*

There is very little concrete information on the cost of caring for chronic ventilator patients. The Gallup organization conducted a survey to document the number of chronic ventilator patients, the cost of those patients in the hospital, the discharge setting for those patients, and the cost burden absorbed by our health care system. The chronic ventilator patient was defined as one needing mechanical ventilation for at least six hours a day for 30 days or more.

Among the most important findings from this survey are:

- There are 11,119 chronic ventilator-dependent patients being treated in our hospitals at any time.

- The daily cost of caring for those patients is $9,012,332.

- Hospitals must absorb 46% of the cost of care for those patients.

- After it is determined that a chronic ventilator patient can be sent to a post-acute care location, the patient must wait approximately 35 days before a bed opens at a qualified facility.

- While waiting, the patient is incurring an additional $27,615 of cost.

Most ventilator-dependent patients are between the ages of 18 and 64. Although the majority of chronic ventilator-dependent patients were estimated to be hospitalized for medical reasons, department directors said that 39.51% of their patients were hospitalized because of reimbursement obstacles; the patients would only receive reimbursement for their care if they were hospitalized. An additional 17.28% of patients were hospitalized while they were waiting for placement in a qualified post-acute care location.

Regarding reimbursement issues, the study found:

- Approximately 60% of chronic ventilator-dependent patients are covered by Medicare/Medicaid.

- Medicare/Medicaid reimburses 47% of the cost of care for ventilator-dependent patients.

- Most ventilator-dependent patients (45%) are discharged to skilled nursing facilities, 43% go to some other type of long-term care facility, and 12% are sent home.

- After it is determined that a chronic ventilator-dependent patient can be discharged to a post-acute care location, it takes approximately five weeks for an opening to occur.

- Not enough beds or facilities was cited as the most frequent reason for incurring a wait.

2. *Waivers*

As an alternative to hospital care for catastrophically ill, but medically stable, individuals, the federal government adopted special funding programs called Waivers. States can apply for special program funding for home and community based services for catastrophically injured individuals. The application for waiver funding must be submitted to, and approved by, the Health Care Financing Administration. Most states have applied for waiver funding and have programs in existence.

In Pennsylvania, as in most states, the Department of Welfare was granted a three-year waiver program for several technology-dependent children. For waiver purposes, technology-dependent children are identified as those with continued dependence on a medical device to replace or compensate for a vital body function and to avert immediate threat to life. Many states supply necessary equipment, home nursing care, and case management to individuals approved for waiver services. These individuals are also eligible for all compensable Medicaid benefits.

In most states, to qualify for the waiver program, an individual must meet the following criteria:

- Must be a resident of that state;

- Must be under 21;

- Must need skilled nursing services on a continuing, daily basis;

- Must be technology-dependent.

3. *Finding Adequate Health Insurance Coverage*

Finding adequate health coverage for a ventilator-dependent patient is a monumental task. Governmental and private insurance have enacted legal, contractual and practical obstacles which make it very difficult, if not next-to-impossible, to transfer an individual from a hospital into a skilled nursing facility (SNF) in a timely manner. To overcome these problems and obstacles, you must consult with an attorney and other professionals knowledgeable in dealing with the myriad regulations concerning reimbursement for chronic ventilator-dependent individuals. It is often necessary to marshall a team approach of doctors, your attorney, hospital administrators, insurance representatives, and your legislators, to overcome all of the problems associated with appropriate placement of an individual on a ventilator.

4. *National Association for Ventilator-Dependent Individuals, Inc. (NAVDI)*

The National Association for Ventilator-Dependent Individuals, Inc. (NAVDI) is an organization which assists ventilator-dependent individuals and their families, and is located at:

> **NAVDI**
> 2500 Metrohealth Dr.
> Pulmonary Div., H-323,
> Cleveland Ohio 44109
> Telephone 216-778-3612.

B. *AMPUTATIONS*

Approximately 50,000 amputations are done each year in the United States. 85% of amputations are of the lower extremity, and the majority are as a result of vascular deficiency. Most upper-extremity amputations are the result of accidents. Traumatic amputations caused by accidents should be investigated to determine whether or not the accident could have been prevented; for example, many work-place amputations occur as the result of defectively designed machinery. The rehabilitation community has made tremendous advances in the design and manufacture of prosthetic devices for amputees. Many health insurance policies and worker's compensation insurers will pay for only the first prosthetic device.

C. *MUNICIPALITIES*

1. *Suits Against a Municipality, County, Borough or State*

The Legislature of most states, including Pennsylvania, have abolished the doctrine of sovereign immunity. Citizens have been granted the right to sue a state or governmental agency for personal injuries. The Legislature granted this right to individuals to sue a state, municipality or a governmental agency only in certain limited, factual situations.

The most common claims against a municipality, state, county or borough, are as a result of automobile accidents. The number and types of road design problems that can be claimed against a municipality are too numerous to mention, but most claims are in the following areas:

- Improper location of telephone poles;

- Improper highway design (Improper highway design is a leading cause of accidents resulting in head trauma and other catastrophic injuries);

- Improper drainage to roadways leading to the accumulation of water and ice;

- Poorly designed on- and off- ramps;

- Lack of warnings—Failure to install proper signs to warn of highway dangers, i.e. "Slippery When Wet", "Reduce Speed", "High Accident Area".

As soon as possible after a serious accident, the facts and circumstances surrounding the accident should be investigated by a trained investigator and engineer to determine what caused the accident. A prompt inspection of the accident scene is important because Pennsylvania law requires that a municipality or governmental unit receive a notice that a lawsuit may be filed against them within **_six months_** from the date of the injury.

The Legislature's rationale for requiring that the municipality receive notice of the accident within six months from the date of the injury was because the Legislature wanted to give the municipality sufficient time to investigate an accident before the evidence was destroyed and the scene of the accident materially changed.

The Legislature requires that a governmental unit receive notice by certified mail that an injury occurred on a certain date, at a certain location, and that the injury was, for example, a head injury. A family does not have to institute a lawsuit against a governmental unit within the first six months following the injury, but they must give a notice to the municipality that suit might be brought against them.

Unfortunately, many one-car collisions caused by improper road design could have been successfully litigated against a governmental unit but were never investigated by the family of the catastrophically injured person. This is because the family is usually unaware that the true cause of the accident was the improper road design.

D. *HERPES, SEXUALLY TRANSMITTED DISEASES AND AIDS LITIGATION*

According to the Centers for Disease Control and Prevention, one in 300 Americans are infected with HIV. The total number of infected persons is estimated to be from 650,000 to 900,000. Treatments and complications from this disease are placing a heavy strain on medical and social services in both the public and private sectors. Millions more people are infected with what health officials call "the other sexually transmitted diseases"; Chlamydia, genital herpes, genital warts, gonorrhea, hepatitis B, and syphilis. Up to 45 million people carry the virus that causes genital herpes.

Litigation involving AIDS and the sexual transmission of diseases has exploded in the 1990's. Countless suits have been filed based on the following theories: (1) Duty to inform - a duty arises when a person knows, or has reason to know, that they have, or are carriers of, a particular diseases; (2) Duty to screen blood supply - Unfortunately, many persons such as hemophiliacs or those needing blood for surgical procedures, have received tainted blood due to lack of adequate blood screening and testing procedures. Other theories of liability have included seduction, trespass, negligence, battery, deceit, fraud, misrepresentation, and violation of statutes relating to the conduct of people with contagious diseases. Some courts have allowed individuals to recover damages for "a reasonable fear of contracting AIDS", without proving exposure to the AIDS virus.

Appellate courts are still at odds concerning whether or not blood banks can be held liable for infecting patients with the AIDS virus by distributing contaminated blood in the early 1980's. Plaintiffs who had contracted the virus through blood transfusions in 1983 claimed that the blood banks had not adequately screened donors or the donated blood. The test to screen blood for the human immunodeficiency virus (HIV) which causes AIDS, was not licensed until 1985.

The infected individuals argued that the industry had known enough before 1985 about the possibility of HIV transmission through blood transfusion that blood banks should have done more to protect patients. It was argued that blood banks should have directly questioned donors about their sexual practices and intravenous drug abuse. The issue of whether or not blood banks can be held liable for infecting the patients with the AIDS virus by distributing contaminated blood in the early 1980's has not been decided by the United States Supreme Court.

Because of the delay between exposure to a sexually transmitted disease and the onset of the disease, the statute of limitations or the period of time within which a claim must be filed may expire before victims even know they have AIDS. The area of sexually transmitted diseases imposes troublesome ethical, moral, and legal issues for the health care community, which are likely to continue into the next decade.

E.   *DPT - VACCINE INJURY COMPENSATION ACT*

On October 8, 1988, the National Vaccine Injury Compensation Program became effective. Congress passed this Act to provide for a system to compensate those children injured as a result of adverse vaccine or toxoid reactions. The vaccines and toxoids currently covered under this program are: diphtheria toxoid, pertussis vaccine and tetanus toxoid (DPT); measles, mumps, and rubella (MMR); oral poliovirus vaccine (OPV) and inactivated poliovirus vaccine (IPV), administered individually or in usual combinations. Effective August 6, 1997, hepatitis B, Haemophilus influenzae type B, and varicella (chicken pox) vaccines have been added for coverage under the program. Eight years' retroactive coverage from the effective date will be provided for vaccine-related adverse affects associated with the three new vaccines.

Medical records will be reviewed to determine if the vaccine given to the child or adult caused or aggravated the alleged injury. Important factors in determining causation are: assessment of the individual's health status prior to administering the vaccine, the type of vaccine, and the date given, and the date, onset and extent of injury occurring after receiving the vaccine.

The deadline for filing a claim for injuries which occurred after October 1, 1988, are as follows:

- For an *injury* which occurred after October 1, 1988, the claim must be filed within three years of the first symptom;

- For a *death* which occurred after October 1, 1988, the claim must be filed within two years of the death, and within four years of the first symptom.

For further information, contact:

The National Vaccine Injury Compensation Program
Park Lawn Building - Room 8A-35
5600 Fishers Lane
Rockville MD 20857

Valid claims which occur after October 1, 1988, are entitled to request reasonable compensation for past and future unreimbursed medical, custodial care, and rehabilitation costs, damages for actual and projected pain and suffering and emotional distress, and lost wages. If there is a vaccine-related death, up to $250,000 compensation for the estate of the deceased may be recovered.

The Act provides for a no-fault system to compensate those injured as a result of adverse vaccine reactions. It is not a requirement that you have an attorney represent you during this process, however, because the rules and the time limits set forth by the U.S. Claims Court are specific and must be strictly followed, many petitioners have made a decision to have an attorney represent them during this process. The Act provides for the payment of reasonable attorney's fees and costs, regardless of the court's decision on compensability, providing the case is brought in good faith and there is a reasonable basis for the claim.

F. *FALLS*

According to the American Trauma Society, falls are the second leading cause of accidental deaths for all persons ages 45 to 75 and the number one cause of unintentional death for persons 75 years of age and older. Falls are the most common cause of non-fatal injury in the United States and the second leading cause of both spinal cord and brain injury. The National Safety Council reports that 7.6 million people were treated in hospital emergency rooms due to accidental falls. In 1996, 13,500 people died due to falls, 76% of whom were age 65 or older.

Since falls often cause spinal cord, head, and other disabling injuries, it is prudent to investigate whether or not your fall was caused by inadequate lighting in a hallway, a broken sidewalk or a wet or slippery walkway. In proving what caused your fall, it is important to have photographs of the particular condition or object that may have caused your fall. Photographs and statements of any witnesses obtained as quickly as possible after your fall will enable you to document for the insurance company how your fall occurred.

G. *PREMISES LIABILITY*

In Pennsylvania there is a **Recreational Land Immunity Act** which grants a broad immunity to owners of land whose land is open to the public for recreational purposes. Essentially, there are only limited situations in which an individual who suffers a serious injury can make a claim for long-term medical benefits against the owner of recreational land in Pennsylvania.

The **Recreational Land Immunity Act** does not apply and you would be able to make a claim for benefits in the following circumstances:

1.   Immunity does not apply to a suit against a city for injuries suffered when a child goes into a public swimming pool;

2.   Immunity does not apply with respect to injuries sustained on a municipal playground;

3.   Immunity does not apply to Penn's Landing, an area of urban redevelopment in Philadelphia, since it is improved land;

4.   There is no immunity for a school district's lacrosse field, since it is improved land.

If you suffer a serious injury while engaged in a recreational activity on any land in Pennsylvania, you should immediately discuss with your attorney whether or not you have the right to bring a claim for personal injuries and what requirements must be met under the **Recreational Land Immunity Act.**

H.   *ALCOHOL - DRAM SHOP CLAIMS*

1.   *Alcohol/drunk driving injuries - Statistics*

According to the American Trauma Society, the greatest single cause of death for those between the ages of 5 and 44 is motor vehicle accidents. About 41% of these fatalities are alcohol-related. Alcohol-related traffic fatalities are highest for persons 21 to 24 years old. For drivers in this age group in fatal crashes in 1995, 28% were intoxicated. 46,800 males and 15,400 females were involved in fatal incidents in 1990. Drivers under 30 years old account for more than half of all drinking drivers who are fatally injured in crashes.

Approximately 43,600 people died in motor vehicle incidents in 1995. 41%, or 16,589, were alcohol-related. In 1995, more than 1.5 million drivers were arrested for driving under the influence of alcohol. Two out of every five drivers will be involved in an alcohol-related accident at some time in their lives. In 1994, 22% of all drivers killed in accidents on weekdays were intoxicated, compared to 43.4% on weekends. The annual cost of alcohol-related incidents in 1995 was 24.4 billion dollars.

2.   *What is a Dram Shop or alcohol claim?*

A Dram Shop or alcohol claim is a claim brought against an establishment, usually a bar or restaurant, for selling alcoholic beverages to an individual that exhibited visible signs of intoxication.

3.   *How do you prove an alcohol or Dram Shop claim?*

a.   Witnesses

Witnesses who saw the individual drinking at the bar or restaurant can provide statements that the person's speech was slurred, that they were loud, that their eyes were red, and they were not able to walk properly, etc. Witness testimony will be accepted by the courts to show that an individual exhibited visible signs of intoxication.

202

b.   Blood alcohol

Breathalyzer tests and tests of an individual's blood can be used as evidence that an individual exhibited visible signs of intoxication.

c.   Toxicologist

A toxicologist is an expert who is able to testify that based on an individual's breathalyzer test results, blood alcohol tests results, descriptions by witnesses of an individual's behavior that the person in question did exhibit visible signs of intoxication on the night they consumed the alcoholic beverage. Toxicologists are used when there are no witnesses who personally witnessed the individual exhibit visible signs of intoxication.

d.   Minors

In many states, it is illegal to sell or provide alcoholic beverages to minors. If a bar, restaurant, or other business does sell or provide alcoholic beverages to a minor and they seriously injure themselves the business facility is not only subject to criminal penalties but also, suit can be maintained against them for civil damages in a Dram Shop or alcohol claim.

4.   *Alcohol claim vs. relatives - host theory*

In some states, neither individuals nor businesses are permitted to provide alcoholic beverages to persons who exhibit visible signs of intoxication. For example, if you have a private party at home, in states that have adopted the "host theory", the host of the party is not permitted, and would be responsible, if an individual leaves the home of the host after consuming too many alcoholic beverages and seriously injures himself/herself or innocent third parties.

5.   *A review of Pennsylvania liquor liability laws*

This section will review the most common types of Pennsylvania liquor liability cases to assist health care providers in identifying benefits.

To determine whether or not there is a valid "dram shop" or liquor liability claim, you must first look at the statute which imposes liability upon a liquor licensee. The dram shop statute states in pertinent part:

"It shall be unlawful ...

"(1) For any licensee or the Board, or any employee, servant or agent of such licensee or the Board, or any other person to sell, furnish or give any liquor or malted

203

or brewed beverages, or to permit any liquor or malted or brewed beverages to be sold, furnished or given, to any person visibly intoxicated, or to any insane person, or to any minor, or to habitual drunkards, or persons of known intemperate habits....

"No licensee shall be liable to the third persons on account of damage inflicted upon them off the licensed premises by customers of the licensee unless the customer who inflicts the damages was sold, furnished or given liquor, or malted or brewed beverages by the said licensee or his agent, servant or employee when the said customer was visibly intoxicated."

The two most common types of liquor liability cases are:

- A customer becomes intoxicated as a result of consuming alcoholic beverages at the defendant's restaurant, bar, tavern, etc., leaves and is involved in an accident which catastrophically injures another person;

- A customer becomes intoxicated at the tavern, bar, restaurant, etc., leaves and is involved in an accident and is seriously injured.

In Pennsylvania, there is no cause of action against a social host for serving alcohol to adults who are visibly intoxicated, insane, drunkards, or persons of intemperate habits. If a social host serves a minor to the point of intoxication and the minor then proceeds to injure a third person in an automobile accident, the social host may be held liable for the third person's injuries. If a minor is served alcohol either by a liquor licensee (bar, restaurant, etc.) or social host and becomes intoxicated and then injures himself, there is a cause of action against the liquor licensee or social host.

The trend in the Pennsylvania Legislature is to expand the rights of victims injured by drunken drivers. Under the Pennsylvania automobile insurance law effective July 1, 1990, the general rule is that unless the injury sustained in the automobile accident is serious, each person who chooses the limited tort alternative would not be allowed to sue for pain and suffering (non-economic loss). However, even if an individual unwisely chooses to give up the right to sue for non-serious injuries, they will still retain the right to file a lawsuit for damages suffered in a motor vehicle accident if the person at fault is convicted of driving under the influence of alcohol or a controlled substance.

With dwindling governmental and private insurance benefits for individuals catastrophically injured in automobile accidents, it is imperative that the health care community be aware of the type of automobile accidents involving alcohol which typically lead to a recovery under state liquor liability statutes. Carefully identifying liquor liability/dram shop cases at the acute care level will enable injured persons to have access to health care benefits to pay for their medical and rehabilitation needs.

6.   *Trends*

The clear trend in all states is to discourage individuals from consuming too many alcoholic beverages. Legislatures and the courts have strengthened criminal penalties against individuals who are arrested for drunk driving and broadened civil penalties by allowing individuals to maintain claims against private persons and businesses for damages to pay their cost of medical and rehabilitation expenses. There are a few cases that have been filed against manufacturers of alcoholic beverages on the theory that they have failed to warn of the dangers of alcohol and that this failure has resulted in children born with birth defects after their mothers consumed alcoholic beverages during the pregnancy.

I.   **GROUP B STREP**

Group B Streptococcus (GBS) bacteria, according to the Group B Strep Association, will infect 15,000 to 18,000 newborns and adults each year in the United States. Group B Strep can result in blood stream, respiratory, and other devastating infections. GBS is considered the number one infectious killer of newborns. About half of GBS disease occurs in newborns and is acquired during childbirth, when a baby comes in direct contact with the bacteria carried by the mother. GBS causes infections in pregnant women - in the womb, in amniotic fluid, in incisions follow caesarian sections, and in the urinary tract. Each year there are over 50,000 cases of such infections in pregnant women.

The Group B Strep Association advocates that every pregnant woman be screened for GBS. One third, or 1,200,000 pregnant women carry GBS bacteria. Doctors should culture at 35-37 weeks of pregnancy.

What are the mother's risk factors for developing GBS disease?

•   Positive culture for GBS colonization at 35-37 weeks

•   Having already had a baby who had a GBS infection

•   GBS bacteria in urine (bacteriuria, either with or without symptoms)

•   Membrane rupture more than 18 hours before deliver

•   Labor or membrane rupture before 37 weeks

- Fever during labor higher than 100.4

- Black race (2 times the risk than for non-blacks)

- Age less than 20 years

If discovered through culture or risk factor, GBS can be treated with antibiotics.

J.   *GUILLAIN BARRÉ SYNDROME*

Individuals who are afflicted with Guillain Barré Syndrome have important bodily functions, such as breathing, blood pressure, heart rate, swallowing, airway clearance, and bladder control that can be affected. The long-term cost of caring for a Guillain Barré patient can be astronomical and tax the resources of most families. It is important that a person who is diagnosed with Guillain Barré Syndrome receive prompt medical care and, often, hospitalization. According to the Guillain Barré Foundation, "During the early stages of the illness, especially for the patient in an intensive care unit, events can be quite frightening. Most patients with Guillain Barré Syndrome were formerly healthy, so that finding themselves suddenly paralyzed, helpless, with intravenous lines, a bladder catheter, and a heartbeat monitor that continuously and monotonously beeps, can be emotionally upsetting... It is helpful for both family and patient to keep in mind that most Guillain Barré patients get better, most eventually walk, and many can ultimately resume a normal life."

K.   *REFLEX SYMPATHETIC DYSTROPHY (RSD)*

Patients with RSD suffer skin and muscular atrophy, lose mobility in their affected limbs, and the affected limbs become extremely sensitive to touch. RSD is caused by injury or other trauma to an individual's arms or legs. There is no widely-accepted medical theory to explain why some individuals suffer an injury and develop RSD, while others do not. RSD is a progressive disease. Medical literature describes three stages:

Stage I: The acute stage;

Stage II: The dystrophic stage;

Stage III: The atrophic stage.

In the acute stage, an affected limb can become paralyzed, and the pain is much more severe than would be expected from this type of injury. In the dystrophic stage, the joints, especially hand joints in arm injury cases, can become stiff. Atrophy (weakening muscle tissue and loss of strength) usually occurs. In the atrophic stage, muscle atrophy and reduced range-of-motion becomes more severe, and individuals who have leg injuries must often rely upon the use of a cane, walker or wheelchair. Doctors often misdiagnose RSD sufferers as "malingering" because the symptoms are difficult to quantify. Many persons who suffer RSD become totally disabled and unemployable.

In a recent case, I was able to demonstrate through the use of medical reports, physiatrists' reports, objective testing, psychiatric testimony, rehabilitation nurses' lifecare plans, and vocational evaluation that a client's RSD took away her ability to walk independently. The evidence also showed that an individual suffering from severe RSD would require numerous hospitalizations, operative procedures, and millions of dollars worth of future medical care and assistive technology. The jury in this case returned a verdict in excess of Nineteen Million Dollars ($19,000,000.00).

XXII. RECREATIONAL INJURIES

A. TRAUMA STATISTICS

Trauma is the medical term for any kind of injury. About 40% of all hospital emergency department visits in the United States are injury-related, according to information from the National Hospital Ambulatory Medical Care survey. Approximately 36.5 million people are treated at hospital emergency rooms for injury-related problems. Falls and motor vehicle accidents are the leading cause of injury-related emergency department visits.

Motor vehicle crashes, falls, drownings, fires, and firearms account for most trauma deaths in the United States. According to the National Safety Council, unintentional injury deaths increased in 1995 for the third year in a row. The 1995 death total was 93,300, an increase of 1,900 from 1994. The motor vehicle death rate also increased in 1995 for the third consecutive year. Unintentional injuries are the leading cause of death among all persons aged 1 to 38. In general, unintentional injuries are the fifth leading cause of death.

The cost of unintentional injuries is immense. $75.1 billion is spent annually in medical expenses, and $222.4 billion in wage and productivity losses.

In future years, 100 million workdays are expected to be lost due to trauma.

In order to adequately fund medical and rehabilitation costs, accidents need to be thoroughly investigated and any available sources of funding need to be found. The case examples given here indicate creative methods I have used to locate such funding.

B. WATER ACCIDENTS - INHERENT DANGERS

The inherent dangers in swimming pools can cause many types of catastrophic injuries. The number of serious head injuries and spinal cord injuries have continued to mount because of these dangers. Statistics show that the leading types of injuries from diving accidents are paraplegia and quadriplegia, and from drowning accidents, anoxia or death.

1. Drowning Accidents

According to the American Trauma Society, drowning rates are highest among individuals ages 15 to 24. Drowning is the fourth most common cause of unintentional injury death for all ages and ranks second for ages 5 to 44. In 1995, there were 4,500 drownings from boat incidents, swimming, playing in, or falling into, the water (this excludes drownings in floods). An additional 400 deaths occur each year due to suicidal drowning.

For drownings not related to boats, the rate is highest among children ages 0 to 4. About 85% of drownings result from falling into water. In 1995, about 300 children ages 0 to 4 drowned in pools, predominately home pools. This accounts for more than one-third of all drownings. The male:female ratio of drowning rates is about 12:1 for those related to boats and 5:1 for others.

2. *Backyard Swimming Pools*

Back yard pools hold a particular hazard for young children, says the Consumer Product Safety Commission (CPSC). In 1995, 78,336 people were injured in backyard pools. Of 550 residential pool deaths in 1995 (the most recent year statistics are available), 320 involved children under the age 5, most often children ages 1-2. Annually, about 2,300 infants, toddlers and preschoolers are treated in emergency rooms for pool-related injuries, often to their heads and spines. About 2,000 children up to age 19 drown each year, according to the National Safety Council, which ranks drowning as the third leading cause of death from injuries for those under age 5 and second among unintentional injuries for older children.

Because of their energy and curiosity, children are at great risk around water. Experts indicate that reducing the number of child drownings requires increasing the number of protective barriers around a pool, insuring constant supervision of children in or near the water, and being prepared for an emergency.

The inherent dangers in pools resulting in drowning accidents are:

a.   No safety gates or locking mechanism to prevent access or entry to the swimming pool (especially for young children);

b.   Inadequate safety gates which give the appearance of protection, but can be easily disarmed by a mischievous child. Experts suggest a layered approach, using multiple barriers, including fences, locks, etc., which would all have to be overcome before a child could enter a swimming pool;

c.   Inadequate warnings on the pool and in the literature provided with the pool at the time of purchase. The literature should include warnings to parents indicating that a ladder should never be left next to an above-ground pool when the pool is not in use, since it invites children to climb it; toys should never be left in a pool, since they also will attract children to a pool; a cover or tarp for a pool should be strongly suggested or required when a pool is not in use.

In May, 1993, the CPSC issued voluntary safety standards for all residential pools, calling for:

- A four-sided fence, at least 4 feet high, around the pool. It should be non-climbable and offer no spaces that a child can pass through;

- Fence gates that are self-closing and self-latching;

- Alarms on every house door leading to the pool to signal if a child has gone outside;

- A motor-driven safety pool cover to securely cover the water area.

Experts also recommend keeping objects that might attract a child out of the pool area, and draining standing water off spa or pool covers, because children can drown in as little as two inches of water. It is important to have a phone at poolside, with emergency numbers posted, keep rescue devices readily accessible, and make sure everyone responsible for your children knows cardiopulmonary resuscitation. Delay in administering CPR, or incorrectly giving CPR, can result in anoxia - a lack of oxygen to the brain - causing severe brain damage to the victim. Every lifeguard and caregiver should be trained by certified personnel. Parents should not permit their young children to swim or play near pools without proper supervision.

3.   *Diving Accidents*

Recently, after I gave a talk at a regional rehabilitation facility, I was greeted in the elevator by a patient in a wheelchair. During an exchange of pleasantries I asked him how he was doing, and he responded that he was "Not too good...*I hurt myself by diving into a pool,* and I'm paralyzed." He believed the myth that persons who receive spinal-cord injuries as the result of a dive into a pool are responsible for their own injuries. This belief is shared by the public at large, the insurance industry, and the health care community.

According to a 1989 United States Consumer Product Safety Commission study, 7,700 people were injured after striking the bottom of a pool when diving. About 60% of these injuries resulted from a head-first dive into shallow water. The American National Standards for Recreational Swimming Pools defines shallow water as "portions of the pool or spa with water depth less than five feet".

MYTH 1: *EVERYONE KNOWS THAT DIVING INTO SHALLOW WATER IS DANGEROUS.*

REALITY: The most common response from beginning lifeguard students who were asked how shallow pool water could be in which to safely execute a dive, was "four feet." A few even suggested three feet was safe. Many other persons, when asked, admitted that they have dived into water of less then five feet, and that they honestly did not think they were doing anything unreasonably dangerous or foolish. In a study of 360 shallow-water diving accidents, it was found that 67.8% of diving-injury victims were visiting the pools for the first time and 62.2% of those hurt were injured on the first dive. These studies refute the myth that most persons know that diving into shallow water is dangerous. A shallow dive from the edge of the pool can result in head impact with the pool bottom in less than 5/10ths of a second after the diver's head enters the water. Most people do not realize how little force is needed to cause a cervical spinal injury.

MYTH 2: *THE DANGERS OF SHALLOW WATER DIVING ARE OPEN AND OBVIOUS.*

REALITY: Even experienced divers can underestimate the dangers of shallow water diving due to inaccurate optical estimation, or the diver's inability to accurately perceive the pool's depth.

MYTH 3: *MOST PEOPLE INJURED IN SHALLOW WATER DIVING ARE CHILDREN.*

REALITY: A major analysis of 360 shallow-water diving accidents conducted in 1990 found that not a single injured person was under the age of 10, the reason being that young children are too small and weigh too little to strike the bottom of a pool at an unreasonable speed. According to an article, _Danger Lurks in Shallow Water_, "After children undergo growth spurts during adolescence, they weigh substantially more and are much taller, so they will strike bottom more readily when diving into shallow water. Still, they remember diving safely into shallow water from their childhood experiences, and expect to do so as they get older."

MYTH 4: *MOST POOLS CONTAIN WARNING SIGNS PROHIBITING DIVING.*

REALITY: A recent study found that 331 of the 360 pool sites visited, or 91.2%, had no signs warning pool users not to dive into the water where the injury occurred. This reality is stark, but true—most individuals who are rendered spinal-cord injured as a result of diving accidents are not warned.

MYTH 5: *IF A DIVING BOARD IS LOCATED NEXT TO A SWIMMING POOL, IT MUST BE SAFE FOR DIVING.*

REALITY: Pool manufacturers and installers of diving boards are not required to warn unsuspecting consumers about how deep a pool must be in order to dive safely.

MYTH 6: *MOST PERSONS INVOLVED IN DIVING ACCIDENTS FILE LAWSUITS.*

REALITY: Most people do not file lawsuits because the overwhelming majority of persons who are injured in diving accidents incorrectly assume that their injury is their own fault.

According to a section on diving injuries contained in **Mechanisms of Head and Spine Trauma**, edited by Anthony Sances, Jr. et al, the physical data pertaining to traumatic cervical spinal cord injuries (TCSCI) reveal that more than 700 injuries resulting in quadriplegia occur in the United States annually as the result of diving accidents. "Constructed pools, both in ground and above ground, account for as much as 50% of diving TCSCI. Inappropriate diving boards, improper design, inadequate warnings, deficient standards and insufficient education are the cause. Young males 15 to 25 years old are generally the victims, with flexion-compression injuries to the mid and lower cervical spine..." The most common cause of the traumatic spinal cord injury is diving into shallow water. The individual will usually become a complete quadriplegic. According to the article,

"The unseen hazards and dangerous conditions associated with head-first entries into shallow water are the result of insufficient time and strength to ward off an unintended head impact with the bottom. Contact with the bottom generally occurs as the result of a delayed pullout or unexpected downward rotation due to an asymmetrical water entry.

"In spite of the startling statistics, society's attitude toward this problem seems to be one of apathy. Diving-related TSCI [traumatic spinal cord injuries] apparently are believed to be the result of horseplay, injudicious behavior, or just plain 'fooling around.' Analysis of the mechanics of diving reveals otherwise. Because of increasing strength, weight, and length, children grow into danger without their knowledge. What was safe for them to perform last year may not be safe this year. Additionally, the unsafe design of most swimming pools and an industry's desire to promote diving and the sale of related equipment expose the unaware and untrained person to an unseen and unrecognized hazard and dangerous condition. Recreational divers are in danger because they don't know they are in danger."

Above-ground swimming pools are the most dangerous type of pool. The inherent dangers in these pools are shallow water, defective designs and inadequate warnings:

•   They are too shallow to allow for safe diving. Usually, the pools are no more than a maximum of four feet in depth;

•   The color of the liner of the pool makes it difficult or impossible to judge accurately the depth of the water;

•   The top rails of the pool are wide platforms and invite diving;

•   Promotional advertising by the manufacturers of pools encourage diving;

•   Users of pools do not properly appreciate the hidden dangers of diving, and believe they can safely do a "flat dive" into any pool. Studies have shown that even if individuals attempt to make a flat dive with their hands stretched out in front of them, they may not be able to control their dive in order to prevent injury. Other studies have shown that diving or sliding head-first into shallow water is very dangerous and should be discouraged. Tragically, the biomechanics of diving head-down and impacting with an immoveable object result in the body being driven into the neck of the diver, with catastrophic consequences.

The circumstances of each diving accident should be carefully reviewed to determine whether or not the injury was caused by lack of warning, lack of education, unsafe diving practices, or unsafe conditions at the diving site.

4.   *Safety Protection*

The argument by the manufacturers of swimming pools that the risk of spinal cord injury from diving into an above-ground pool is obvious and therefore should be avoided, is discounted by many studies which show that individuals believe that pools are safe for diving, not inherently dangerous.

Since it is clear that the swimming pool industry is aware of the inherent dangers of swimming pools, it should be mandated that they take steps to drastically reduce head injuries and spinal cord injuries resulting from pool accidents. Educating the public by presenting advertisements which discuss the dangers and demonstrate how to swim safely, and not advertisements which show individuals diving into swimming pools, would be a major step in the right direction. Clear and adequate warnings should be permanently affixed to the pools and described in the pool manuals.

Attractive nuisance injuries where minors are attracted to certain dangerous conditions, such as a swimming pool without a fence, can be avoided through better safeguards by the pool industry and increased vigilance by parents and pool owners. In 1995, the National Safety Council reported that more than 300 children age 4 and under died from drowning accidents.

All homeowners and commercial pool owners should be warned to fix broken ladders, have properly trained lifeguards, discourage untrained divers, and inspect their pools for dangerous conditions at regular intervals.

Many safety changes have occurred as a result of litigation by spinal cord and head injured survivors, but more needs to be done to make swimming safe and not inherently dangerous, so catastrophic water injuries can be prevented.

C.   *PLAYGROUND ACCIDENTS*

Every day in the United States, over 500 children have their day of fun on a playground cut short by a visit to an emergency room. Between 20 and 50 children die each year from injuries due to playground equipment. The Consumer Product Safety Commission stated that in 1995 an estimated 150,000 children required emergency room treatment for playground injuries. 75% of the injuries involved falls. Death from short falls onto asphalt or concrete are not uncommon; in fact, a direct fall onto the head from a height as low as a foot can be fatal.

According to the Consumer Product Safety Commission, playground equipment is fifth on their list of the 100 most hazardous consumer products.

In 1981, the Consumer Product Safety Commission issued guidelines for playground equipment and surfaces. Unfortunately, falls to inappropriate playground surfaces are the leading cause of serious playground accidents and injuries.

Other playground accidents have occurred when minors are injured on swings, merry-go-rounds, spin-a-rounds, jungle gyms and sliding boards that are poorly constructed, inadequately maintained, or defectively designed by a manufacturer. Also, numerous serious injuries have occurred when minors were inadequately supervised at a playground or recreational area.

According to the U.S. Consumer Product Safety Commission, the key to preventing children from falling in playgrounds is to make sure the equipment is "age-appropriate". It may be safe for a sixth grader to hang from monkey bars, but very dangerous for a 5-year-old. Where a child is climbing equipment, the height of each step should be no more than knee-high to the child, and the maximum height of any piece of equipment should be no more than six feet from the ground. There also should be a shock-absorbing surface such as sand, wood chips, etc., beneath all equipment. Merry-go-rounds, wildly swinging tires, and other equipment that can cause dizziness and disorientation increase the chances of a fall. Trampolines should never be used by children without supervision. The swing is the most common playground equipment involved in children's injuries. In addition to falls, a swing with a heavy seat can accidentally deliver a dangerous blow to an unsuspecting child.

D. *ATTRACTIVE NUISANCE INJURIES*

Minors who are attracted to certain dangerous conditions, such as: a swimming pool without a fence, kites stuck on high-voltage electric wires, or other conditions that look safe and invite or attract a small child, can cause very serious injuries.

The law imposes a high standard of care on homeowners, businesses, municipalities and others, to protect children from areas and conditions that are known to be dangerous.

XXIII. PRODUCT LIABILITY CLAIMS

A. *VEHICLES*

1. *Crashworthiness*

A manufacturer cannot guard against all dangers associated with riding in an automobile, but the courts have held that a manufacturer can foresee many dangers that a person will encounter while driving an automobile, and can design safety features to guard against these dangers. The failure to guard against these dangers has led to a theory under the law called "crashworthiness".

Our courts have said: "Traffic accidents from a wide variety of causes are foreseeable to the auto manufacturer, and the absence or inadequacy of design features which might protect vehicle occupants may be a sufficient reason to hold the manufacturer liable for injuries attributable to unsafe design..."

Usually a crashworthy theory is brought against a manufacturer of an automobile when a car has been recalled because of a design defect, or because the vehicle does not meet the minimum standards of safety necessary to protect an occupant or passenger during an automobile accident.

The trend is that crashworthiness theories are being successfully litigated in more jurisdictions. An example of a crashworthiness case: A vehicle is rear-ended by another vehicle and a person who is wearing a seat belt is thrown against the dashboard and suffers a closed head injury because the front seat came apart on impact. It would be claimed in a factual situation such as this that the car was not "crashworthy".

2. *Seat belts - Seatbelt Act - Pennsylvania*

On November 23, 1987, the **Pennsylvania Seat Belt Act** was signed into effect and requires all occupants to wear seat belts during the operation and use of a motor vehicle. Included in the law is a provision which contains language prohibiting the introduction into evidence in a civil case of the fact that the victim was not wearing a seat belt at the time of the accident. This "seat belt defense" has been applied arbitrarily in the past to deny innocent and injured persons their rightful medical benefits and monetary recovery. For example, often when a drunk driver has struck an innocent victim who was not wearing a seat belt, the insurance company would argue that the person not wearing the seat belt was partially responsible for his or her own injury, and thereby deny or substantially reduce the victim's right to compensation.

The courts have begun to address the issue of whether rear-seat lap belts are defective. A study by the National Transportation Safety Board of fifty people wearing lap belts who were in accidents found that they would have fared "substantially better" if they had been wearing a lap/shoulder combination. The report found two problems with lap belts: first, all the force restraining the body occurs in one area, creating greater stress; second, the lap belt creates a whipping effect, which can cause injuries if the passenger's head strikes any object. Also, if the belt is worn too high, it can damage internal organs and fracture the spine. It is likely that most manufacturers will offer, not only as an option but probably as standard equipment, a lap/shoulder combination in place of a single lap belt system.

Substantial recoveries have been obtained as a result of litigation against manufacturers of defective seatbelts. Claims have been brought against manufacturers of defective seatbelts on the following theories:

• Rear seat lap belts defective;

• Failure to provide shoulder restraints;

• Too much slack or give in a seatbelt;

• Failure of the seatbelt to lock or restrain the individual when an accident occurs.

a.   Defective Seat Belts and Seat Backs

Sir Isaac Newton first formulated the theory that for every action there is an equal and opposite reaction. Newton's theory is the basis for today's occupant containment theory in motor vehicles. In a frontal collision, seat belts and air bags protect motorists from striking steering wheels, windshields, and dashboards. Seat backs and head rests provide protection in the opposite direction, preventing motorists from catapulting rearward and breaking their necks and backs. It is clear that defectively designed seat belts, seat backs, head rests, shoulder belts and lap belts can not only fail to protect from serious injury but they may cause additional injury in specific cases.

The following is an overview of the most common hazards.

Rear Lap Belts: In July 1986, the National Transportation Safety Board and other experts revealed that rear lap belts can be a deadly menace in automobile accidents, especially to children. These experts had warned for many years that "lap belts may induce injury, ranging in severity from minor to fatal, to the head, spine, abdomen, intra-abdominal viscera and its connecting tissue and blood vessels, and intra-thoracic viscera and its connecting tissue and blood vessels. Such injuries may occur singly or in

217

combination." The experts went on to say that rear lap belts promote head injury by allowing the upper torso to swing forward, and inflict abdominal and spinal cord injury by overloading the lower torso with crash forces. Automobile manufacturers have known for many years that properly designed lap/ shoulder belts would eliminate the hazards caused by rear lap belts.

Shoulder-only Belts: Because there is no lap belt to restrain the torso, drivers and passengers can suffer internal neck injuries.

Excessive Slack: Normally, a lap/shoulder seat belt must be reasonably snug across the chest and pelvis area to minimize forward motion. Unfortunately, many belts are designed with too much slack. Properly designed seat belts without excessive slack are technologically available, however, they are currently available only on higher priced automobiles.

"Window Shades": Automobile manufacturers have been aware since the 1970's that lap/shoulder belts were so poorly designed that they squeezed the wearer's body uncomfortably. Rather than redesigning the belts, the manufacturers simply equipped them with a tension-relieving device known as a "window shade". This device allows for several inches of slack to be introduced into the belt system. Unfortunately, a loose lap/shoulder belt is a significant hazard in a crash. According to the National Highway Transportation Safety Administration, as little as two inches of slack can substantially raise head injury force levels, and these few inches of slack can effectively eliminate a belt's protection. In addition, a slack belt can promote or allow ejection or "submarining" (the occupant sliding out from under the belt). Although some manufacturers appear to have begun phasing out "window shades", their refusal to recall them in cars already out on the highway leaves countless drivers and passengers at risk for serious head and spinal cord injuries.

Door-mounted Belts: This type of belt fastens with no help from the user. If a door opens during a crash, the occupant whose belt is anchored to the door may be ejected, leading to catastrophic injuries. Auto makers continue to equip many new models with door-mounted belts, and have refused to retrofit or recall vehicles equipped with door-mounted belts, or warn the automobile owners about the dangers.

Seat Backs: Seat backs were designed to protect occupants when there is a rear end collision. When a car is struck from the rear, the car is propelled forward and the occupants are thrown backward. The seat back should remain upright while cushioning and containing the occupant's body. If a seat back collapses, the driver can be ejected from the vehicle or lose control, often with tragic results. In addition, poorly designed adjustable head restraints can cause the upper torso to react in a slingshot fashion to a rear end collision, resulting in severe spinal injury, including quadriplegia.

Auto shoulder belts: Safety engineers have known for years that lap-only belts do not prevent injuries as well as the lap-and-shoulder combination and could actually cause injuries in certain situations. "The Seat Belt Syndrome", a 1962 report, described injuries caused by lap belts rupturing the soft tissue of the abdomen. Spinal cord and other serious injuries have been documented. A National Highway Traffic Safety Administration report estimates that, at the current rate of use in the United States, some 25 lives would be saved and 500 people would avoid injury each year if all cars had rear shoulder belts. In July 1989, under pressure from Congress, the National Highway Traffic Safety Administration adopted a rule requiring three-point belts in rear seats by December 1989. Light trucks, including minivans, were given until September 1991 to comply, though some manufacturers were voluntarily installing them. Auto makers have introduced retrofit kits that convert lap belts into lap-and-shoulder belts, but few drivers buy them because the manufacturers are not paying the cost of the kit and installation, which is approximately $150. It would have been relatively simple and inexpensive, $20 a belt or less in today's dollars, to have required rear lap-and-shoulder belts as standard equipment in 1968, the year auto makers were required to install them in the front seat. It would have been easier still in 1972, when regulators went so far as to require car makers to install anchor points for rear shoulder belts, but neither the government nor the manufacturer took the final step and required the rear lap-and-shoulder belts as standard equipment.

3.   *Airbags*

It is irrefutable that airbags reduce serious head injuries and other catastrophic injuries by protecting the occupant from striking his head on the window or dashboard, or being thrown from the automobile. During a crash, the airbag is designed to deploy within seconds. However, the tremendous force exerted by the expanding bag on any object in its path could prove to be fatal for a small child or an infant in a car seat in the front passenger seat of an automobile with this supplemental restraint system (SRS).

SAFETY AGENCY ISSUES WARNING ON AIR BAG DANGER TO CHILDREN

The National Highway Traffic Safety Administration (NHTSA) has repeatedly issued warnings of the dangers of placing a rear-facing infant car seat in the front seat of a motor vehicle equipped with an air bag. Unfortunately, there are no uniform instructions in automobiles or on infant car seats to warn parents of the dangers of improper placement of a rear-facing infant car seat in front of an air bag. I am presently representing a family whose child, strapped in a rear-facing infant car seat in front of an air bag, was killed when the air bag deployed.

On October 27, 1995, NHTSA warned that children who are not pro-tected by a seat belt could be seriously injured, or killed, by an air bag, and in the strongest possible terms NHTSA urged parents to insist that their children ride belted in the **BACK SEAT** whenever possible.

The safety agency considers air bags to be supplemental frontal crash protection. The seat belt, which provides protection in all kinds of crashes, is the primary, and most essential, item of safety.

In summary, NHTSA is warning:

1. **Parents should never place a rear-facing infant car seat in the front seat of a vehicle equipped with air bags;**

2. **All children should ride belted in the BACK SEAT whenever possible;**

3. **All children in back seats should use both lap belt and shoul-der harness to prevent lap-belt-induced injuries in the event of an accident.**

Currently, more than 15 million vehicles are equipped with air bags on both the driver and passenger sides. By law, all new cars and trucks must have dual air bags by the 1999 model year. NHTSA knows of 25 deaths related to air bag deployment. The six cases under scrutiny now, including my case, are of special concern because they involve small chil-dren, and because they involve crashes at speeds under 20 miles an hour. Investigators believe that the children may have slipped from the front seats when the driver slammed on the brakes (or when the impact occurred) and an air bag was deployed—inflating at more than 100 miles an hour—forcing the child against the roof or other parts of the vehicle.

Manufacturers also have the technology to install a "lock-out sys-tem" which would enable a parent to turn a switch to prevent the passen-ger side air bag from deploying. Air bag and auto manufacturers are also working on so-called "smart air bags" that, with the help of computers, would be able to detect the height, weight and position of occupants and adjust deployment accordingly.

4. _Rollover_

The National Highway Safety Administration is considering a feder-al motor vehicle safety standard associated with rollovers of utility vehicles, pick-up trucks, vans, and passenger cars. Statistics show that rollover fatalities in utility vehicles and pick-up trucks have risen more than 29% since the mid-1980's.

Lawsuits have been filed against the manufacturers of Jeeps (Jeep CJ-5's) and other recreational vehicles (Suzuki Samurai), since they have a tendency to roll over. The rollover is caused by the defective design of the vehicle which, at high speeds and quick turns, causes the vehicle to tip and roll over. Families should not allow an insurance company to destroy, alter, repair, or modify a vehicle involved in an accident without first contacting an attorney so that an expert may inspect the vehicle to determine the cause of the accident.

5. *Roof Collapse - Automobile*

Crashworthiness claims have been successfully litigated when the roof of vehicles collapse during a rollover. Vehicles are defectively designed because they do not have roll bars or other devices which would prevent roof collapses.

6. *Collapsible Steering Column*

A collapsible steering column will prevent many serious injuries such as spinal cord injuries caused when an individual is thrown against the steering column during an accident. Cars that are equipped with airbags prevent a driver or passenger from being thrown into the steering column.

7. *Side Impact*

The Coalition for Consumer Health and Safety recently recommended ways to improve consumer safety through changes in side-impact standards. The Coalition urged the National Highway Traffic Safety Administration to amend its current crash side-impact standards by:

a. adding a side-impact crash-test standard;

b. releasing crashworthiness test results;

c. including side-impact test results in the new car assessment program;

d. extending side-impact standards to light trucks, vans and utilities vehicles;

e. formulating strength parameters for sides of cars.

It has been estimated that side-impact crashes annually account for approximately 8,000 deaths and 23,000 serious injuries. The National Highway Traffic Safety Administration's current side-impact protection standards vary with the weight of the car and require less protection for lighter cars, which are more vulnerable in side-impact crashes.

8.   *Exploding Gasoline Tank*

Almost every car manufacturer has been involved over the years with suits involving gas tank fires. Every accident where there is a gas tank fire should be investigated, since design defects can play a role in the cause of a gasoline fire. The automobile companies have made great efforts to reduce the number of exploding gas tanks by making modifications to their design as a result of lawsuits that have been successfully litigated against them by injured claimants.

9.   *Multipiece Rims*

These truck tire rims have a habit of exploding when the tire is being assembled or disassembled. The trend is for the manufacturer to require a tire cage to be used which encloses the tire and reduces the number of serious injuries during this process

B.   CHILDREN'S CAR SEATS

With shocking frequency, the child car seats which are designed to restrain and protect children from injury in an auto crash become the instrument which inflicts catastrophic injuries. Every state requires children to travel in safety seats, and there are three types of child safety seats used in the United States:

1.   Rear-facing seats for infants from birth up to about 20 pounds or 27 inches tall;

2.   Seats that convert from rear-facing to forward-facing for children from birth to 40 pounds or 40 inches tall;

3.   Booster seats for those 30-50 pounds. According to the experts, rear-facing seats give the most protection, by spreading the force of a head-on crash over the baby's entire back, and protecting the head and neck. Research experts have found that about 30% of infant seats are used incorrectly, facing forward rather than rearward.

Thousands of dangerous car seats have been recalled and manufacturers have designed safer car seats because families have complained to consumer groups and attorneys. More than 20 million car seats have been recalled in the 12 years since wide-scale testing provisions were enacted. In the last few years, nearly a million Century Products seats were recalled because their latch mechanisms can jam in a crash; in addition, if a defective latch releases, a child may be ejected from the seat and thrown against the vehicle's interior. Almost half a million Fisher-Price seats have been recalled because their shoulder straps may come loose and fail to provide adequate protection in a collision.

Manufacturers continue to sell car seats that are poorly designed, and fail to provide adequate information regarding the proper installation for the safe use of the car seats. Studies have shown that over 60% of car seats are unsafe because of the way they are used.

Millions of automobile child-restraint seats that have been recalled or failed to pass government tests are still being used or sold. The Center for Auto Safety has placed part of the blame on the federal government.

In the last decade, 622 children were killed while strapped into child-safety seats. Among the problems cited in the report were:

- Belt fasteners that did not hold;

- Belts that were too loose;

- Buckles that popped open;

- Seat shells that cracked;

- Seats that inclined too far to hold the child;

- Seats with choking hazards.

Consumer Reports has published an excellent study of the leading car seats, and rates the best and worse type of child-restraint seats. Consumers can call the Transportation Department's Auto Safety Hotline - 800-424-9393 - to learn whether the child-restraint seats they own or want to purchase have been recalled.

In a recent case that I investigated, a child's car seat was provided for the child at the time the family purchased an automobile, but there were no instructions concerning the proper mounting of the car seat, nor any instructions insuring the safe use of the car seat. In this particular case, the child was improperly placed into the car seat, and as a result of a collision, the child was thrown from the car seat and suffered catastrophic head injuries.

In another case I investigated, a child became a paraplegic as a result of a "whiplash" injury, when the child was thrown forward and the lap belt of the car seat exerted pressure on his torso, causing pancreatic and spinal injuries. Numerous pancreatic and spinal injuries have been reported as the result of defectively designed car seats.

Any time a child is seriously or catastrophically injured in a car seat (especially head and spinal cord injuries), the car seat should be examined by a qualified expert to determine if the design of the car seat caused or contributed to the child's injury, and whether or not it is safe to continue to use the car seat.

C.   *ALL-TERRAIN VEHICLES (ATV's) - UNKNOWN DANGERS*

According to the American Trauma Society, about 40% of fatalities caused by all-terrain vehicle (ATV) incidents have been children younger than 16 years of age. 125,000 ATV injuries were severe enough to require emergency room visits in 1994. Injuries from ATV accidents are usually multiple and severe. Head injury, combined head and spinal cord injury, and internal injuries are common ATV injuries. Here are the answers to some common questions on ATV's:

1.   What are ATV's?

All-Terrain Vehicles are 3-wheeled or 4-wheeled vehicles designed for recreational use. ATV's were first imported from Japan into the United States in the early 1980's.

2.   How many ATV's have been sold in
        the United States?

Today there are more than 2.5 million ATV's in the United States.

3.   Who are the major manufacturers
        of ATV's in the United States?

ATV's are manufactured by Honda, Yamaha, Suzuki and others.

4.   Are ATV's unsafe to ride?

Manufacturers of ATV's advertise that they can go anywhere and can be driven by anyone. Unfortunately, thousands of youngsters who believed in the manufacturers' claims have been killed or maimed in off-road accidents.

The Consumer Product Safety Commission has held extensive hearings on the inherent dangers of All-Terrain Vehicles (ATV's) and All-Terrain Cycles (ATC's) for children. The Commission found that 3-wheeled ATV's were "eminently dangerous" since the ATV's would tip over, throwing the riders off the ATV or pinning the riders under the ATV.

5.   Have 3-wheeled ATV's been
        recalled?

In 1988, as a result of pressure from attorneys, parents, and consumer groups advocating children's rights, the Consumer Product Safety Commission filed suit against five major ATV manufacturers. The manufacturers agreed to stop selling 3-wheeled ATV's in the United States, and to halt the sale of adult-sized 4-wheeled ATV's to children under 16. The federal government bowed to the pressure of the ATV manufacturers and did not impose a recall and a recent survey of over 215 dealers contacted in 19 states found that ATV dealers are still promoting the use of ATV's by youngsters.

6.   Are manufacturers required to fix
        the ATV's instability problems?

Manufacturers and distributors of ATV's are required to do nothing to correct the ATV's instability problem, which has caused thousands of ATV's to roll over, pinning the rider under the vehicle. Manufacturers have argued they will provide free training for ATV users, but only for new purchasers. Training courses will not be mandatory, despite the Consumer Product Safety Commission's finding that the incidence of injury is 13 times higher for untrained drivers in the first month of use.

7.   Have families of catastrophically
        injured children successfully sued
        ATV manufacturers?

Yes, families have sued ATV manufacturers and have won judgments for millions of dollars in compensatory damages to pay for lifetime medical costs and punitive damages, to punish the manufacturers for selling inherently defective vehicles. My office is presently litigating several ATV cases on behalf of children who have suffered catastrophic head injuries and spinal cord injuries.

CONCLUSION

The Consumer Federation of America, the U.S. Public Interest Research Group, Public Citizen, and The American Academy of Pediatric Groups have asked the court to prohibit the sale of ATV's for children and to direct the Consumer Product Safety Commission to comply with its obligation to keep in its public reading room a complete file of materials relating to an agreement that was made between the nation's top ATV distributors and the U.S. Consumer Product Safety Commission. The 57 page consent decree outlined a series of initiatives and procedures intended to improve public knowledge of operating hazards, to provide warning and training to vehicle operators, and to prevent solicitation of orders for certain ATV's for use by children. In 1988, the court ruled that the agreement between the nation's top ATV distributors and the Consumer Product Safety Commission should not be modified. The court refused to grant the request of the groups seeking to prohibit the sale of ATV's for children.

The only sensible protection remains with the consumer. Parents must not allow their children to ride on ATV's, but too few parents realize the dangers that attend the use of ATV's by children, most of whom lack both the judgment and coordination to control the vehicle safely.

D.   *TOYS - CHOKING HAZARDS*

A new law, aimed at preventing small children from choking on toys or toy parts, took effect on January 1, 1995. ***The Child Safety Protection***

Act of 1994 requires manufacturers to put labels that specifically warn of choking hazards on small balls, latex balloons, games, and vending machines that contain toys. Current federal regulations prohibit the marketing of toys with small parts to children under age 3. According to the Consumer Product Safety Commission (CPSC), the law requires manufacturers to state the reason why the toy is dangerous. Choking on small toy parts and balloons ranks among the most common causes of toy-related deaths among children ages 6 months to 12 years, the Commission said, citing statistics compiled between January 1, 1993, and September 30, 1994. During that period, the CPSC reported, 11 children died from choking on deflated or burst balloons, and 8 choked to death on balls.

The law specifically bars the sale of any ball or marble that measures less than 1.75 inches in diameter that is intended for use by children under the age of 3. Latex balloons must carry a choking warning for children under age 8. The law requires toy manufacturers and retailers to report to the CPSC any choking incidents that result from toys. The trial lawyers were very active in working with the CPSC in having this new law passed. Any serious injury involving choking hazards with toys should be investigated by your attorney and reported to the CPSC.

E. BABY WALKERS

The manufacturers of baby walkers face another run-in with the government concerning safety. The Consumer Product Safety Commission is considering design change proposals for baby walkers to reduce injuries. According to the agency, walkers, typically used by children under 15 months of age, were associated with 20 deaths and 22,900 emergency room visits in 1995. Most of these accidents occurred on stairs.

The American Academy of Pediatrics supports a ban on the use of baby walkers because "the risk of injury is very significant", and walkers used for long periods "delay the development of motor skills in many children", according to Dr. Marilyn Bull, Indiana University. Dr. Bull states, "It's a misconception that they help [babies] learn to walk....that's one thing they don't do."

Authors of a 1997 study on baby walkers are arguing that the government should require that the devices should be built wider than a standard doorway — 35.4 inches. Canadian manufacturers voluntarily adopted that standard eight years ago. According to the study, about 3 million walkers are sold each year, and they are associated with an estimated 25,000 injuries treated in hospitals annually. The injury rate is increasing, and 75% of injuries occur in falls down stairs, despite warning labels and wide publicity about potential dangers.

F.   TELEPHONE POLES

This is a relatively new area of litigation and concerns placing a telephone pole too close to the edge of a highway in violation of certain standards. The standards require that a telephone pole be placed at a safe distance from the edge of the highway so that vehicles which may leave the roadway do not impact or strike the telephone pole.

Failure to place telephone poles in their proper place along the highway is the second greatest cause of run-off-road fatalities.

G.   LADDERS, SCAFFOLD AND CRANES

Injuries have resulted from the use of these products caused by lack of cross-bracing, inadequately constructed ladders, unbalanced steps, and ladders moving or slipping while an individual is using one.

Cranes are often involved in work-related or construction accidents. These are caused when the cranes have a boom or bucket which collapses, the crane touches a high voltage or electrical wire, or the crane is improperly operated by the workman or engineer.

H.   HELMETS

More and more cases are being litigated against helmet manufacturers for failing to guard against head injury, spinal cord injury and other injuries. In the past, motorcycle manufacturers and ATV manufacturers have argued that serious injuries were caused because minor children and adults were not wearing helmets, and they have often prevailed on this theory in the courts. Recently, with many states adopting helmet laws, individuals have been wearing helmets for protection, but the helmets they have been wearing have been defectively designed, lack sufficient strength and durability, have cracked, and often give a parent or an adult a false sense of security that they can safely operate a motorcycle or all-terrain vehicle.

If an individual suffers a head injury or a spinal cord injury while wearing a helmet, the helmet should be examined by an expert to determine exactly how the injury occurred and whether or not the helmet should have prevented or lessened the injury.

I.   JET SKIS AND RECREATIONAL BOATING

The jet ski is a very powerful recreational device, and unless one is using the jet ski unimpaired and with proper training, serious and disabling injuries can occur. In 1995 there were 836 deaths attributed to improper use of jet skis and recreational boating, and countless injuries requiring in-patient hospitalization.

J.   SLEDS, TOBOGGANS

Sleds and toboggans which are defectively designed have caused numerous catastrophic injuries. Usually, the sleds and toboggans are defectively designed because they do not have an adequate steering mechanism and they tend to tip over, causing the occupant to be seriously injured.

K.   SNOWMOBILES

Snowmobile accidents have been caused because children are not properly trained to drive snowmobiles, which have a tendency to become airborne and roll over.

L.   GARAGE DOOR OPENERS

According to information released by the National Safety Council, nearly 20,000 people have been injured in 1994 as a result of accidents involving automatic door openers. A typical scenario involves children playing with the devices, either racing to exit after starting the closing action, or playing "chicken" with others to see who can most nearly evade the descending door. Often, the child loses. The door strikes, then pins the youngster to the ground, causing crush injuries. Consumer groups have urged the Consumer Product Safety Commission to require fail-safe auto/reverse systems and limit the amount of force that a door unit can generate.

M.   WINDOW SCREENS

Windows with faulty or missing screens present a life-threatening hazard, particularly to active children and curious toddlers. Brain injury, spinal cord injury, multiple fractures and death are often the result when a window screen gives way as a child pushes against it, or when a screen is absent in the window of a multi-story building and a child falls out. Thousands of claims throughout the country have been filed against apartment owners, building owners, and manufacturers of screens by parents. In some of the successfully litigated cases, the theories were:

- An apartment owner provided unsafe window screens - screens could be easily pushed out, leaving the window unguarded;

- A family lived on the second floor and had left windows open because the air conditioning system in the apartment complex was not working. Some of the windows had no screens and residents had complained to the apartment manager about both the lack of air conditioning and the absence of screens, but no repairs were made. A child fell from an unscreened window and suffered significant injuries;

- "Pop out" screens released when a toddler pushed against the window, causing the screen to fall out and the child to be severely injured;

- Failure to supply windows with adequate tolerance to permit locking;

- Failure to replace missing window screens;

- "Insect screen" gave way when a child leaned his head against it;

- The clips holding a screen came loose, causing a child to fall;

- Failure to supply windows with "limit stops" to prevent windows from being open more than 3-5 inches as specified in many building contracts and building codes;

- Housing authority failed to provide window screens after tenants had complained - a child fell out of an unscreened window and suffered serious injuries;

- A child fell through a window ventilator placed in an improper location on the sill of a bay window.

In some instances, apartment owners are required by BOCA (Building Officials & Code Administrators National Property Maintenance Code) to have screens in the windows of their rental properties. Building codes in each municipality vary, and the determination of whether or not the owner of an apartment or other rental unit is in violation of a particular building code depends on the facts and circumstances of each particular case.

An investigation should be undertaken immediately after a child is seriously injured. If the window was screened, the screen involved in the accident should never be discarded, since it will be necessary for the screen to be examined by experts for the manufacturer of the screen as well as by an expert retained by the attorney who represents the injured child. Photographs of the window and screens should be obtained. It is important for families to realize that, even though an apartment owner or housing authority may have complied with a local building code by having screens in the window of the building involved in the accident, the screens may be unsafe or defective, since building codes and BOCA codes do not mandate the design of screens in a particular building.

Consumer groups are attempting to have uniform standards enacted throughout the country which will require housing authorities and apartment owners to have proper window screens in place in all buildings. Unfortunately, laws requiring safe window screens could take many years to be enacted, while there currently are millions of unsafe window screens in houses and apartment buildings throughout the country.

N.   *ROLLERBLADES - IN-LINE SKATES*

Rollarblading is a very popular sport. In-line skates have been manufactured for adults and children. According to the Consumer Product Safety Commission, there were more than 83,000 in-line skating injuries in 1996. Children under 15 will suffer more than half of the broken limbs and bruises. More than 49,000 children are expected to receive emergency room treatment for in-line skating injuries in 1996, including 22,000 for broken bones and 7,000 for head injuries. Most injuries and deaths from in-line skating occurred because people skate without helmets, and they skate before learning proper techniques, such as how to properly brake. Some have argued that rollerblades are inherently dangerous, especially for young children, since the braking mechanisms may be inadequate and the braking pads wear out frequently.

O.   *ESCALATORS*

According to a 1997 study, escalators are a significant source of childhood injury, especially for young children. Escalator experts have indicated that better design and maintenance, including warning signs and easily accessible emergency shut-off buttons, would substantially reduce the risk of injury.

XXIV. MINORS' LEGISLATION

A. BICYCLE HELMET LAW

According to the National Safe Kids' campaign in Washington, each year 400 children under the age of 14 are killed in bicycle accidents in the United States, 70% from head injuries. Young bicycle passengers are required to wear helmets in California, Massachusetts, New York and Pennsylvania, as well as New Jersey.

1. *Pennsylvania*

The Pennsylvania bicycle helmet law, which previously applied only to children up to age 5, was amended on March 1, 1995 to raise the age limit to age 12. The law now requires a child under 12 years of age to wear a helmet while operating or riding as a passenger on a bicycle, and includes passengers in a restraining seat on a bicycle or in a trailer towed by a bicycle.

While Pennsylvania does not require that helmets be worn by adults, certainly it makes sense to do so.

2. *New Jersey*

Effective July 1, 1992, New Jersey requires that children under the age of 14 wear an approved helmet when bicycling. This is the first such law of its kind in the nation.

Guidelines for selecting and using an appropriate and safe helmet for children and adults include: Purchase a helmet from someone who is well-versed in size, fit and adjustment; Select a helmet certified by both the *American Society of Testing and Materials (ASTM)* and *American National Standards Institute (ANSI)*; Choose a model that is comfortable, and which suits your needs, riding style and experience; Store your helmet in a cool, dry place (not in a car); An impact on the helmet could diminish or deplete its usefulness—send it to the manufacturer for inspection following an accident.

If a person suffers a serious head injury while wearing a bicycle helmet (or any other kind of helmet), the helmet should be preserved, without alteration, modification or any other change, to be examined by a qualified expert to determine whether or not the helmet is defective.

B. CHILD ABUSE

1. **Pennsylvania Child Protective Services Law**

The purpose of this section is to delineate the rights and obligations of a hospital and its staff when confronted with a minor patient who is suspected to be the victim of child abuse.

231

The question that is most often asked by hospital personnel and social workers is: Must a written consent be obtained from a family member or a parent before a child may be treated in a child abuse situation?

In suspected child abuse cases, it is unnecessary to obtain the consent of a parent or other family member to commence treatment of the child. Courts have consistently held that special circumstances exist when a suspected victim of child abuse is presented to a hospital for treatment.

The **Pennsylvania Child Protective Services Law** constitutes the legislative response to this issue. Section 2209 appears to actually transform the issue from that of authority to treat to that of a mandate to treat. The **Pennsylvania Child Protective Services Law** states as the following:

> "Children appearing to suffer from any physical or mental trauma which may constitute child abuse shall be admitted to and treated in appropriate facilities of private and public hospitals on the basis of medical need and shall not be refused or deprived in any way of proper medical treatment and care."

Therefore, it is clear that the consent of the abused child's parent or other family member need not be obtained in Pennsylvania prior to a hospital's treating of "children appearing to suffer any physical or mental trauma which may constitute child abuse."

Most states have laws similar to Pennsylvania's **Child Protective Services Law**. All health care providers should immediately contact the appropriate local or state agency when they believe a child may have suffered physical and/or mental trauma which may constitute child abuse.

Recently, my office has been asked to represent a child to make a claim against a health care provider who repeatedly ignored objective signs of child abuse, and failed to contact the local and state authorities. As a result, in addition to a civil lawsuit being filed against the treating health care provider, the State of Pennsylvania filed formal criminal charges against the doctor.

2. *Private foster care agency can be sued*

In a recent 1997 case, the Federal District Court in Pennsylvania ruled that although foster parents cannot be sued under the Civil Rights law, private foster agencies can be. In *ESTATE OF ADAM EARP VS. DOUD ET AL*, Judge Fullam ruled that Best Nest Inc., a foster care agency under contract with the City of Philadelphia, should be treated as a "state actor", because its contract called for it to perform functions that are traditionally "the exclusive prerogative of the state." Adam Earp was taken from his mother and placed in foster care in October 1994. He was eighteen months old when he was killed in a fire at a foster home that was apparently started by another child playing with matches. The court ruled:

> "The state removed Adam Earp from his home. It had a duty to provide him with a safe haven. The defendant (Best Nest Inc.) undertook to carry out that governmental obligation and became a state actor for purposes of Section 1983 liability."

XXV. PLANNING FOR THE FUTURE

A. *STRUCTURED SETTLEMENTS: BENEFITS AND DISADVAN-TAGES*

    1. *What is a structured settlement?*

        a. **Structured settlements** are devices used to resolve a personal injury claim. A defendant liability insurance company will purchase an insurance annuity which will pay the injured plaintiff certain specific benefits. These monetary and medical benefits are paid in more than one installment throughout the life of the injured individual.

        b. **Lump sum settlements** are settlements where an individual, his family, or his court-appointed guardian receives one lump sum cash payment to be used to pay for the individual's medical expenses, lifetime care, lost wages, and pain and suffering.

    2. *What are the advantages of a structured settlement versus a lump sum payment?*

The advantages of a structured settlement are:

        a.   Protection from undue influence

Many persons who receive large sums of money in one installment do not know how to properly invest the money and are influenced by their family members or other persons, and may unnecessarily dissipate their funds. The structured settlement, once it is approved, cannot be changed, and protects disabled individuals from themselves and others who would give them poor advice, or take advantage of them.

        b.   Security

The structured settlement guarantees that there will be funds necessary to meet the lifetime medical needs of the injured party. Persons who are disabled have security in knowing that they will not have to become wards of the State, and that they have input over the kinds of medical care they will receive and where the medical care will be rendered, since they know that the money will be available to them on a specific basis, such as monthly, quarterly, twice a year, etc.

        c.   Professional Management

In a structured settlement, the money is usually managed by a bank, an insurance company, or someone who is qualified in managing substantial sums of money.

d.   Flexibility

The structured settlement can be written so as to accomplish the specific needs of the injured individual in each and every case.

e.   Contingent Medical Fund

A structured settlement can fund future medical needs by setting up a contingent medical fund so that if future medical advances are made which can assist an individual's disability, there will be funds available to pay for such care. If an individual accepts a lump sum cash payment, and either dissipates or poorly invests the money, there may be insufficient funds to pay for medical advances in the future.

3.   *What are the disadvantages of a structured settlement?*

a.   Finality

Once a structured settlement is accepted it cannot be changed. For example, if an individual accepts a structured settlement to pay $2,000 a month in income and $50,000 a year in medical expenses, and five years later wants to purchase a house for $250,000, the individual cannot go back to the insurance company and change the structured settlement proposal. The structured settlement is flexible while being negotiated, and can be designed to meet the needs of the individual, but once it is accepted and put in writing, its flexibility ends.

b.   Cash in hand

Many family members believe that the best type of settlement is a cash settlement which allows them to do their own investing. For individuals who have a background in investing and are prudent money managers, this cash-in-hand approach may be in the best interest of the disabled person, depending on the investment market, interest rates, and the ever-present problem of inflation.

4.   *Can a structured settlement include cash payments?*

Normally a structured settlement agreement will include a lump-sum payment of cash up front, plus an annuity which will pay benefits according to an agreed timetable.

5. *Is the money used to fund a structured settlement tax-free?*

All proceeds from a lawsuit, whether recovered from a settlement or trial, and either paid as a lump-sum cash payment or used to fund a structured settlement, are tax free. In a lump sum settlement, once the individual receives the cash and then makes an investment, the interest earned on that money is taxable. In a structured settlement agreement, the periodic payments which an individual may receive throughout the course of his or her lifetime are tax free upon receipt, and only the interest generated after the money is invested is taxable.

6. *Can structured settlement payments be paid to designated individuals upon the death of the injured individual?*

Generally, structured settlement benefits are guaranteed for a period of time, and if the injured person dies before the guaranteed period has been exhausted, then the benefits will be paid to the named beneficiary. For example, if a structured settlement guarantees monetary benefits to be paid each month for 30 years, and the injured person dies one year after the structured settlement agreement has begun, the benefits will be paid to the beneficiary for the remaining 29 years.

7. *Who decides what should be included in the structured settlement agreement?*

Usually, once settlement negotiations are undertaken, an insurance company will present several structured settlement proposals for discussion and review. These proposals should be examined by individuals who are familiar with the costs of funding such proposals, so that the family and the disabled individual can be assured of what it costs the insurance company to buy or fund a specific settlement proposal.

Prior to any settlement negotiations the attorneys should review with the medical professionals future medical costs so that these needs can be incorporated into any structured settlement proposal. Inflation and cost of living increases should be a part of a properly drafted structured settlement annuity.

8. *When should a structured settlement be considered?*

A structured settlement proposal should always be considered when representing a catastrophically injured adult or minor. The disabled individual or the court-appointed guardian should be urged to evaluate many different proposals to determine which one will best meet the financial and medical needs of the catastrophically injured person.

CONCLUSION

Attorneys, in representing a catastrophically injured individual, have a dual role: To litigate and obtain the best financial settlement, and to assure that the funds are used to meet the financial and medical needs of the injured individual and are not dissipated.

B.   LIFECARE PLANS - COST PROJECTIONS

Attorneys and insurance companies are increasingly relying on rehabilitation nurses, case managers, and lifetime planning experts to pre-pare reports setting forth the lifetime needs of persons with catastrophic injuries or illnesses.   These lifecare plans or future cost assessment reports should include the following:

- **The purpose of the report**

- **The facts of the case**

- **Biographical information, including school and work history**

- **Prior health history**

- **Diagnosis of the medical problem or medical condition**

- **List of all hospitals and treating physicians**

- **List of medical records reviewed**

- **Itemized cost of all durable medical equipment**

- **Medications**

- **Therapies**

- **Annual doctor visits**

- **Nursing care**

- **Home evaluation**

- **Family support system**

- **Home modifications**

- **Future medical care**

- **Respite care**

- **Prognosis**

- **Recommendations**

Increasingly, insurance companies are reviewing medical charts and submitting cases for peer review before paying medical benefits. If the treating professional has underestimated the catastrophic illness or injury (traumatic brain injury or spinal cord injury), this can increase the difficulties in receiving medical reimbursement from an insurance company for future care, and in proving the injury or illness at trial.

C. *LONG-TERM CARE - CUSTODIAL CARE AND REHABILITATION*

1. *Custodial Care vs. Rehabilitative Gains*

Two issues which consistently arise in connection with the medical treatment of catastrophically injured persons are: whether or not they can continue to make rehabilitative gains, and whether or not the care they are receiving is "custodial care". The provisions of most insurance policies will either deny payment for custodial care, or will pay very limited benefits.

During the next decade, insurance companies will increasingly press the issue of whether or not medical services contribute substantially to the improvement of the injured person's medical condition. The position of most insurance companies is that they will not pay for medical services which do not substantially contribute to the improvement of the injured person's condition.

In *YOUNG V. EQUITABLE LIFE ASSURANCE SOCIETY OF THE UNITED STATES*, an injured person was receiving care in a hospital and suffering from pre-senile dementia. The insurance company asked the Court to rule that it did not have to provide coverage, since the medical care the injured person was receiving was "custodial care" and there was an exclusion in the policy denying payment for custodial care services. The Superior Court in Pennsylvania ruled that the "custodial care" limitation in a group health policy was inapplicable where an injured person received medicine to control seizures and psychosis, engaged in various therapeutic programs, and received psychiatric assistance.

Essentially, the Court ruled that if custodial care is given, but is accompanied by medical services, i.e. medication, etc., which substantially contributed to the improvement of the insured's medical condition, then a limitation in the policy refusing coverage for custodial care is not applicable, and the insurance company must pay for expenses under the terms of its particular policy.

238

It is very important that health care professionals and families be aware that in a catastrophic injury case, the issue of whether care is custodial or rehabilitative must be addressed by both the legal and the health care community. It can be anticipated that insurance companies will attempt to utilize the "custodial care" clause more often, to deny medical treatment.

The medical rehabilitation community should anticipate that within the coming year insurance companies will seek a determination that a person has plateaued, or cannot make significant rehabilitative gains, or that the treatment they are receiving is "custodial care".

2.   *Long-Term Care - Is anyone responsible?*

An issue which consistently arises in connection with the medical treatment for both catastrophically injured persons and the elderly is: Is anyone responsible for the payment of adequate care? During 1998, it is anticipated that the government will attempt further cutbacks in benefits for long-term home care and nursing home care. Most private insurance policies will either not pay for nursing home care and long-term care for the catastrophically injured, or will pay very limited benefits.

A recent study by the United Seniors Health Cooperative found that six out of ten people with private nursing home insurance are likely to receive no benefits because of restrictions in their policies. The most common restriction, found in 77% of the plans, was that a person must first be hospitalized for a medical problem that leads to the nursing home admission before being permitted to collect benefits for nursing home care. The study found that 54% of nursing home admissions do not come directly from a hospital and will not qualify for benefits under a plan with this restriction. The other major limitation, included in 40% of the surveyed insurance plans, was that a person must first receive skilled-level nursing home care before they can qualify for lower levels of long-term care. Such a requirement excludes an additional 40% of nursing home residents. The effect of these exclusions in private insurance policies is even more dramatic and troubling when combined with waiting periods and other restrictions, such as the definitions of "durable medical equipment", "rehabilitation gains", "pre-existing conditions", etc.

It is crucial that all insurance policies be studied very carefully when someone has received a catastrophic injury or needs long-term home care, so that proper documentation and reports can be provided to the insurance company or government agency. These reports need to be focused so that exclusion definitions and restrictions do not permit an insurance company the opportunity to deny benefits.

3. *Long-Term care insurance*

If you are 45 years of age or older, the odds are nearly 50/50 that eventually you will spend some time in a nursing home. The current cost of nursing home care can be as much as $50,000 a year. Americans spend approximately $50 billion a year for long-term care, $41 billion of this for nursing home care. Nursing home residents and their families pay for about 51%; Medicaid, on behalf of poor patients, pays 42%; other governmental programs, such as the Veterans' Administration, pay 5%. As previously indicated Medicare pays very little of the cost of long-term nursing home care, slightly over 1%, and private insurance pays less than 1%. Lack of available governmental programs has given rise to nursing home insurance sold by private industry. It is estimated that 1.5 million insurance policies for nursing home care or long-term care, have been purchased.

All experts agree that a good nursing home policy should provide benefits that will be paid longer than a single year, have a reasonable waiting or elimination period before payments start, and inflation protection. In addition, in evaluating the proper long-term care policy for your family, you should consider the following:

- Coverage of all three levels of care in a nursing home: Skilled, intermediate and custodial. Most nursing home patients need only custodial care, however those individuals who are catastrophically ill or injured as the result of accidents often need all three levels of care. Insurance policies, that are not specifically long-term care insurance policies, will normally exclude the cost of custodial care.

- The insurance policy should cover Alzheimer's Disease, should you develop the disease after purchasing the policy.

- The policy should allow you to enter at any level of care, without prior hospitalization.

- The policy should have provisions for the coverage of care received in your home.

- A guaranteed renewable clause. It should have a guarantee that the policy cannot be cancelled, non-renewed or otherwise terminated because you get older or suffer deterioration in your physical or mental condition.

In years past, long-term care meant only one thing: a nursing home. Fortunately, because consumer groups, advocacy groups, non-profit foundations and the medical community have lobbied for a wider range of choices, the following are some of the services that are available to provide care for an individual who is catastrophically ill or injured:

- Skilled nursing care.

- Intermediate nursing care.

- Custodial care.

- Nursing home care.

- Transitional living care.

- Life-care centers - apartments/cottages.

- Home health care.

- Homemaker services.

- Adult day care.

- Adult foster care.

- Respite care.

- Hospice care.

- Community skills care.

D.   *HINTS IN CHOOSING A NURSING HOME*

The Illinois Council for Long-Term Care has published guidelines in choosing a nursing home, as follows:

- Is the home licensed? Ask. If the answer is yes, ask to see the license.

- Does the administrator have a current state license? Again, ask to see it.

- Is the nursing home Medicare and Medicaid approved?

- What other insurance plans are accepted?

- Are there any additional charges, i.e. laundry, therapy, etc.? If so, what is the cost?

- Are residents allowed to furnish their rooms with their own furniture? Can residents have their own radios or televisions?

- Can a husband and a wife share the same room?

- Are residents permitted to smoke in their rooms? If so, are they supervised? What about alcohol?

- Are there restrictions on making or receiving phone calls?

- What are the visiting hours?

- Where is the resident's money kept? Are there provisions for personal-banking services?

- When was the last state or local inspection, and what were the results?

- How often are fire drills held for staff and residents?

- What types of recreational activities are available to residents? Don't hesitate to ask to see the schedule of activities.

- How are residents' medical needs met? Does the nursing home have an arrangement with a nearby hospital to handle emergencies?

- Are special diets available for those who need them? Is there a professional dietician on the staff who is available as a consultant?

These are all valid questions. Don't hesitate to ask.

Generally, families pay for nursing home care through one of the following ways:

- Medicare coverage, which is limited to skilled care services provided in a skilled nursing facility

- Medigap insurance

- Private health insurance, such as Blue Cross/Blue Shield

242

- Major medical will usually pay for a nursing home as long as the patient has skilled nursing needs

- Veteran's Administration benefits

- Long-term care insurance policy - statistics show that only 5% of those older than 65 who are in a nursing home are covered by a long-term care insurance policy

- Private payment

- Funds from a lawsuit/settlement

- Medicaid - Medical Assistance grant

E.   *RESPITE CARE*

In many cases, family members are the primary caregivers for their catastrophically ill or injured loved one. Family members are often the primary caregivers because they want their loved one home and there is no health insurance coverage, or inadequate health insurance coverage, to pay for attendant or nursing care. It is unreasonable to expect families to accept the burden of 24-hour-a-day care, seven days a week, for months and years. Respite care is a concept which allows the family member to "take a break". Some health insurance companies and governmental agencies will pay for respite care for a limited period of time each calendar year.

F.   *HEALTH INSURANCE, ACCIDENT INSURANCE: PLANNING*

1.   *Medical payment coverage*

Medical payment coverage is often called "med pay coverage". Many insurance policies, such as homeowner's insurance policies, provide for med pay coverage regardless of how a person was injured at your home. For example, if a guest falls and injures himself climbing your steps, regardless of whether or not you were negligent, medical payment coverage would pay your injured guest's medical bills. Most insurance policies provide medical payment coverage for a specified amount. These amounts are very small. Insurance companies will not voluntarily send you a check for medical payment coverage - you must ask the insurance company whether or not there is medical payment coverage to cover your particular claim. If you have a copy of the declaration sheet or insurance policy, examine it carefully to determine all the coverages available to pay your medical bills.

The health and accident policy should be examined to determine the following:

a.   Limit of lifetime benefits

Example: $1 million lifetime maximum;

b.   Deductible

Will the policy not pay, for example, the first $10,000 in medical bills?

c.   Exclusions

Does the policy only pay for acute care or does it pay for care in a rehabilitation facility, transitional living program, skilled nursing care or long-term care in a nursing facility?

d.   Definitions

What is the definition of rehabilitation services? Does the insurance company have an option of terminating coverage if they or their doctor determine a person is no longer making substantial rehabilitative gains, i.e. they have "plateaued", or their care is "custodial" in nature?

e.   Coordination of benefits

Is there a section in the policy which requires that the health or accident insurance be coordinated with any other insurance that you may have so that, in effect, when you have two insurance companies one becomes primary and one is secondary? Your bills will first go to the primary carrier, who will pay according to their insurance contract. Any remaining bills will be sent to the secondary carrier. It is often difficult to determine which carrier is primary and which is secondary, especially when there is a catastrophic injury and neither insurance company wants to assume payment of the medical bills for the injured person.

Most people have Blue Cross and Blue Shield, a major medical plan, HMO or some type of private health or accident insurance which may pay medical bills if you have a catastrophic injury or illness. As soon as possible after the injury or illness, you should get a copy of the insurance policy and plan booklet to see whether or not it will cover rehabilitation expenses, skilled nursing care, etc. This policy should be reviewed by your attorney so that you can make adequate discharge planning decisions, and properly fill out the application or proof of claim forms requesting medical benefits for a catastrophically injured person. Great care should be taken in filling out the application forms requesting medical benefits for a catastrophically injured person.

2. *Homeowner's insurance*

A homeowner's insurance policy should be carefully examined to determine whether or not there is medical coverage under the terms and provisions of the particular policy. Many homeowner's policies provide coverages which pay a certain amount of medical bills, regardless of how the injury occurred, so long as it happened on the premises of the home-owner, or if other provisions are met. The homeowner should carefully review the policy after an injury occurs, since many policies contain language requiring a notice of the injury or proof of claim within a specified period of time.

3. *Excess - Umbrella Insurance*

An excess or umbrella policy is an insurance policy which usually covers an individual under the following situations:

a   An individual is negligent;

b.   The negligent individual seriously injures a third party;

c.   The liability insurance to cover the injuries of the third party is insufficient.

In the above situation, if you have excess liability insurance, then your excess liability insurance would cover any claim the injured individual has against you individually for an amount that exceeds your primary liability insurance. An attorney, when representing a catastrophically injured person, will make a diligent search to determine whether or not there are any excess or umbrella insurance policies.

4. *Buying Insurance: A gamble*

Buying insurance need not be a gamble. Some tips from the National Association of Professional Insurance Agents on purchasing insurance are:

a.   **Shop for the best insurance agent**. Shop for agents as you would shop for stockbrokers or banks. Choose one that offers the best combination of price, coverage and service;

b.   **Shop for the best insurance company**. Check the independent rating services to see how they grade the companies. For example, Standard & Poor's Corp. of NY rates the financial strength of many insurance companies;

c.   *Make sure your insurance policy is covered by the State Guaranty Fund.*

Make sure the policy you buy is covered by your state's guaranty fund, which pays claims for insolvent insurers.

d.   *Check to see if your insurance company is an admitted or non-admitted carrier.*

Know the full name of your company and the state where it is based. Ask whether the company is an "admitted" or "non-admitted" carrier. Non-admitted insurers usually cover "high risk" insureds, but are not protected by state guaranty funds. If your carrier is non-admitted, make sure it is approved to operate in your state.

G.   *ESTATE PLANNING*

1.   *Estate planning documents*

a.   Wills

A Will is a legal expression of what you want to happen to your estate and your children when you die. A Will should include an Executor, Guardian, and Trustee. It is also good practice to name an alternate Executor, Guardian and Trustee, in the event of death, incapacity or unwillingness to serve. A Will is a document that can always be modified to meet changing financial and medical needs.

(1)   *Executor*

The duties of an Executor include: responsibility for filing (probating) the Will; seeing that taxes are paid; that beneficiaries receive their inheritance; that the guardian or alternate guardian named in the Will assumes responsibility for the care of the children, and assuring that the wishes of the parents are carried out according to the terms and provisions of the Will.

(2)   *Guardian*

The choice of a guardian or alternate guardian, especially for a disabled child, is one of the most important decisions a parent can make. The guardian or alternate guardian who is named in the Will has the legal responsibility to act in place of a parent, making all decisions that a parent would make. Before parents name a guardian for their minor children, they should discuss with the prospective guardians whether or not they are willing to serve in the event of the parents' death. In the case of a catastrophically injured child, it is particularly important that the parents select a person who is aware of the special needs of the child. Some factors to consider are:

- Does the proposed guardian have a relationship with the minor?

- Does the proposed guardian have children? If so, what are their ages, their sex?

- How is the stability of the marriage of the proposed guardian?

- How is the health of the proposed guardian?

- What is the education and financial expertise of the proposed guardian?

(3) *Trustee*

A trustee is the person responsible for controlling the manner in which any trust funds are invested. This is often the same person named as guardian and/or executor in the Will. It is advisable to choose a trustee who has expertise in money management and who also has a relationship with the child. Frequently, parents will choose a bank to act as co-trustee with a family member when there are substantial assets.

b. Intestacy

If you have no Will at the time of your death, you die intestate. You have given up the right to determine three important matters: First, you cannot decide who gets your property at your death; second, you cannot select the manner in which that property is given; and third, you cannot name a guardian, executor and trustee for your children.

c. Trusts

A trust is a document which sets up funds and provisions to benefit your heirs or designees upon your death. It is normally a part of your Will and estate planning documents.

(1) *Discretionary Trusts*

Discretionary trusts are used for children with disabilities, since the financial needs of a minor can change substantially as the child reaches majority or as governmental insurance benefits are reduced or modified. A discretionary trust is the most flexible estate planning document. It gives the trustee or co-trustees broad discretion.

(2) *Mandatory Trusts*

A mandatory trust does not allow flexibility, since it requires that the trustee make certain payments to a child in certain specific amounts at certain specified times. The attorney setting up the mandatory trust should examine state laws carefully to insure that the trust does not disqualify the minor child from state and federal governmental benefits.

d. Outright gifts/bequests

The manner in which property is given to a child with disabilities also requires considerable thought and expertise. Usually, an outright gift or bequest to a child with disabilities is not practical or feasible since it may disqualify the child from receiving certain benefits such as Medicaid, Supplemental Social Security income, and state welfare benefits. One way to avoid this problem is to leave property to another beneficiary or individual and ask him/her to use the funds for the child. This is called a "morally obligated gift" but there is no guarantee that the individual will comply with the deceased parent's request that the funds be used for the child with disabilities.

e. Life Insurance

Life insurance is an instrument which can be used to create an estate for catastrophically ill or injured individuals and children with disabilities. A life insurance policy is a contract between the owner of the policy and the life insurance company under which the life insurance company is legally obligated to pay the proceeds to the named beneficiary of the policy. The proceeds are paid to the beneficiary named in the insurance policy, and not to persons named in a Will. Through the use of life insurance, and especially life insurance combined with trusts, an individual or a parent can create a large estate to provide the funds for future medical treatment.

f. Disinheriting a child

In many states it is legally permissible to disinherit a child. One reason a parent might disinherit a child with disabilities is that the disinherited child could then be eligible for public assistance and governmental benefits. Parents may, in some instances, choose to disinherit their non-disabled children to allow their limited funds to be used for the financial and medical needs of the child with disabilities.

g. Power of Attorney

A power of attorney is an instrument authorizing one person to act as another's agent. In addition to a guardian named in their Wills, parents of a child with disabilities should each have a power of attorney, since if they themselves become ill or disabled, the person named in the Power of Attorney has the right to assist the disabled parent.

h.   Durable Power of Attorney

A durable power of attorney is a document in which a competent individual, a parent, names another person to act on his or her behalf in the event the parent becomes unable to manage his or her own affairs. The person named in the durable power of attorney will serve as the guardian of the incapacitated parent without the necessity of petitioning the court. An attorney should be consulted in drafting any powers of attorney to be sure specific state requirements are met.

i.   Guardianship

If a child is still disabled when he becomes an adult, and is unable to manage his own affairs and money, then the parents must petition the court to have a guardian appointed. The court will name a guardian of the person, who handles the medical decisions, and a guardian of the estate to handle financial decisions. Usually, the proposed guardians are one or both parents, or family members. The guardian of the person and the guardian of the estate can be the same individual, although if there are large sums of money to invest for the child with disabilities, the courts generally require a bank as a corporate co-guardian. Section III, Guardianship, beginning on page 9, discusses in detail adults who require court-appointed guardians.

2.   _Family Assets_

The cost of long-term care in a nursing home for a person with a catastrophic injury can be astronomical. It may be possible through a guardianship or power of attorney or other legal device for the assignment of assets between spouses, to allow a person to qualify for state-supported long-term care. Such devices avoid the unpleasant alternatives of either divorce or family bankruptcy in an effort to avoid expending all of the family assets on nursing home care. An attorney can advise you whether such a plan is proper in your situation.

H.   _SETTLEMENT TRUST (SPECIAL NEEDS TRUST)_

An issue often arises as to whether or not an individual's governmental benefits or eligibility for governmental benefits can be maintained if the person receives substantial sums from a personal injury settlement or verdict. In many cases, even though the personal injury recovery is substantial, the funds awarded are not sufficient to meet the long-term medical and rehabilitation cost of the catastrophically ill or injured person. In such circumstances, properly drafted settlement trusts (special needs trusts) may allow an individual to receive governmental benefits in addition to the money received in the personal injury lawsuit. The advantages and disadvantages of using a settlement trust in your particular case should be discussed with your attorney before resolving your personal injury claim.

XXVI. <u>MEDICAL PROVIDERS AS EXPERT WITNESSES</u>

One of the most fundamental tenets of American litigation is its insistence upon the most reliable sources of information at trial. "One of the earliest and most pervasive manifestations of this attitude is the rule requiring that a witness who testifies to a fact.....must have actually observed the fact."[1] However, the law has also long recognized that many human under-takings involve complex disciplines which the average layman cannot hope to comprehend without additional guidance from those who are learned in the field. Therefore, the law acknowledges that where a controversy involves a science, profession, or occupation which is "beyond the ken of the average layman"[2], expert testimony is admissible to assist the fact finder in resolving the dispute.

In order for the court to permit such expert testimony, the witness must have sufficient skill, knowledge, or experience in his or her field to make it probable that his or her opinion will aid the fact finder in its decision. While the court may rule that a certain subject area will require that a member of a given profession, such as a physician, be utilized as the expert witness, a specialist in that particular field is not always legally required, although such expertise is frequently desirable. Finally, the courts generally will not allow the introduction of expert testimony in areas of science which are only experimental, but rather will require that the subject matter of the expert's testimony "be sufficiently established to have gained general acceptance in the particular field to which it belongs."[3] Therefore, opinion evidence will not be admitted if the state of scientific knowledge in a field is not so advanced as to permit a reasonable opinion to be asserted, even by an expert.

Opinion evidence of a traumatic brain injury will be admitted based on computer tomography (CT) scans, x-rays, electroencephalograph (EEG), and magnetic resonance imaging (MRI). Some courts have allowed expert testimony based upon positron emission tomography (PET) scans, evoked potentials, and brain electrical activity mapping (BEAM) tests.

"Objective" neuropsychological testing is in fact little more objective than the psychologist running the tests and is subject to the same contextual bias as the other forensic examinations. Just as one neurologist can find clear evidence of brain damage in a patient whom a second neurologist finds entirely free of impairment, very often "objective" neuropsychological testing will reveal precisely what the examiner hoped to find.[5] Nevertheless, opinion evidence based on "objective testing" will be viewed more favorably by the courts and gives the trial attorney more ammunition in trying to prove or disprove the residual effects of the traumatic brain injury.

As previously mentioned, to the lay person as well as the court, the damages of a spinal cord injured individual are more obvious than those of an individual who has suffered traumatic brain injury. Just as it is generally difficult to obtain insurance reimbursement for services for the traumatically brain injured, such as group homes, computer programs, and transitional living programs, insurance companies are also reluctant to pay for programs and services for the spinal cord injured, such as computerized adaptive living devices for the home, motorized wheelchairs, state-of-the-art vans, and other durable medical equipment. Insurance companies will reimburse for, and courts will usually allow testimony concerning, any medical testing or advance if the state of scientific knowledge in the field is so advanced as to permit a reasonable opinion to be asserted by an expert.

When an attorney has determined that the use of a medical expert is strategically valuable and legally admissible, counsel frequently will prepare the case with substantial emphasis upon the anticipated testimony of the expert. A medical expert should expect to be required to answer questions within a particular legal framework in accordance with rules of admissibility and evidence. Since the witness's expertise must first be accepted by the court in order to allow the witness to offer an expert opinion, the witness initially will be asked to testify as to academic and employment credentials, including educational background, relevant work experience, publications authored, and ongoing professional training. Opposing counsel will then be permitted to cross-examine the expert regarding these credentials, and counsel may object to an acceptance of the witness as an expert by the court. Since the standard for acceptance of the qualifications of an expert is generally quite modest, it is relatively rare for a proffered expert to be rejected by the court. However, as the leading scholar on the law of evidence has noted, "The witness must have sufficient skill, knowledge or experience in that field or calling as to make it appear that his opinion or inference will probably aid the trier in his search for truth."[6] If a witness has any reasonable pretension to specialized knowledge on the subject under investigation, he/she may testify, and the weight to be given to this evidence is for the jury to determine.[7]

After a witness in a traumatic brain injury or spinal cord injury case has been accepted as an expert by the court, counsel generally will then provide a factual basis for the witness's opinion. For example, counsel will inquire into the witness's familiarity with the patient and his/her medical condition, the witness's involvement in the treatment of the patient, and the records/documentary materials that the witness reviewed and relied upon in preparing the opinion. After establishing the factual foundation for the expert witness's opinion, counsel will either: (1) ask the witness a direct question to obtain an opinion in the relevant area; or (2) fashion a "hypothetical question" that asks the witness to assume certain facts already presented at trial, and to state an opinion based upon those facts. The former method generally is utilized where the expert witness has first-hand knowledge of the material facts (e.g., the witness was the victim's treating physician), so that the witness may describe his or her own observations and provide an expert opinion therefrom. A hypothetical question is typically used in circumstances where the expert witness does not possess first-hand knowledge of the facts of the case, but rather is presenting an opinion based upon the observations and evaluations of other individuals. Finally, after the witness has stated his or her expert opinion, the witness may be asked to relate those facts that support the conclusion reached.

An issue which frequently arises when substantial reliance is placed upon expert testimony is the extent to which the expert may rely upon the reports or statements of others who have not testified in court. This situation occurs when a treating physician is unavailable to provide an expert opinion at trial. In such circumstances, the court must determine whether another physician qualified in the field of inquiry may provide an opinion with regard to the medical condition of the patient that is based only on reports of others, without ever having examined that patient. The clear trend of the law is to permit such an expert opinion to be presented.[8] The Pennsylvania Supreme Court permitted "medical witnesses to express opinion testimony on medical matters based, in part, upon reports of others which are not in evidence, but which the expert customarily relies upon in the practice of his profession."[9] The court also held that expert medical witnesses may rely on reports of laypersons, provided such reports are customarily relied on by experts in the medical field. Consequently, an expert may generally render an opinion based upon the reports of others, so long as the expert is prepared to testify that the reports are of the type customarily relied upon by colleagues in the field.[10]

When the testifying witness is someone other than the initial treating physician, the witness will have a better foundation upon which to base his or her final conclusion of traumatic brain injury if the initial treating physician made a prompt, factually correct, thorough investigation of the circumstances of the accident and the patient's prior medical history and has clearly documented these in his/her notes.

In preparation of testimony, an expert must also be aware that he or she will be expected to state that the opinion rendered is held to a reasonable degree of medical certainty.[11] Consequently, the expert witness must carefully avoid the use of such conditional words as "probably" or "maybe", as the expert is required to express his opinion to a higher degree of certainty. In one case, a doctor was asked whether the plaintiff's condition was caused by the automobile accident which gave rise to the lawsuit.

The doctor testified that the accident was "consistent with the injury", and that "there is probably a cause and effect relationship". The Court held this testimony to be inadmissible:

> "The issue is not merely one of semantics. There is a logical reason for the rule. The opinion of a medical expert is evidence. If the fact finder chooses to believe it, he can find as fact what the expert gave as an opinion. For the fact finder to award damages for a particular condition to a plaintiff, it must find as a fact that the condition was legally caused by the defendant's conduct. Here, the only evidence offered was that it was 'probably' caused, and that is not enough. Perhaps in the world of medicine nothing is absolutely certain. Nevertheless doctors must make decisions in their own profession every day based on their expert opinions. Physicians must understand that it is the intent of our law that if the plaintiff's medical expert cannot form an opinion with sufficient certainty so as to make a medical judgment, there is nothing on the record with which a jury can make a judgment with sufficient certainty so as to make a legal judgment. Because Mrs. McMahon's testimony was not made with sufficient certainty, it was not legally competent evidence...."[12]

This "certainty requirement" has evolved into a key phrase where counsel will ask an expert to express his or her opinion "to a reasonable degree of medical certainty". It is not required that the expert express an opinion with absolute certainty.

Attorneys are increasingly relying on rehabilitation nurses, case managers, and lifecare planning experts to prepare reports setting forth the lifetime needs of persons with catastrophic head or spinal cord injury. These future cost assessment reports should include: the purpose of the report; the facts of the case; biographical information; diagnosis of the medical problem; school background; work history; family support system; home evaluation; list of all hospitals and treating physicians; list of medical records reviewed; prior health history; itemized cost of all durable medical equipment; medications; therapies; annual doctor visits; nursing care; home modifications; future medical care; recommendations; and prognosis.

Increasingly, insurance companies are reviewing medical charts and submitting cases for peer review before paying medical benefits. If the treating professional has underestimated the traumatic brain injury or spinal cord injury, the difficulties increase in receiving medical reimbursement from an insurance company for future care and in proving the injury at trial.

[1]McCormick on Evidence, 2d, Section 10, at 20.

[2]McCormick on Evidence, 2d, Section 13, at 29.

[3]Frye v. United States, 293 F. 1013, 1014 (1923) (the first case to consider and reject—the admissibility of the results of a lie detector examination). McCormick on Evidence at 29-31, 489.

[4]Rimel et al "Disability Caused by Minor Head Injury" Neurosurgery (1981) 9-221-228; Psychiatry in the Everyday Practice of Law, Blinder (2nd Ed. 1982).

[5]Psychiatry and the Everyday Practice of Law, Blinder, 2nd Ed. (1982), p 40.

[6]United States v. Viglia, 549 F.2d 335 (5th Cir. 1977) (physician with no experience in treating obesity could render an opinion regarding the use of a controlled substance allegedly used for controlling obesity).

[7]McCormick on Evidence, 2d, Section 15, at 34-36; Federal Rules of Evidence, Rule 703.

[8]Commonwealth v. Thomas, 444 Pa. 436, 445, 282 A.2d 693, 698 (1971).

[9]Commonwealth v. Daniels, 480 Pa. 340, 390 A.2d 172 (1978); See also McCormick on Evidence, at 34-36.

[10]75 A.L.R., 3d 9, "Admissibility of Expert Medical Testimony as to Future Consequences of Injury as Affected by Expression in Terms of Probability or Possibility."

[11]McMahon v. Young, 442 Pa. 484, 486, 276 A.2d 534, 535 (1971-).

[12]Hamil v. Bashline, 481 PA. 256, 392 A.2d 1280 (1978); Restatement of Torts, Section 323.

XXVII. RECALL AND REINSTATEMENT OF DRIVING PRIVILEGES OF MENTALLY OR PHYSICALLY UNQUALIFIED DRIVERS

The ***Pennsylvania Motor Vehicle Code*** and the regulations of the Pennsylvania Department of Transportation provide for the recall of the driving privileges of individuals who are believed by the Department to have become physically or mentally unqualified to be licensed.

The Department of Transportation has promulgated, through its Medical Advisory Board, detailed regulations regarding physical and mental qualifications of drivers. In addition to establishing visual standards for licensed drivers, these regulations provide ten areas of physical or mental impairment which can result in the recall of any individual's driver's license. These ten areas are as follows:

A.   *EPILEPSY*

An individual suffering from epilepsy <u>may</u> <u>not</u> drive unless his or her personal licensed physician reports that the individual has been seizure-free for a period of at least one year immediately preceding, with or without medication.

An applicant between the ages of 16 and 18 years applying for his or her first license shall have been free from seizure for a period of at least two years immediately preceding, with or without medication.

Waiver of the freedom from seizure requirement may be made upon specific recommendation by a licensed physician who specializes in neurology or neurosurgery if:

1.   A strictly nocturnal pattern of the condition has been established over a period of at least three years immediately preceding, with or without medication; or

2.   A specific prolonged aura accompanied by sufficient warning has been established over a period of at least five years immediately preceding, with or without medication.

The Motor Vehicle Code provides for nine other areas of physical or mental conditions which may result in recall, as follows:

B.   *OTHER PHYSICAL AND MEDICAL STANDARDS*

1.   *General*

A person afflicted by any of the following conditions may not drive if, in the opinion of the examining physician, the conditions are likely to interfere with the ability to control and safely operate a motor vehicle:

(a)   Loss or impairment of the use of a foot, leg, finger, thumb, hand or arm, as a functional defect or limitation;

(b)   Unstable or brittle diabetes or hypoglycemia, unless there has been a continuous period of at least six months freedom from a related syncopal attack;

(c)   Cerebral vascular insufficiency or cardiovascular disease, including hypertension, with accompanying signs and symptoms;

(d)   Periodic loss of consciousness, attention or awareness from whatever cause;

(e)   Rheumatic, arthritic, orthopedic, muscular or neuromuscular disease;

(f) Mental deficiency or marked mental retardation in accordance with the International Classification of Diseases. For diagnostic categories, terminology and concepts to be used in classification, the physician should refer to the Diagnostic and Statistical Manual of the American Psychiatric Association and the Manual on Terminology and Classification in Mental Retardation of the American Association on Mental Deficiency;

(g)   Mental or emotional disorder, whether organic or functional;

(h)   Use of any drug or substance, including alcohol, known to impair skill or functions, regardless of whether the drug or substance is medically prescribed;

(i)   Any other condition which, in the opinion of the examining licensed physician, could interfere with the ability to control and safely operate a motor vehicle.

C.   DOCTOR'S RESPONSIBILITY

The **Pennsylvania Motor Vehicle Code** mandates that all physicians report in writing to the Department the name of any individual over 15 years of age who has been diagnosed as suffering from one of the disabilities or disorders previously listed in this article if, in the doctor's opinion, the doctor believes that the condition will impair the person's ability to drive safely.

If the Department of Transportation has cause to believe that a licensed driver may not be physically or mentally qualified to be licensed, the Department of Transportation shall appoint one or more individuals to determine the competency of the driver, and may order a physical examination of the driver by a physician.

D.   *INCOMPETENCY*

The **Motor Vehicle Code** mandates the recall of the operating privileges of any person whose incompetency has been established.   If a decree of incompetency has been withdrawn by the Court, that evidence should be submitted to the Department of Transportation with a request to reinstate the person's driving privileges.

E.   *REINSTATEMENT OF DRIVING PRIVILEGES*

When an individual whose license has been recalled believes he or she is now competent to operate a motor vehicle, he or she should be examined by a physician of his or her own choice, with regard to the previously disqualifying disability.

If the physician believes that the condition is no longer likely to interfere with the individual's ability to control and safely operate a motor vehicle, the physician should obtain a form relating to the particular condition from the Bureau of Driver's Licensing at the following address and phone number:

PA Department of Transportation
Bureau of Driver Licensing
P.O. Box 68682
Harrisburg, PA 17106-8682
(717) 787-6309

After the Department of Transportation has reviewed the doctor's information, it will determine whether a special driver's examination must be taken by the individual prior to reinstatement of the license.

The Department of Transportation will give great weight and emphasis to a treating doctor's opinion concerning the issue of whether or not a person is mentally or physically capable of driving safely.   Generally, the Department of Transportation will reinstate driving privileges on the basis of a doctor's letter setting forth his opinion that the person is able to drive safely.

CONCLUSION

I have often been asked whether or not an individual who has lost his or her driving privileges should tell an insurance company about the head injury or other disabling injury which led to the informal or formal revocation of driving privileges. The individual should answer any questions truthfully, honestly and fully on any application for insurance, but should not volunteer any information if not asked. In other words, if an application for insurance asks whether or not there is any reason, medically, why you are unable to drive safely, and you have just been cleared by your doctor, who has written a report to the Department of Transportation or has given you a report indicating that you can drive safely, you can honestly answer that question "no". Some applications for insurance will ask whether or not you have ever been treated for epilepsy or ever had a seizure problem and this question also must be answered truthfully, fully, and in as much detail as required by the application.

If an individual's driving privileges have been revoked improperly or the individual has medical evidence that these privileges should be reinstated by the Department of Transportation, but the Department has failed to do so, this denial may be appealed through the Courts of Pennsylvania.

XXVIII. **CONCLUSION**

In this book I have highlighted many of the legal, medical and insurance issues affecting the catastrophically ill and injured and their families. Family members, treating doctors, rehab nurses, social workers, consumers, attorneys — All of us must fight for the benefits to which our loved ones, our patients, and our clients, are entitled.

BE AN ADVOCATE — YOU CAN MAKE A DIFFERENCE!

XXIX. INFORMATION SOURCES: WHERE TO CALL FOR DISABILITY RELATED AND NON-PROFIT ORGANIZATIONS AND AGENCIES

The following are agencies you can contact for helpful information:

- About-Face National Organization for Persons with Facial Disfigurement
  215-491-0602

- Access Board, U.S. Architectural & Transportation Compliance Board
  800-USA-ABLE

- ADA Answer Line at the Equal Employment Opportunity Commission
  800-669-EEOC
  800-669-4000

- ADA Accessibility Guidelines
  Voice: 800-872-2253
  TDD: 800-993-2822

- ADA Disability and Business Technical Assistance Centers
  V/TDD: 800-949-4232

- ADA Disability Rights Education and Defense Fund
  V/TDD: 800-466-4232

- American Association of Kidney Patients
  800-749-2257

- American Council of the Blind
  800-424-8666

- American Foundation for the Blind
  800-232-5463

- American Foundation for Urologic Disorders
  800-242-2383

- American Hearing Research Foundation
  800-638-8299

- American Kidney Fund Information
  800-638-8299

- American Liver Foundation
  800-223-0179

- American Paralysis Association
  800-225-0292

- American Syringomyelia Alliance
  903-236-7079

- American Trauma Society (ATS)
  800-556-7890

- Amputee Coalition of America
  615-524-8772

- Amyotrophic Lateral Sclerosis (ALS) Association
  800-782-4747

- Better Hearing Institute
  800-327-9355

- Books on Special Children (BOSC)
  914-638-1236

- Canadian Paraplegic Association
  416-422-5644

- Captioned Films for the Deaf
  Voice/TDD: 800-237-6213

- Children's Craniofacial Association
  800-535-3643

- Children's Hospice International
  800-242-4453

- Cleft Palate Foundation
  800-24-CLEFT

- Cornelia de Lange Syndrome
  Foundation   800-223-8355
  CN: 800-753-CDLS

- Computer-Disability News
  312-667-7400

- Council of Citizens with Low Vision
  800-733-2258

- Crohn's & Colitis Foundation of
  America
  800-932-2423
  NY: 212-679-1570

- Cystic Fibrosis Foundation
  800-344-4823

- Drug Abuse Hotline
  800-662-HELP

- Dystrophic Epidermolysis Bullosa
  Research Association
  212-693-6610

- Epilepsy Foundation of America
  800-332-1000

- Family Resource Center on Disabilities
  Voice: 312-939-3513
  TDD: 312-939-3519

- Foundation for SCI Prevention
  800-342-0330

- Functional Electrical Stimulation
  InformationCenter
  800-666-2353

- Hear Now - National Hearing Aid Bank
  Voice/TDD: 800-648-HEAR

- Higher Education and Training for
  People With Handicaps
  800-54-HEATH
  DC: 202-939-9320

- Hospice Education Institute - Hospice
  Link 800-331-1620

- Huntington's Disease Society
  800-345-4372

- Impotence Information Center
  800-843-4315
  800-543-9632

- International Medical Society of
  Paraplegia, National Spinal Injuries
  Centre, Stoke Mandeville Hospital,
  Aylesbury, Buckinghamshire, England

- International Office of Orton Dyslexia
  Society
  800-222-3123

- International Polio Network Gazette
  International
  314-534-0475

- International SCI Network
  800-548-2673

- Job Accommodation Network
  800-526-7234
  WV: 800-526-4698

- Job Opportunities for the Blind
  800-638-7518

- Learning Disabilities Association of
  America, 4156 Library Rd., Pittsburgh
  PA 15234 - 775 local chapters
  412-341-1515

- Library of Congress Handicapped
  Hotline
  800-424-8567

- Lupus Foundation Information Line
  800-558-0121

- Medicare Telephone Hotline
  800-638-6833

- Miami Project to Cure Paralysis
  800-782-6387

- Multiple Sclerosis 24 Hour Information
  Line   800-344-4867

- National Adoption Center for Special
  Needs and Physically Disabled Children
                          800-TO-ADOPT

- National AIDS Hotlines
                 English 800-342-AIDS
                 Spanish 800-344-SIDA
                    Deaf 800-AIDS-TTY

- National Alliance for the Mentally Ill
                          800-950-6264

- National Association for Ventilator
  Dependent Individuals
                          216-459-3612

- National Brain Injury Foundations
  Family Helpline   800-444- NHIF
  PA: South Central Brain Injury
  Chapter   610-286-9776

- National Burn Victims Foundation
                          800-803-5879

- National Captioning Institute
           Voice/TDD: 800-533-WORD

- National Center for Youth with
  Disabilities
                          800-333-6293

- National Coordinating Council on
  Spinal Cord Injury
                          617-338-7777

- National Down's Syndrome Congress
                          800-232-NDSC

- National Down's Syndrome Society
                          800-221-4602

- National Easter Seal Society
                          800-221-6827
                       IL: 312-726-6200

- National Health Information
                          800-336-4797

- National Hearing Aid Society Helpline
                          800-521-5247

- National Hospice Organization Helpline
                          800-658-8898

- National Information Center for Children
  & Youth with Disabilities
                          800-695-0285

- National Information Clearinghouse for
  Infants with Disabilities
                          800-922-9234

- National Kidney Foundation
                          800-622-9010

- National Organization for Rare Disorders
                          800-999-6673

- National Paralysis Foundation
           800-925-CURE

- National Rehabilitation Information Center
                          800-34-NARIC

- National Reye's Syndrome Foundation
                          800-233-7393

- National Spasmodic Torticollis Association
                          800-487-8385

- National Special Education Alliance
                          800-732-3131

- National Spinal Cord Injury Association
                          800-962-9629
       Website: HTTP://www.spinalcord.org

- National Spinal Cord Injury 24-hour Hotline

  800-526-3456

- New Jersey Catastrophic Illness in Children Relief Fund Commission, 363 W. State St. - CN 364, Trenton NJ 08625-0364

  609-292-0600

- Paralyzed Veterans of America, 801 - 18th St. NW, Washington DC 10006

  202-USA-1300

- Phoenix Society for Burn Survivors

  800-888-BURN

- Rehab Dimensions, 365 Plum Industrial Court, Pittsburgh PA 15239, Edward Kachurik or Patrick Aydelott

  412-733-1333

- Sickle Cell Disease Association of America

  800-421-8453

- Simon Foundation for Incontinence

  800-23-SIMON

- Spina Bifida Association

  800-621-3141

- Stroke Connection of the American Heart Association

  800-553-6321

- Stuttering Foundation of America

  800-992-9392

  DC: 202-363-3199

- Tourette Syndrome Association

  800-237-0717

- United Cerebral Palsy

  800-USA-5-UCP

  NY: 202-842-1266

  PA: 412-683-7100

- United Ostomy Association

  800-826-0826

- United Scleroderma Foundation

  800-722-4673

- United States Consumer Product Safety Commission Hotline

  800-638-2772

XXX. GLOSSARY OF MEDICAL TERMS *

A

ABSCESS:- A cavity filled with pus.

ABSTRACT THINKING:- The ability to reason and to solve problems.

ACCESSIBLE:- Free of barriers which prevent use (See Architectural Barriers).

ACTIVITIES OF DAILY LIVING (ADL):- Routine activities, such as bathing, dressing, feeding, etc.

ADVANCE DIRECTIVE:- Documents (such as a Living Will or Health-Care Power of Attorney) that allow you to state your preferences regarding your medical treatment, in the event you become incapacitated.

AGITATION:- Behavior pattern of restlessness and increased activity intermingled with anxiety, fear and/or tension.

ALERT:- State of being watchful or ready.

AMBULATION:- Walking.

AMNESIA:- Memory loss.

   Retrograde:- Inability to remember information prior to the injury.

   Anterograde:- Inability to consistently remember events since the injury; associated with inability to remember and learn new material.

ANEURYSM:- A bubble-like deformity in a blood vessel wall which is prone to bleeding.

ANOXIA:- Generalized lack of oxygen supply - may be due to poor blood flow to the brain or low oxygen in the blood.

ANTICOAGULATION:- Process of "thinning the blood." Medication (Heparin, Coumadin) is used to slow down normal blood clotting and thus prevent blood clots or thrombophlebitis from forming in the veins.

ANTICONVULSANT:- Medication used to control or decrease the possibility of seizure (e.g., Dilantin, Phenobarbital, Mysoline, (Tegretol).

ANTIDEPRESSANTS:- Drugs which help treat depression.

APHASIA:- An impairment of communication, caused by damage to an area of the brian, which can involve not only speaking, but understanding of spoken language, writing, reading and use and understanding of gestures.

> **Expressive**:- Problems in communicating with others.

> **Receptive**:- Problems in the individual's understanding what others attempt to communicate.

APRAXIA:- Disorder of the voluntary control and organization of movements.

ARCHITECTURAL BARRIERS:- Features that prevent a disabled person from using a facility (e.g., steps, narrow lavatory doors and stalls, high telephones and drinking fountains, curbs, etc.).

ARTERIOVENOUS MALFORMATION (AVM):- A "tangle" of blood vessels present from birth which may be prone to bleeding.

ASPIRATION:- When food or liquid goes into the windpipe (trachea) and lungs instead of the esophagus and then the stomach. This can cause lung infection or pneumonia.

ASSISTANCE:-

> **Dependant/Maximum**:- Person is unable to perform the task.

> **Moderate**:- Person can participate somewhat, but still requires a good deal of help.

> **Minimum**:- Person does most of task himself/herself, but requires some help.

> **Contact Guard/FBI (finger-in-belt)**:- Person requires no real help. A hand is placed on him/her for safety precautions (e.g., for balance or lack of attention).

ASSOCIATED REACTION:- A non-purposeful movement that accompanies another movement (e.g., patient's arm may bend involuntarily when he/she yawns.)

ATAXIA:- A type of muscular incoordination.

ATTENTION SPAN:- The amount of time a person can concentrate on a particular task.

ATTORNEY-IN-FACT:- Person you choose to make decisions on your behalf if you become disabled.

ATROPHY:- Deterioration or loss of tissue.

AUTOMATIC SPEECH:- Items said without much thinking on the part of the speaker. These included songs, social communication (e.g., "Hello" or "How are you?") or can be items previously learned through memorization. Spontaneous swearing in individuals who did not do so pre-injury is another example.

B

BALANCE:- The ability to use appropriate righting and equilibrium reactions to maintain an upright position. It is usually tested in sitting and standing positions.

BED MOBILITY:- The ability to move oneself in bed.

BEHAVIOR MODIFICATIONS:- Interaction with a person in a way which either decreases, increases or maintains specific behavior. The techniques of behavior modification are generally intended to facilitate improved self-control by expanding the individual's skills, abilities and independence.

BILATERAL:- Both sides.

BLOOD LEVELS:- Amount of medications or other substances in the blood. Blood tests must be done regularly when a person is on certain medicines to ensure that proper levels are maintained.

BOWEL MOVEMENT:- BM, Feces, move your bowels.

BOWEL PROGRAM:- A routine to help a person have regular BM's at a set time every one or two days. (May included medications, suppositories, diet, timing, etc.) This prevents or at least cuts down on the possibility of accidents.

BRAIN STEM:- The lower extension of the brain connected to the spinal cord. Neurological functions located in the brain stem include those necessary for survival - being awake or alert.

CARF:- Commission on Accreditation of Rehabilitation Facilities.

CATHETER:- A narrow tube. Frequently used to drain the bladder. Tube inserted into the bladder to drain urine.

CEREBELLUM:- The portion of the brain (located at the back) which helps coordinate movement. Damage may result in ataxia.

CEREBRAL INFARCT:- When the blood supply is reduced below a critical level and the brain tissue in that region dies.

CEREBROSPINAL FLUID:- Liquid which fills the ventricles in the brain and surrounds the brain and spinal cord.

CIRCUMLOCUTION:- Use of other words to describe a specific word or idea which cannot be remembered.

CLONUS:- Rapid muscle contraction and relaxation. Can be an indication of central nervous system impairment.

CLOSED HEAD INJURY:- Trauma to the head which does not penetrate the skull but which damages the brain.

COGNITION:- "Thinking" skills such as being able to organize, solve problems, follow directions, etc.

COGNITIVE DEFICIT:- A reduction in one or more "thinking" skills which include:- attention, concentration, memory, sequential thought organization, judgment, reasoning and problem-solving.

COGNITIVE REHABILITATION:- Therapy programs which aid people in the management of specific problems in thinking and perception. New strategies and skills are taught to help people improve function and/or compensate for remaining deficits.

COMA:- A state of unarousable unresponsiveness with eyes closed.

COMMUNITY SKILLS:- Those abilities needed to function independently in the community. They may include: phone skills, money management, pedestrian skills, meal planning and cooking, use of public transportation, etc.

COMPENSATION:- Utilizing strengths to make up for weaknesses (e.g., a person with a visual field cut can learn to compensate by turning his/her head to take in his/her surroundings)

COMPUTERIZED AXIAL TOMOGRAPHY (CT SCAN OR CAT SCAN):- Cross sectional x-ray of brain, skull or other body parts.

CONCRETE THINKING:- Thinking limited to what is seen or to one specific example (e.g., a proverb can be interpreted in an abstract or concrete way). Proverb: don't cross the bridge until you get to it. Abstract interpretation: don't worry about troubles until they come. Concrete interpretation: the bridge is a long way off.

CONCUSSION:- Brief loss of consciousness.

CONFABULATION:- Making up facts or events. It differs from lying in that the individual is not attempting to deceive.

CONFUSION:- A state in which a person is bewildered, perplexed or unable to orient him/herself.

CONGENITAL:- Condition usually existing at or before birth.

CONTINENT:- The ability to control urination and bowel movements.

CONTRACTURE:- Loss of full movement of a joint.

CONTRALATERAL:- Opposite side.

CONTRECOUP:- Injuries on the side of the brain opposite the point of impact.

CONTUSION:- Bruise.

COPING PATTERN:- Behaviors, attitudes and/or emotions used to deal with or overcome problems or difficulties.

COUNSELING:- Communications between a therapist and an individual with goals that may include adjusting to changes in one's life and attaining a higher level of understanding of oneself, dealing with emotions, improving relationships and life situations and appreciating one's strengths.

CUE:- A signal or direction used to assist a person in performing an activity (e.g., you give a person a cue when you tell him the initial of your first name when he cannot remember your name).

DECUBITUS:- Pressure area, bed sore, skin opening, skin breakdown. A discolored or open area of skin caused by pressure. Common areas most prone to breakdown are buttocks or backside, hips, shoulder blades, heels, ankles and elbows.

DEEP VEIN THROMBOSIS (DVT):- A blood clot in a vein, most commonly seen in the calf or thigh.

DEFICIT:- A problem area in a person's functioning.

DEPRESSION:- A feeling of sadness brought about by loss. Usually a natural process in brain injury recovery. On occasion, professional treatment may be necessary.

DIFFUSE:- Brain damage which involves many areas of the brain rather than one specific location.

DIPLOPIA:- Double vision.

DISCRIMINATION:- The ability to detect differences between similar objects or events.

DISINHIBITION:- Inability to control or inhibit emotions and impulses.

DISPOSITION:- Plans for where the person will live after discharge from the hospital and who will be able to help him/her.

DO-NOT-RESUSCITATE (DNR) ORDER:- An order in a patient's medical record, directing the treating doctors and health care professionals to withhold cardio-pulmonary resuscitation. Another term for a DNR order is "No Code".

DORSIFLEXION:- When applied to the ankle, the ability to bend at the ankle, moving foot upward.

DYSARTHRIA:- "Slurred" speech due to paralysis or weakness of tongue, lips, soft palate and/or other facial muscles involved in the production of speech.

DYSPHAGIA:- Problem with or absence of the ability to chew and/or swallow.

DYSTOCIA:- Difficult labor.

E

EDEMA:- Swelling.

ELECTROENCEPHALOGRAM (EEG):- A medical test which studies "brain waves" or electrical activity of the brain. Useful for diagnosing seizure disorders.

ELEVATIONS:- Steps, curbs or ramps.

EMBOLUS:- A clot which travels from one part of the body to another.

EPILEPSY:- Seizure disorder.

EQUILIBRIUM:- Normal balance reactions and postures.

EVOKED POTENTIALS:- Recording electrical activity in the brain in response to specific visual, auditory or sensory stimulation. may help further determine the damage. (See EEG)

EXTENSION:- Straightening a joint or body part. (Example: when the arm is held out straight, the elbow is extended.)

F

FIGURE-GROUND:- The differentiation between the foreground and the background; this refers to all sensory systems, including vision, hearing, touch, etc. (e.g., auditory figure-ground is at work when you are able to listen to a conversation in a noisy room.

FLEXION:- Bending a joint.

FOCAL:- Restricted to one region (as opposed to diffuse).

FOLEY/FOLEY CATHETER:- Catheter designed to stay in bladder for a period of time to drain urine; empties into a bag.

FRONTAL LOBE:- Front part of the brain; involved in planning, organizing, problem-solving, selective attention, personality and a variety of "higher cognitive functions."

G

GAIT:- Pattern of walking.

GASTROSTOMY TUBE:- Tube placed into the stomach through an incision in the abdomen. It is used to feed people with long-term swallowing problems.

H

HEMATOMA:- Blood clot.

Regarding the brain:-

Epidural:- Outside the brain and its fibrous covering but under the skull.

Subdural:- Between the brain and its fibrous covering.

Intracerebral:- In the brain tissue.

HEMIANOPSIA:- Visual field cut. Blindness for one half of the field of vision. This is not the right or left half of vision.

HEMIPLEGIA, HEMIPARESIS:- Refers to varying degrees of loss of control or weakness of either the right or left half of the body, resulting from injury to the opposite side of the brain. (See paresis, plegia) Bilateral hemiplegia can result from injury to both sides of the brain.

HEMISPHERE:- One of the two halves of the brain.

Right:- Controls left side of the body and is involved with visuospatial abilities.

Left:- Controls the right side of the body and is involved with language.

HEMORRHAGE:- Bleeding that occurs following trauma.

HOYER LIFT:- Mechanical device for lifting and transferring individuals.

HYDROCEPHALUS:- Enlargement of fluid filled cavities in the brain.

I

IMPACTION:- A blockage in the intestines by hardened feces, this can result from no BM for several days. It sometimes can be treated with medicine. If not treated, it can cause an obstruction which needs surgery.

IMPULSIVE:- Acting too fast without thinking whether it is safe or appropriate.

INCOMPETENT:- Some states use the word **incompetent**, but some states use the words **incapacitated person** instead of incompetent. A person is incapacitated if they lack the ability to understand and appreciate the nature and consequence of medical and other legal decisions.

INCONTINENT:- The inability to control one's bladder and/or bowel. Many people who are incontinent can become continent with training.

INDEPENDENT:- The ability to perform a task without assistance or supervision.

INDEPENDENT LEISURE FUNCTIONING:- The ability to identify one's leisure time, decide how one wishes to constructively use that time, gather the resources necessary for the activity chosen and successfully "recreate."

INTELLECT:- Used to refer to many of the higher functions of the brain.

INTELLIGENCE QUOTIENT (IQ):- Refers to a test score to measure general intellectual ability.

INTERMITTENT CATHETERIZATION PROGRAM (ICP):- Bladder training program where a catheter is inserted to empty the bladder at regular time intervals.

INTRAVENOUS FEEDING (IV):- A needle placed into a vein for the purpose of giving liquids and/or medications.

IPSILATERAL:- Same side.

ISCHEMIA:- A reduction in the blood supply.

J

JARGON:- Spoken language that has a normal rate and rhythm but is full of nonsense words

JEJUNOSTOMY TUBE (J TUBE):- A type of feeding tube surgically inserted into the small intestine.

JUDGMENT:- The ability to make appropriate decisions. This is closely related to abstract thinking because one must be able to reason to arrive at good judgment. It is listed separately because faulty judgment is easy to identify and is an indication that the thinking processes are impaired (e.g., a patient with poor judgment might try to go up to bed down stairs despite the fact that his/her balance is not steady.

LABILITY:- State of having notable shifts in emotional responses (e.g., uncontrolled laughing or crying.

LATENCY OF RESPONSE/RESPONSE DELAY:- The amount of time it takes a person to respond after the stimulus has been presented.

LEARNING:- The process which produces changes in a person's knowledge and/or behavior and allow him/her to perform activities.

   Old:- The ability to perform an activity based on numerous repetitions: habit performance.

   New:- The ability to perform or understand familiar activities.

LEG BAG:- A small, thick plastic bag that ties onto the leg and collects urine. It is connected by tubing to a urodrain.

LEISURE COUNSELING:- The exploration of how a person felt about leisure/recreation before his/her injury and how he/she feels about it now, how to make the best of leisure time, what recreational resources are available in the community and how to take advantage of them, and what changes have to be make to continue past leisure pursuits.

LOGBOOK:- A diary-like listing of the individual's daily activities which can help him/her remember what happened during the course of the day, who he/she came in contact with and the order in which events occurred. The brain injured person, his/ her family and staff are encouraged to make entries. Used to compensate for memory deficits.

LOWER EXTREMITY:- Leg.

M

MEMORY:- The process of storing and retrieving information, sometimes categorized according to the mode in which it is received (e.g., visual vs. auditory).

   Immediate:- being able to recall something within a few seconds of its presentation. Relies on concentration and attention.

   Short-term:- lasts longer than immediate memory, for several minutes.

   Long-term:- refers to the person's ability to store information. In neuropsychological testing, this refers to recall thirty minutes or longer after presentation. - The term "Remote Memory" is sometimes used to refer to events remembered from years ago. (See Amnesia)

MOTOR:- Regarding movement.

N

NASOGASTRIC TUBE (NG TUBE):- A tube passed through the nose into the stomach. It is sometimes used to keep the stomach empty when attached to a pump. More often in rehabilitation, it is used to feed people with swallowing problems.

NEGLECT:- "Forgetting" or not paying attention to the body or the environment.

NEOLOGISM:- Nonsense or make-up word used when speaking. The person often does not realize that the work makes no sense.

NPO:- Latin initials that stand for "Nothing by Mouth". This means no food or liquids for a set time, usually in preparation for certain tests or when the person cannot safely swallow.

NYSTAGMUS:- Involuntary rapid movements of the eyeball(s).

O

OCCIPITAL LOBE:- Area in the back of the brain whose primary function is processing visual information. Damage to this area can cause visual deficits. (See Hemianopsia)

ORIENTATION:- Accurate awareness of self, time and place.

ORTHOSIS:- Brace.

AFO:- Ankle foot orthosis (stops below the knee).

KAFO:- Knee ankle foot orthosis (includes the knee and thigh).

MAFO:- Molded ankle foot orthosis (made of heavy duty plastic).

OVERNIGHT DRAINAGE BAG (ONDB):- A large thick plastic bag that is connected to a urodrain. It hangs on the bed and is used to collect urine at night or when someone needs to be in bed during the day.

P

PARAPHASIC ERROR:- Substitution of an incorrect sound (e.g., tree for free) or related word (e.g., chair for bed.)

PARESIS/PLEGIA:- Mild, moderate weakness or total lack of control.

Hemi:- Refers to one side of the body.

Para:- Refers to both sides from the trunk down.

Quadri:- Refers to both sides from the neck down.

PARIETAL LOBE:- One of the two parietal lobes of the brain.

Right:- Damage to this area can cause visuospatial deficits (e.g., the patient may have difficulty finding his/her way around new or familiar places).

Left:- Damage to this area may disrupt a patient's ability to understand spoken and/or written language.

PERCEPTION:- The ability to make sense of what one sees, hears, feels, tastes, or smells. Perceptual losses are often very subtle, and the patient and/or family may be unaware of them.

PERSEVERATION:- Repeating the same response (verbal or motor) when it is no longer appropriate.

PHLEBITIS:- Vein inflammation.

PLATEAU:- A temporary or permanent leveling off in the recovery process.

POSEY ROSS:- A bar placed on the wheelchair to prevent a person from standing up or falling out.

POSEY VEST or JACKET/HOUDINI JACKET:- A vest worn to keep a person in bed or in a wheelchair because he/she forgets he/she can't get up alone. This is for a person's safety.

PRONATION:- Position of the arm with palm downward.

PRONE:- Lying on one's stomach.

PROPRIOCEPTION:- The sensation that allow a person to know the position of his/her body parts.

PSYCHIATRY:- The medical specialty which deals with psychological and biological treatments of emotional problems.

R

RANGE OF MOTION (ROM):- Refers to movement of a joint (important to prevent contractures).

Active ROM:- The muscles around the joint do the work of moving it.

Passive ROM:- The muscles are not working and the person or someone else moves the joint.

REFRIG BAG:- Device used to help keep males dry when they are incontinent. It is a small plastic bag filled with absorbent tissue that is secured around the penis.

REMEDIATION:- The process of decreasing a handicap by challenging the individual to use and improve deficient skills.

RESPIRATOR:- Sometimes called a ventilator, it is a mechanical device that aids a patient's breathing.

RIGHTING AND EQUILIBRIUM REACTIONS:- High level reflexes that allow us to maintain balance.

S

SCANNING:- The active search of the environment for information usually refers to "visual scanning", which is a skill used in reading, driving and many daily activities.

SCOTOMA:- Area of blindness of varying size anywhere within the visual fields.

SEIZURE:- An uncontrolled discharge of nerve cells which may spread to other cells nearby or throughout the entire brain. Usually lasts only a few minutes at most. May be associated with loss of consciousness, loss of bowel and bladder control and tremors. May also cause aggressive or other behavior change.

SELECTIVE ATTENTION:- Ability to focus on the most important aspect of a situation without becoming distracted.

SENSATION:- Feeling pain, movement of body parts, touch, temperature, etc. Also seeing, hearing, smelling and tasting.

SENSORIMOTOR:- Refers to all aspects of movement and sensation and the interaction of the two.

SHUNT:- A surgically placed tube running from the ventricles to deposit fluid into either the abdominal cavity, heart or large veins of the neck. The purpose is to drain the ventricles in the brain when the normal "drainage" system is not working.

SKULL FRACTURE:- The term used to describe the breaking of the bones surrounding the brain. A depressed skull fracture is one in which the broken bone(s) exert pressure on the brain.

SOFT SIGNS:- Fine and gross motor abnormalities.

SPASTICITY:- Hyperactivity of stretch reflexes (such as a response to tapping the knee with a hammer); may or may not get in the way of functional activities, may be associated with increased tone or tension in muscles, usually in a pattern such as flexion or extension.

STRUCTURE:- To outline, define or simplify.

SUBLUXATION:- Partial dislocation or separation of a joint.

SUPERVISION:- Refers to the assistance provided when a person requires no physical help but requires a person nearby for safety.

> **Close**:- Assistant stands close to person, ready to give assistance if needed.

> **Distant**:- Assistant can see the person and offer verbal assistance but is not close enough to touch him/her.

SUPINE:- Lying on one's back.

SUPPOSITORY:- Medicine inserted into the rectum to help stimulate the muscle to push the feces out. This can be a small solid material or liquid.

STATUS EPILEPTICUS:- Continuous seizures; may produce permanent brain damage.

STIMULUS:- That which causes sensation (i.e. light vision, salt for taste, sound for hearing, etc.

> When a person first comes out of a coma he/she needs a great deal of controlled stimulation of all kinds.

> When he/she becomes agitated, he/she needs very limited stimulation (e.g., only one task for one sense at a time).

SYNERGISTIC MOVEMENT:- Refers to movements that occur together in set patterns and may be difficult to isolate.

T

TDD:- Telecommunication device for the deaf.

TEDS:- Antiembolic stockings or support hose. Tight knee or thigh high stockings that support the leg muscles and help the circulation in the legs.

TELEGRAPHIC SPEECH:- Speech which sounds like a telegram. Only the main words of a sentence (nouns, verbs) are present; the small words (ifs, ands, buts) are missing. This type of speech often gets the message across.

TEMPORAL LOBES:- There are two temporal lobes, one on each side of the brain.

Right:- Mainly involved in visual memory (i.e. memory for pictures and faces).

Left:- Mainly involved in verbal memory (i.e. memory for words and names).

THROMBUS:- Clot.

TIME VOID:- Bladder training program where the person goes to the toilet at regular intervals whether he/she feels the urge to urinate or not. The goal is bladder continency through better control and timing.

TRACHEOTOMY/TRACH:- A surgical opening (hole) at the front of the throat providing access to the trachea or windpipe.

TRACKING:- Visually following an object as it moves through space.

U

UNILATERAL:- One side.

UNILATERAL NEGLECT:- The tendency to ignore things on one (the affected) side.

UPPER EXTREMITY:- Arm.

URINARY TRACT INFECTION (UTI):- When a foreign organism has grown to a large number in the bladder. This can cause fever, chills, burning on urination, urgency, frequency, incontinence, foul smelling urine.

URODRAIN:- A type of external urine collecting device for men.

V

VENTRICLES:- Fluid filled cavities inside the brain.

VERBAL APRAXIA:- Difficulty producing the correct sounds or sequences of sounds in words even though there is no paralysis of the speech muscles. The individual usually knows what he/she wants to say but cannot initiate the sounds or put them in the correct order to form words.

VERBAL FLUENCY:- Ability to produce words.

VISUAL FIELD CUT:- See Hemianopsia.

VISUAL IMAGERY:- Use of mental pictures to aid in recall.

VOID:- Urinate, pass water.

VOLUNTARY or VOLITIONAL MOVEMENT:- Refers to movement purposefully made by the person.

W

WORD RETRIEVAL DEFICIT:- Difficulty recalling a specific word or words.

* Reprinted with the permission of
**The Brain Injury Program at
Magee Rehabilitation Hospital
6 Franklin Plaza
Philadelphia, PA 19102**